DISCARD

D1558185

REPAIRING COMMUNITIES THROUGH RESTORATIVE JUSTICE

JOHN G. PERRY, EDITOR

FOUNDED 1870

American Correctional Association
Lanham, Maryland

Copyright 2002 by the American Correctional Association. All rights reserved. The reproduction, distribution, or inclusion in other publications of materials in this book is prohibited without prior written permission from the American Correctional Association. No part of this book may be reproduced by any electronic means including information storage and retrieval systems without permission in writing from the publisher.

Printed in the United States of America. Coordinated by Magnet Print Brokers, Alexandria, Virginia.

For information on publications and videos available from ACA, contact our worldwide web home page at: http://www.aca.org.

ISBN 1-56991-152-5

This publication may be ordered from:

American Correctional Association
4380 Forbes Boulevard
Lanham, Maryland 20706-4322
1-800-222-5646

Library of Congress Cataloging-in-Publication Data

Repairing communities through restorative justice / edited by John G. Perry
p. cm.
Includes bibliographical references and index.
ISBN 1-56991-152-5
1. Restorative justice ? Criminal justice, Administration of. I. Perry, John G., 1943-
HV8688 .R46 2002

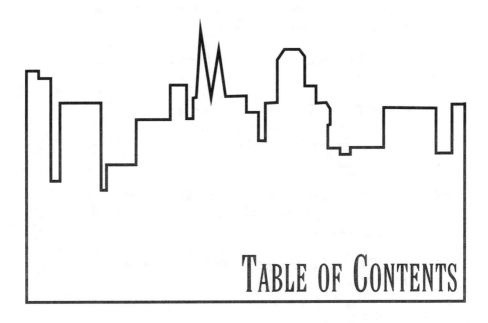

TABLE OF CONTENTS

Foreword by James A. Gondles, Jr., CAE. v

1. Introduction: Challenging the Assumptions 1
   JOHN PERRY

Theoretical Issues

2. Moral and Philosophical Foundations
   of Restorative Justice 19
   FRANCIS J. SCHWEIGERT

3. Community Is Not a Place:
   A New Look at Community Justice Initiatives. 39
   PAUL MCCOLD AND BENJAMIN WACHTEL

4. Linking Crime Prevention to Restorative Justice 55
   JOHN BRAITHWAITE

5. A Comparison of Four Restorative Conferencing Models
   by the Office of Juvenile Justice
   and Delinquency Prevention 67
   GORDON BAZEMORE AND MARK UMBREIT

Practical Concerns

6. Community Conferencing as Conflict Transformation. . . 107
   JOHN M. MCDONALD AND DAVID B. MOORE

7. The Psychology of Community Conferencing 123
   LAUREN ABRAMSON AND DAVID B. MOORE

8. Building Peace: The Victim Offender
   Reconciliation Program Approach
   and Its Growing Role in Communities 141
   RON CLAASSEN

9. Grossly Negligent Operation with Death Resulting:
   A Conferencing Case Study 153
   CHRIS DINNAN

10. Some Practical Examples of Restorative Justice 169
    JOHN PERRY

Assessment

11. Community Justice Sanctioning Models:
    Assessing Program Integrity 185
    GORDON BAZEMORE AND DAVID R. KARP

Concluding Vocabulary and Questions for Further
Consideration 213

About the Authors 215

Index 219

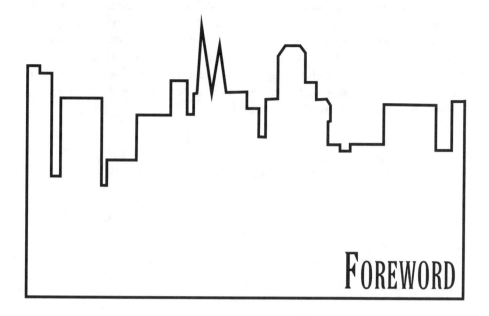

FOREWORD

W e talk a lot about communities, but what exactly is a community? You could define it as a group of people with similar traits or interests or in a specific geographical area. We all live in a community; in fact, we are part of many communities that revolve around the aspects of our daily lives—neighborhoods, work, schools, places of worship, families, friends, and clubs. Communities are enormously diverse, but they have one thing in common: they are all formed by relationships between people. The strength of a community depends on the quality of the relationships that bind it together.

When a crime is committed, it is more than just a violation of the law or an assault against a person or property—it affects the whole community. It threatens the integrity of the relationships that make up the community. For instance, the victim's faith in the community may be shaken because it failed to protect him or her from the crime. Of course, the offender loses the trust of the community because of the crime, and there is often a host of friends, neighbors, and family of the victim and the offender who are affected. All these people or communities represent vital links in a chain that are being weakened by crime.

Restorative justice deals with the damage to communities that is often not addressed by traditional law enforcement and corrections. It recognizes that many parties are injured when a crime is committed, and it attempts to repair those injuries with the participation of everyone involved, including the offender.

Repairing Communities through Restorative Justice is a collection of thoughtful essays on this alternative response to crime. Edited by John Perry, from the Vermont Department of Corrections, this book examines restorative justice from several angles—its theoretical foundations, practical applications, and assessment of its many types of programs. The book also includes vocabulary terms and questions at the end of each chapter to help the reader become more acquainted with the important themes of restorative justice. Finally, Perry provides some practical examples that give the reader vivid illustrations of restorative justice in action.

James A. Gondles, Jr., CAE
Executive Director
American Correctional Association

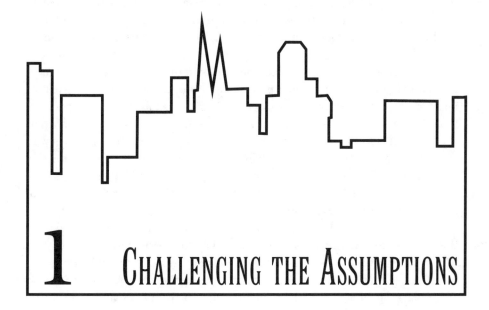

1 CHALLENGING THE ASSUMPTIONS

JOHN G. PERRY
DIRECTOR OF PLANNING
VERMONT DEPARTMENT OF CORRECTIONS
WATERBURY, VERMONT

The crime problem in America involves the fear of crime, and the lack of confidence among the citizens in the criminal justice system. That fear has created a decade of increased reliance on incarceration as the dominant response to crime, and the quadrupling of the corrections budget. Yet, the total number of crimes committed on victims in this country has been going down, steadily, for thirty years. Even the number of crimes reported to police, despite a steady diet of cops and drug dealers on television is dramatically lower. A few politicians claim credit for the decline due to the massive increases in incarceration, despite the logic (causes usually precede effects).

Nevertheless, a major source of citizen frustration is the inability to define what is being achieved by the justice system, both on an individual case basis and from the perspective of the community. As the media focus on the spectacular failures and the extremes of the normal spectrum, government is caught between overwhelming caseloads of minor criminals and the need to target resources to protect the public from the dangerous ones. In the rush to efficiency, the government bypasses the most effective agents, the community and the family, instead focusing on the individual cases that squeak the loudest.

To understand what is wrong with government, it helps to think of what we do as if it were a twenty-first century business. If business leaders wanted to improve the bottom line, they would not merely add more bells and whistles to the product. Effective businesses would look at their market and meet the market demand with whole new product lines. If we look at the justice business as a market, we can recognize that it is subject to market forces. What has been selling in the criminal justice market recently are nifty new products with catchy names like "three strikes and you're out," or names with the moral authority of a victim, like "Megan's Law."And if you think Social Security is the third rail of politics, try being "Soft on Crime!" These ideas have been selling, and legislators have been buying, but the taxpayer has to pay for all the rhetoric, and it is getting expensive.

America leads the world in many arenas in which we should take pride. But one area not worthy of pride is our leading the world in the incarceration of our citizens. We also lead the world in the number of citizens who are under direct government supervision and control. Nevertheless, the United States is spending $120 billion at last count for this imprisonment and supervision (Bureau of Justice Statistics, 1996). Two million people are in jail or prison, four million on probation or parole (Bureau of Justice Statistics, 2000).Yet, we have done this without any stated goal or any type of measure of success.

This spending and the high incarceration rate might be acceptable if we were accomplishing some purpose, unless, of course, the intended outcome is simply to do what we are doing—incarcerating 2 million human beings, and watching 4 million others. Very few other industries can create their own market.

Here is what we do now. We take a nineteen-year-old kid who is whacked out on crack who steals a $500 television set and sells it for $25 to get high but makes his buy from an undercover narc who busts him and because he does not have anyone to roll over on, he gets a year in the slammer, which costs taxpayers $25,000—for a $500 TV.

This might be somewhat tolerable if it worked. However, what is mind-boggling is that not only does it not work, it makes him worse! He is *more* likely to reoffend after a stint among real criminals than if we had just left him alone. And what about the victim? She gets to have her taxes go up to pay for him to be in prison where he gets to sit in the day room and watch TV.

In the economics of scale, for the cost of his prison term, we could buy forty computers and give them away to kids, and pay for their first year of Internet access. Here is another perspective. Say the same nineteen-year-old gets a better lawyer and pleads guilty to the burglary, but since it is his first felony, and the crime is not serious (certainly not compared to buying crack), he gets probation. When that does not work, we put him on probation, this time with mandatory treatment once a month. Then, when that does not work, we put him on probation again. When that does not work, we put him in jail for a short term, to teach him what he is facing, but since it is his first time in jail and the offenses are all nonviolent, and we are crowded, we let him out early.

This teaches him an important lesson. It teaches him that we do not care. It also teaches him that he is a victim of the system and allows him to forget about his responsibility to the victim and his community. The adversarial system (his attorney and the plea bargaining system) nearly forces him to deny responsibility to minimize consequences. In other words, he pleads guilty to something he did not do, in return for a sentence he does not deserve. This process disconnects the offender from the victim. In fact, this is intended. The adversarial system presumes that the victim or her survivors will only want vengeance and will commit further crime. The adversarial system demeans the ability of the victim, as it separates the offender from the community. Then, when the offender finally does something really serious, and hurts someone in the process, we put him in prison for a long time. When that teaches him some new skills, and he reoffends, we employ three strikes and he is out.

If we taught kindergarten the same way, we would tell you to learn how to read, once. Then, we would have you read in front of the class, and when you stumbled, we would give you the book that tells you how to read, and then when that did not work, we would give you a dictionary to look up the words you did not know. After that, when that did not work, we would hit you over the head with the dictionary. Finally, when you still did not know how to read, we would throw the book at you, and throw you out of school. So, if what we are doing so patently does not work, why on earth do we do it?

Diane Gordon[1] calls it "The Justice Juggernaut." We are now recycling two-thirds of the prison graduates back to prison. We are getting ready to recycle a third of the probationers into prison to teach them a lesson. The system feeds on its own failures.

The law of supply and demand is in operation. The problem is that there is more crime than there will ever be capacity to deal with it. We put 700,000 people in jail or prison last year, out of a reported 30 million crimes. That is just more than 2 percent of the potential market. The supply (prison) will never catch up with demand (crime). This is good news for those in the private prison business, or in a criminal justice union, but it is really bad news for those of us who have to pay for it.

What do we do about it? Restorative justice presents part of the answer. This book on restorative justice and other writing that is beginning to appear in professional circles is a start.

The current American system of justice is based on a retributive model that focuses on meting out punishment to offenders in proportion to the harm that they have perpetrated on victims or on the social order. It presumes that punishment is justified and is the right thing to do, even though we all know that it is not.

For justice to be just, it must be certain, swift, fair, transparent, and predictable. However, for justice to be affordable, it also must be efficient and adequate, and it must deceive the public into believing it is working. The best way to do that is to be totally uncertain, unfair, and to accomplish this all in secret. We do it best in prison.

Prison is a terrible place to be. Prison not only ruins your life and your identity, it ruins the lives of all of your family, and if we imprison enough people, it ruins your community, your culture, and your friends. If we wanted to create criminals, we could do no better than to take an angry, vulnerable young man and throw him into a pit with other angry, somewhat older, bitter men. In the science of criminal risk prediction, the risk factor is called "pro-criminal associates."[2]

Thus, the retributive model is a zero-sum game.[3] It presumes that somehow, the punishment the offenders "get" is somehow equivalent to the harm that has been done to the victims. It presumes that the offenders and the victims will never interact again, and even if they do, everything will be hunky-dory because "they got what they deserved" and besides, they are on an electronic monitor, and we will catch them right away if they harm the victims (again).

Despite this set of beliefs about retributive justice, we know that you do not get behaviors you want using punishment.[4] You do, however, get behaviors that you may well *not* want. What you get is resentment against the authority that imposed the punishment and if there is any connection to the victim, it is anger for having testified against the offender.

Nevertheless, for the past 200 years, the fundamental purpose of sentencing and corrections has been retributive. For the past 100 years, judges have had only two choices in sentencing: to punish or not to punish. For the past twenty-five years, we have known that not only does punishment not work, but that it also makes most offenders *more* likely to reoffend. We have attempted to ameliorate the effects of punishment with rehabilitative strategies, and with alternative forms of punishment in the community. None of these has been spectacularly successful in reducing the demand for incarceration.

Sometimes it is instructive to look at things from a fresh perspective. The American Kennel Club has known for years that you do not get your dog to sit up and beg by beating him. What you get instead is a dog that is afraid, who messes on the rug, and who does not protect you from a burglar. If you want the dog to behave in certain ways, you get there by positively reinforcing successive approximations. Why do American correctional experts not know that?

Punishment not only does not work, but it makes most people worse.[5] If you do something to me, I will want to do something back. If you are more powerful than I, I will learn that power is what gets you your way. What I will want to do is to hurt you as you have hurt me. If I cannot hurt you because you are too powerful, I will hurt someone else who is not as powerful as I am.

Thus, the premise of the retributive model is wrong. In addition, the practice is wrong, too. We have based our progress as a civilization (some might quibble with that characterization) on the rule of law, with each ensuing decision based on the precedents of decisions made before. Then, under the retributive model, if you are the victim of a crime, in the American system of justice, you are on your own. The system is designed for the state and what the state feels like doing or affording. So, if you are an unhappy consumer of the American justice (and I know you are[6]) have I got a deal for you.

A new product is on the justice market that is different from the current justice product line. It has many names, including restorative justice, community justice, reparative justice, and reinvented probation. Chief Justice Yazzi of the Navajo Nation says he does not know what all the fuss is about. In his nation, they just call it "Justice."

It is not an accident that these "new" forms of justice are coming to light from aboriginal peoples (Inuit, Maori, and Navajo). Aboriginal peoples are closer to our tribal heritage. Human beings are not designed to function in anonymous cities of glass and steel living among huge numbers of strangers. We are social animals, tribal animals, who were designed to survive best in small hunter-gatherer bands, and who function in a clan structure of related kin.

Additionally, it is not a surprise that these new forms of justice also are emerging from aboriginal peoples in the former colonies of the British Empire. Our Anglo-Saxon forebears conquered by William had a Southern European form of justice imposed on us. This Roman law was designed to be imposed on subject peoples. Anglo-Saxon law[7] was based on the Dane law (itself an import through conquest, but from the Northern Europeans, otherwise known as Barbarians), which was a village and clan-based law, where a crime was an offense against the victims and their family and created a debt that had to be paid by the offenders and their family.

The Norman rule of law imposed the idea that a crime was an offense against the king (since all conquered peoples were the property of the throne, then damage done to the king's property required compensation of the king's treasury) instead of the victim. The Angles and the Saxons spent the next thousand years (almost) trying to restrain the power of the king and to take back their government. This is what the American revolutionaries did in 1776 (except that our founding fathers forgot their tribal roots, because they were steeped in English jurisprudence).

So, this new model of justice is, in reality, a very old model. Francis Schweigert, in his essay in this book, describes some of its philosophical and moral roots, not only in European tradition but also in the tribalism of less "civilized" peoples. Much has been said about the Old Testament jurisprudential roots of the retributive model. Schweigert examines the deeper spiritual tests that create the moral grounding of empowerment, in the establishment of the moral standard of the community and in the redemptive modality of restorative justice as rooted in the same tradition, but stronger.

Until now, justice in America has not been *about* the victim. It has not been *about* the community. It has been about offenders and their relation to the law. The founding fathers did a good job of protecting the offender from the power of the state, but they left out the community, and they left out the victim.

This role of the community was shown clearly when, in 1995, a group of East African jurists visited Vermont for a week to look at our public defense system. We made a presentation to them about our reparative boards, which were just beginning. One of the jurists, the Chief Justice of the Supreme Court of Tanzania, asked to spend the day with us. In the wide-ranging discussion of justice and what we were trying to accomplish with reparative boards, he told us that when they were first designing their justice system after they had achieved independence, they were intent on doing a better job than had been done to them by their colonial masters. So, they drafted laws which were more punitive, built harsher prisons, mandated longer sentences.

Then, one day he was visiting his tribe in the bush when an offender who had served a long sentence in prison came home. Before the offender was allowed to come into the village, he had to undergo the tribal justice ritual. "It was as if," the Chief Justice said, "nothing had happened. Nothing that the state had done was of any consequence to the community at all. The crime was not resolved until the offender had undergone the ritual of the tribe and made amends for his crime to the people he had offended."

Thus, restorative justice is about reciprocity. It is about the fundamental human characteristic of not wanting to hurt people we know. It is about the glue that holds all human societies together—doing favors for one another. Every human being is hardwired for reciprocal behavior. If you do something for me, I will feel a sense of obligation and kinship for you, and I will likely return the favor. If you help me with my math homework when I need it, I will help you with lunch money when you need it. If you do a big favor for me, I will be indebted to you, and when you need help, you can call on me. If, for example, you fall into the river and I throw you a life buoy and pull you ashore, you are likely to remember me when I am in trouble. It is even more dramatic, say, if your two-year-old daughter runs out into the middle of the street in front of a sixteen-wheeler that has lost its brakes and I dash out and grab her and roll out of the way just in the nick of time. In this case, it is very likely that you and I will become lifelong friends, and that the next time I need help, I can count on you, up to and including assistance on a mortgage.

Restorative justice is about making things right, repairing the damage, making amends, returning the stolen, fixing the broken, and healing the wounds. It is about reestablishing the offender and the community and the victim into "right relation" with one another. This requires that the community, victims, and offenders value the process and have the capacity and authority to accomplish justice. This requires a new definition of community. Instead of thinking about community simply as a place where government works, Paul McCold and Benjamin Wachtel describe it in Chapter 3 as a reconceptualized structure of relationship and support.

Restorative justice is not about offenders and the law they have broken. It is about offenders and the harm done to victims, and the damage done to the social contract. It is about repairing that damage, and restoring the victim and the offender to functioning. It is about "healing the breaches in reciprocity."[8] In Chapter 4, John Braithwaite furthers the discussion of the empowerment of community discussing the balance between shaming and punishing, focusing the power of the community on the harm done, not on what the community will do to the offender.

The outcomes from restorative justice are fundamentally different from the outcomes from the retributive model. Howard Zehr's chart below contrasting the retributive and restorative system[9] is a starting point. Restorative justice works in different ways from retributive justice and achieves different ends. The outcomes for victim, offender, and community are each different, though interdependent.

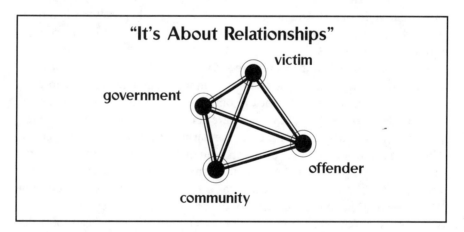

The Process

Restorative justice processes put the participants in the crime in the center—and government in the background. The processes, whether it is a community board structure, a family group conference, a workplace meeting, or a neighborhood problem-solving gathering, share several features. They are structured processes that ensure everyone who wants to participate is heard.

They focus on understanding the harm done, repairing the harm, making amends, and taking responsibility. The process is interactive, and nonadversarial. Each participant affects, and is affected by, all of the other participants.

The methods are not new. They involve taking due deliberation of the wrong done, and righting the wrong. The hallmark of restorative justice is *inefficiency*. Restorative justice processes take the time to discuss, consider, and interact. They are human emotional processes which are difficult both to describe and to proceduralize. In Chapter 5, Gordon Bazemore and Mark Umbreit describe four of the models, each of which share the principles of restoring the victim, the offender, their families, their networks, and the community in which they live to a right relation, each doing it in different ways.

1. The Victim

Being a victim is an intensely emotional state. Even for the most minor of crimes, it can be so upsetting that it can be paralyzing. The effect of suffering a loss of property, a violation of space, or a trauma to self or loved one triggers deep responses in all humans. We all move from the loss or trauma to shock, anger, denial, blame, transference, and revenge. These emotions are strong, and universal.

In addition, the effect on the victim is magnified by the impact of the victimization on others. The stigma of being known to be a victim is itself strong. Knowing a person who is the victim of a crime is emotion ridden. Punishment is the most uncivil response we have developed.[10] Yet, to recognize the urge to punish and not to succumb to it is only possible when there is an effective alternative. Shifting the focus from the offender to the victim is an effective strategy.

The outcomes for the victim are at the center of the restorative process. By focusing on the harm done to the victim and community, the restorative process is about the victim, not the offender. The focus is on what we are going to do for the victim, not what we are going to do to the offender. Victims get to tell their story and to describe the harm done, from their perspective. This changes the definition of the harm from that described by the state in the criminal charge to that which is real to the victim. The sensitivity of the process allows the victim's concerns for safety or fear from retaliation to be met. The confirmation of the community can provide reconciliation.

By telling the story, the victim gets to be heard. The process of telling and being heard is *reification*, making the event real and the loss recognized. The community reaffirms the wrong done and validates the harm. The victim receives empathy from the social network and support from those who are contiguous. The harm is then the subject of the process. Repairing the damage done, returning the value lost, restoring the victims to their former state of well-being, when it is possible (recognizing that it may not be possible), and

Summer Home

The crime was vandalism. Four teenagers were snowmobiling and came upon an unoccupied summer home on a lake in Eden, Vermont. They broke in, lit a fire in the stove, ate some food, found the wine cellar, got drunk, and trashed the place. They did not just trash it, they destroyed it. The wine that did not get drunk got smashed, they defecated on the carpet, smashed the pottery, broke the windows, used the antique furniture for kindling, and what they did not break they threw into the lake.

The judge sentenced all four boys to see a reparative board. The victim came to all four meetings. She drove up from Connecticut each time. She listened to their story and told each of them what the place meant to her, and what the things were that they had destroyed. Each of the boys' stories told the same tale. They were bored, broke, and idle, and it just got out of hand. One of the boys told her he understood what it was like to be a victim. He told of having been "ripped off" when somebody broke into his trailer and stole his stereo.

When the victim was asked if she had received any satisfaction from the process, she said to each of them, "When this first happened, I wanted you to mow my lawn once a week—with your teeth. I don't want that any more. Now, all I want is for you to learn from this, and go and have a good life."

making amends for the losses suffered is all value-adding activity. It is not destructive activity.

When the offender acknowledges responsibility, the victim has the opportunity to make the crime into an event attached to a person, rather than a disembodied evil. In the presence of the community, the safety from retaliation feared is mitigated. The result can be that the victim is reaffirmed in her safety and can feel competent and in control of the occasion. When offenders tell their side of the story, the victim can discover that the malevolence is not personal, or that the severity was unintentional, and that the offenders know they have done wrong.

When the offender apologizes and offers amends, the victim is empowered to judge the sincerity and adequacy of the offer, and with the support of the community, can choose to accept the offering. This interaction can help restore the victim as an empowered member of the community and lead to reconciliation. Justice for the offender is justice for the victim and *vice versa*.

Restoration cannot always and often should not occur instantaneously. Those who look upon restorative justice as instant gratification, easily achieved in a couple of hours, mistake the beginning of the process for its totality. In a recent case in a local court, the offender had killed his best friend in a car accident that was the result of negligent driving. The victim's wife had just given birth, and they were out celebrating. As a result of mediation and pretrial negotiation, the offender offered to provide child support, as if the child were his own, for the entire period of minority, through college. This is a twenty-year obligation, at least, and the offender acknowledged that he could never repair the damage he had done to the child, his mother, and his friend, but he could make amends. The sincerity of the offer, and its scope, are far more valuable to the survivors than any punishment would have been. Contrast this with the likely sentence the offender would have received. In Vermont, the typical sentence for a driving accident fatality is five-to-fifteen years, suspended, with one year to serve. This sentence serves no one. It is a compromise. It is an abject waste.

2. The Offender

The offenders owe a series of debts, not only to the law, but first and primarily to the victim and the victim's family, to their own family, and to their neighbors and community. The law is an attempt to quantify these obligations and regularize the responses to criminal behavior. However, the retributive system of justice, in its efforts to mete out punishment fairly, ignores in large measure, the obligations of the offender to both the victim and the community. Restorative justice focuses on those debts and on taking responsibility for those debts. The debt to the victim is described and defined mainly by the victim, but it is also defined by the community and its moral standard.

The offenders' recognition of the obligations they owe is the first goal of the restorative process. It begins with reaching an understanding of the harm done. Each of the participants describes the events, from his or her own perspective. Offenders get to hear the differences in the effects of the crime on the different people involved. They get to experience the impact of their behavior on the victims, and they get to hear the concern of the community over the risk their behavior poses to them. They also get to be heard by the victims, and by the community. Hearing each other's versions of events moves the process forward, toward a shared definition of the harm done.

The next step for the offender is to acknowledge responsibility for the identified harm done. This step is the most difficult for most offenders, and it is the step on which the adversarial justice process spends the least amount of time (though it has the most procedural safeguards). The American system of justice is, by and large, not a system for determining the guilt of the offender and then meting out punishment commensurate with the offense. In Vermont, for example, some 97 percent of the felony convictions and 99 percent of the misdemeanor convictions are achieved by plea. The process of plea negotiation cannot help but result in the exchange of truths for expedience. The adversarial process mandates that the offender deny responsibility to minimize consequences. This results in the homogenization of justice, with little regard for the particulars of the behaviors and their consequences.

In the restorative process, the offender is given the opportunity to take more responsibility in the light of the emotional definition of the harm done. This is a difficult outcome to quantify. It is measured, after it happens, in the descriptions of satisfaction achieved by the participants. During the process, however, it is measured by the emotional state of the people in the room. The degree to which the process informs the offenders may be inferred by the alacrity and diligence with which they accomplish the tasks of reparation and restoration.

The next step, reintegration, is like the other steps, contingent on the interaction with the community and the victim. The offender cannot morally reenter society in full and good standing until and unless the victim is restored. In many cases, this cannot happen overnight. In nearly all cases, it requires that the offender engage in some activities to make amends, to repair the damage done, and make inroads into restoring the victim. The demonstration of sincerity and remorse is not merely by words, but by creating and adding value.

3. The Community

The role of the community in restorative justice, whether in conferencing, reparative boards, in community courts, community prosecution, or youth courts, is to establish the boundaries for the community, to set the moral norms. The community provides the forum in which justice can occur. Justice occurs when the social contract gets signed. One is supposed to have learned, through growing up in a culture or going to civics classes or from your family, that one has implicitly already signed the contract but no one ever lets you see the document. There is a lot of fine print in the social contract, and for those for whom the contract has been a bad deal, it is difficult to comprehend the benefits accruing to being a party. Restorative justice is about making the contract explicit.

The contract can be made between two individuals who have a conflict (one victim, one offender), and this contract can be mediated. That can result in an agreement between people, which is enforced by the parties themselves. So long as they are accountable to each other and to the community, there is less need for external governmental accountability. The face-to-face encounter and negotiation, either with help or by itself, creates a level of reciprocal binding. However, the more public the process, the more the community is involved in the informal social controls that enforce the agreement.

The definition of community in restorative justice is very broad. As Paul McCold and Benjamin Wachtel say, "community is not a place." One of the common threads among community restorative and aboriginal justice processes is the reliance on elders. The role of the community in the implementation of a restorative process begins by providing the forum for the initial meeting, and participating as elders (not necessarily by virtue of age) and keepers of the community. The forum allows the participation and hearing of the conflict, and the ritual and ceremony for sanctioning the process. The process can take many forms, from a simple negotiated settlement to mediation, facilitation, circle, conference, or board. The forum provides the place, and the community provides the moral and social authority.

The community owes a debt to the victims, for not having protected them from the crime. Providing the means for the offender to repair the damage caused is one way of meeting the obligation, and ensuring that the contract is fulfilled is another. But in a larger sense, the community owes the victims the opportunity to become wholly restored, completely apart from the offenders and their involvement. One of the bitterest consequences of the retributive state system of justice is that victims are set apart from the community and labeled, shamed, and excluded from reintegration, too. By acknowledging the reality of the harm done, and by taking responsibility for the breach in reciprocity with the victim, the community begins to repay the debt it owed to the victim.

The community also owes a debt to the offenders for not having provided the appropriate opportunities to their family for nourishing and supporting their success. Offenders may not have had significant opportunity for success and may not have been allowed the appropriate supports and encouragement. This may be a harsh judgment, but from the perspective of the ecosystem, distributive justice imbalances are at the root of the disconnect between the offender and the community.

The restorative response occurs face-to-face. If anonymity is a root permission for criminality, then one remedy, probably the most important, is to resolve it publicly.[11]

Letter from a Board Member in Springfield

"I have been on the board for two years now with a fairly stable presence of volunteers who serve. I am making no special arguments or pleas of perfection for our group of volunteers, but from the beginning I have been approached in town by people who have been through the Springfield Board. They have either shaken hands or found some positive conversation to share. In fact, in many of the cases there was an assumption (perhaps) that there was a type of bond between us. I think that this is remarkable. When I started, I was dreading seeing the people in town that would have gone through the system. I thought it might be embarrassing for both parties.

I would guess that when out and about in town, I do not present an easily approachable figure, and certainly was initially reticent about dealing with our clients. I no longer behave in this manner. Other board members have experienced the same thing as I have so I remain convinced that we are at least offering an integration back into the community. Something good is going on."

The best outcomes for the community occur when the moral standards are reaffirmed, when the victim and the offender are returned to a useful and productive life in good standing. When this occurs, the costs, social and fiscal, are minimized. The process of achieving these goals is both simple and complex. It is simple to do, and very hard to describe because it is an emotional transformation, in a human encounter. John MacDonald and David Moore, in Chapter 6, discuss conferencing in Australia as a transformative process, and they compare the various restorative programs in America. They discuss the difficulty they have as experts in providing definition to what are essentially natural democratic processes.

Since many of the prototypes for restorative justice are aboriginal or "primitive," places like Vermont where people can be characterized as far more intimate and less civilized than most modern Americans living in cities, it is often a criticism of restorative processes that they cannot work in the modern urban environment. In Chapter 7, Lauren Abramson and David Moore discuss that transformative process as a basic human psychological process and describe the operation of conferencing in an urban setting.

4. The System (Courts, Criminal Justice, Law, and Politics)

Restorative justice will not replace the need for prisons to house the unrepentant, truly violent and dangerous offenders. Restorative justice, however, can replace the felt need among the public, the legislature, and the criminal justice system to use prison simply to punish offenders who have broken

---

Title 28, Vermont Statutes Annotated
Section 2a, Restorative Justice

"State Policy: It is the policy of this State that principles of Restorative Justice be included in shaping how the criminal justice system responds to persons charged with or convicted of criminal offenses. The policy goal is a community response to a person's wrongdoing at its earliest onset, and a type and intensity of sanction tailored to each instance of wrongdoing."

"Policy Objectives

(1) Resolve conflicts and disputes by means of a non-adversarial community process.

(2) Repair damage caused by criminal acts to communities in which they occur, and to address wrongs inflicted on individual victims.

(3) Reduce the risk of an offender committing a more serious crime in the future, that would require a more intensive and more costly sanction, such as incarceration."

---

the law. What is more important, prisons can be sources of restoration, too, if the premise of the institution is shifted, such that the offender's obligation to the victim is paramount and controlling.

The primary role of the justice system in restorative processes is to allow these processes to occur and to sanction their results. A secondary role is to provide an appellate response for parties to the conflict resolution who are not satisfied by the outcome.

The role of the legislature, at least in Vermont, has been to study the outcomes, listen to the participants, and provide the authority. The 2000 session of the General Assembly amended the corrections' statute as shown on page 13.

Victim Restoration, Offender Reintegration

When the victim gets a say in what the offender will do, and the community participates in validating the agreements reached, the victim has a far greater chance of being reintegrated as a whole and restored participant. When the offender does accomplish the amends and makes reparation of the damage done, the victim can choose to be restored. In all regards, the victim can find meaning in the event and hope for the future. If all these are in place, then reconciliation can be achieved.

In the reparative probation program, ordinary citizens of Vermont make sentencing decisions about adult criminal offenders from their community. Board members meet with offenders and victims, resolving their disputes by providing the offenders with the opportunity to acknowledge their wrongdoing, apologize to their victim, and make amends to their community. The offenders are sentenced by the court, having pled guilty to a nonviolent crime. The sentence is then suspended, pending their completion of a reparative agreement.

The boards are focused on the minor crimes—on fixing the "broken windows" in James Q. Wilson's and George Kelling's phrase (*The Atlantic*, 263: 46-57, 1982)—the crimes that are too petty to be dealt with by the system, and which are not only the crimes that diminish the quality of life, but also are committed by the criminals who learn that we do not care enough about their behavior to do something about it. They are the crimes that often are committed by our children and young people. Reparative boards give citizens an opportunity to do something about their neighborhoods and their communities.

By involving citizens directly in decision making about individual cases, they are forced to look at the offenders not as strangers, not as numbers, and not as monsters. The offenders are forced to confront the reality of their offense and its impact on the community and their victims. This confrontation, with a restorative outcome, shifts the paradigm from punishment to reintegration. The offender is held accountable, the victim is restored, and the

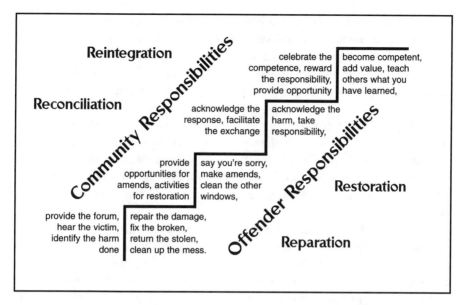

community is repaired. Perhaps even more important, the dispute is resolved by the community, and the community is empowered.

The programs in restorative justice are not fixed in granite. They learn from one another and adapt and evolve. In Chapter 8, Ron Claassen describes the Victim Offender Reconciliation Program (VORP) in San Francisco, which has been in operation for years as a reconciliation process between the offender and the victim as the principals of the conflict. He notes at the end of his chapter that observing the New Zealand model has caused the VORP to restructure to involve conferencing techniques.

Restorative justice is not simply a separate alternative way to resolve conflict. It also can be an integral part of the traditional justice process. Chris Dinnan, in Chapter 9, describes a single case study that involves the recent use in Vermont of conferencing as an alternative technique for presentence investigations.

If crime is a result of anonymity, the solution to crime is to put people face to face.

Signing the Social Contract: Thoughts on the Hypotheses for Restorative Justice

In evolutionary terms, does the human propensity for reciprocity in small social networks within contiguous boundaries break down stereotypical responses to strangers and out-labeled populations, and allow positive value-adding demonstrations of making amends to the victim and community? Does this, in turn, create the opportunity for offenders to reestablish the social contract?

In terms of neurological biochemistry, does the public acknowledgment of wronging behavior in the presence of valued peers and the victim create a change in brain chemistry that is adaptive? Does ritual reinforcement of that acknowledgment in terms of public restitution and mediated communication between disputants in a crime create behavioral habituation become self-reinforcing?

Or, from an economic perspective, is punishment cost effective? Does inflicting a penalty (loss or suffering of a person, rights, or property) on the offender of a crime make any difference on recidivism? If so, at what cost? This is in contrast to affording the offender the opportunity to repair the damage done by the crime, to make amends to the victim, and to learn how to avoid reoffense.

To put it more plainly, providing the community with the opportunity to see and hear offenders' stories of the circumstances and emotions of a crime has a positive outcome. This is especially the issue if such stories are accompanied by the victims' stories of the impact and loss created by the crime, and if community members are allowed to define reparative activities for the offender to make amends and restore the victim, and then offenders are allowed to repair the damage done to community and victims, experience the impact of their behavior on others, and learn ways to avoid criminal responses to life problems, reporting back to the community board on lessons learned. Now, how can you implement some of these principles in your community?

This book attempts to provide some of the answers. Others will be based on experiments that may be relevant to other individuals' settings. In five or ten years, the discussion of these issues should take on new questions based on broader experience in these various settings. The final chapter, by Gordon Bazemore and David Karp, addresses the assessment of what is becoming a movement, and defines the parameters for evaluation. Assessing the efficacy of restorative justice will require new paradigms for evaluation, too.

Endnotes

[1] Diane Gordon. 1990. *The Justice Juggernaut*. New Brunswick, New Jersey: Rutgers University Press.

[2] Don Andrews and James Bonta. 1994. *The Psychology of Criminal Conduct*. Cincinnati: Anderson.

[3] Robert Wright. 2000. *Nonzero: The Logic of Human Destiny*. New York: Pantheon.

[4] Paul Gendreau. 1996. Principles of Effective Intervention with Offenders. In Alan T. Harland, ed. *Choosing Correctional Options that Work*. Thousand Oaks, California: Sage.

[5] Paul Gendreau, op cit.

[6] Shulman, Ronca, and Bucuvalas, Inc. for the Council on State Governments, *What Do We Want (And What Are We Getting) from the Criminal Justice System?* August,

1999. Seventy-five percent of the public in eleven East coast states believe the entire system of criminal justice needs total revamping.

7 Paul Halsall, *Medieval Sourcebook*, "The Anglo-Saxon Dooms 560-975," www.fordham.edu/halsall/sbook-law/560-975dooms.html.

8 Bill Page. 2002. *Natural Democracy.* Unpublished manuscript.

9 Howard Zehr. 1990. *Changing Lenses.* Scotsdale, Pennsylvania: Herald Press.

10 Michel Foucault. 1978. *Discipline and Punish.* New York: Pantheon.

11 MacArthur Foundation. 1999. Project of Human Development in Chicago Neighborhoods, q.v. Robert J. Sampson and Dawn Jeglum Bartusch, "Attitudes toward Crime, Police, and the Law: Individual and Neighborhood Differences," National Institute of Justice Research Preview, June.

Questions

1. Why are citizens frustrated at their inability to define what is being achieved by the justice system? What can be done about this?

2. Contrast the adversarial/retributive system with the restorative justice system in terms of outcome for the criminal offender.

3. What does the author mean by "we know that you do not get behaviors you want using punishment?"

4. Explain the following statements:

   • Restorative justice is about reciprocity.

   • The hallmark of restorative justice is inefficiency.

   • The outcomes for the victim are at the center of the restorative process.

   • The offenders owe a series of debts, not only to the law, but first and primarily to the victim and the victim's family, to their own family, and to their neighbors and community.

   • By involving citizens directly in decision making about individual cases, they are forced to look at the offenders not as strangers, not as numbers, and not as monsters. The offenders are forced to confront the reality of their offense and its impact on the community and their victims.

MORAL AND PHILOSOPHICAL FOUNDATIONS OF RESTORATIVE JUSTICE

2

FRANCIS J. SCHWEIGERT, PH.D.
COMMUNITY LIAISON
NORTHWEST AREA FOUNDATION
ST. PAUL, MINNESOTA

Introduction

Restorative justice did not arise as a centralized or coordinated move-ment, but as a series of innovations and experiments in widely varying places and circumstances—all sharing some common assumptions and principles. The moral and philosophical foundations of restorative justice lie in these social practices and practical experiments. They include the following: mediation and nonviolent conflict resolution, the rediscovery of restitution, community development and empowerment, community justice in non-European cultures, and biblical justice.

Although unraveling the precise historical development of even one of these sources would be difficult, it is possible to discern among them the moral and philosophical understandings that give coherence and direction to this movement. These understandings, embodied in restorative practices, are the guiding and grounding elements in a philosophy or theory of restorative justice. In this chapter, the most influential streams of restorative practice and thought are traced back to their origins, to highlight the key concepts that guided reformers and contributed to the rapid growth of the restorative justice movement in the United States.

Social Practices and Restorative Justice

Mediation and Nonviolent Conflict Resolution

There is a clear continuity between the wide use of mediation in marriage and family counseling, social work, labor disputes, tenant disputes, workplace conflicts, political negotiations, and criminal cases. In all these cases, the parties directly involved in the dispute work together to create a solution that they see as just, and the mediator's role is to provide a process and social space for the conflicting parties to do this work.

Early experiments in victim-offender conferencing built on practices of mediation and nonviolent conflict resolution (Wright, 1991, pp. 53-54). Thus, victim-offender conferencing provides a process of nonviolent conflict resolution in which victims can express how they have been hurt, offenders can take responsibility for their offenses, and victims and offenders together can take responsibility in determining how to remedy the harm done—and even to promote the well-being of the community beyond what it was before.

The mediation process is designed and conducted to be constructive, voluntary, and fair—key characteristics that make this an empowering experience for participants. The process is an exercise of power by participants themselves to create something good from a painful situation or event. It is voluntary and noncoercive because participants choose to participate and settlements are decided by consensus. The process is fair because the mediator assures that both parties will be able to participate equally: voicing their interests, expressing their fears and hopes, and helping to discern the true source of conflict and seeking real solutions.

Empowerment in mediation is made possible through the exercise of freedom within clear and clearly accepted constraints. This is not an imaginary standard of pure individual freedom; the influences of institutions and persons on the lives and decisions of individuals are far too complex to be reduced to such a standard. Rather, freedom is grounded in a process in which all participation depends on a willingness to accept the boundaries of the process and contribute to its success. These boundaries become the vehicle for exercising power within the process. To listen without interrupting is a constraint on freedom, yet within the egalitarian dynamics of negotiation and consensus-building, this constraint frees both parties to speak and listen more carefully, to be understood and to understand, not forced to contribute but drawn into contributing to a shared solution.

Thus, victim-offender conferencing is bound by neutrality in its process but governed by freedom in mutual understanding and the construction of solutions. In this way, it combines the moral authority of law with the moral authority of individual conscience and community norms. The law binds with a kind of rigid universality because it must apply equally to all. This quality influences the rules governing the mediation process. In contrast, the recognition of harm and the construction of solutions call for a keen sensitivity to the immediate circumstances and the flexibility necessary in all the complexities of social existence. The moral authority invoked in this effort must go beyond law to conscience, translating understanding into obligations and consequently into action according to the exercise of individual choice. What makes restorative practices so powerful is this moral grounding, its grip on the conscience of participants—on their choice to be there to try to do something good in these unique circumstances.

The Rediscovery of Restitution

Restitution is a prominent element in many restorative agreements, replacing fines or other penalties to define the offender's obligation in response to crime. Although seen as innovative today, this direct accountability to victims requiring the offender to repair or replace what was damaged or lost in the crime is the rediscovery of practices common in the West since ancient Greece and Rome. Daniel Van Ness notes that Roman law in 449 B.C. was based on repayment to victims, and the Laws of Ethelbert in 600 A.D. articulated detailed reparation schedules for various levels of crime to restore order and peace without recourse to revenge (Van Ness, 1989, p. 2). Aristotle defines this in the *Nichomachean Ethics* (Book V) as "rectifactory justice," restoring social equality by taking away unfair gain from violations of contracts and restoring losses to the victims. In restorative practices, however, this notion of corrective or rectifying justice is extended beyond reparations to incorporate broader possibilities of restoration. Wright credits Albert Eglash with developing the theoretical basis of this broader notion of restitution (Wright, 1991, p. 32).

Eglash defines restitution as a response to crime by contrasting it with reparation in four ways: (1) reparation is a financial obligation, restitution is any constructive act; (2) reparation is limited in its extent, restitution is creative and unlimited; (3) reparation is court-determined, restitution is guided, self-determined behavior; and (4) reparation is an individual act, restitution can have a group basis (Eglash, 1958, p. 619).

Four key notions of restorative justice are embedded in Eglash's notion of "creative restitution." First, by a *constructive* sanction he means "an offender giving something of himself," the action is nonpunitive and open to a broader meaning than simply payment of money. Second, a *creative and unlimited* sanction takes account of the nature of the offense and the kind of damage it inflicted on the victim. It can go beyond simply returning or repairing property, to reconciling the victim and offender, and even beyond reconciliation to social improvement.

"Creative restitution requires that a situation be left better than before an offense was committed . . . beyond what any law or court requires, beyond what friends and family expect, beyond what a victim asks, beyond what conscience or superego demands." Third, the sanction is *self-determined* by the offender, with the help of "a skillful guide." This kind of sanction can remove the stigma attached to criminal behavior and provide a means of personal growth extending far beyond the immediate situation of crime. Fourth, the sanction can be determined and carried out by a *group*, providing a way for offenders to "seek out and to help others in the same boat" (Eglash, 1958, pp. 620-621).

Restitution at its best places offenders in activities valued by their communities, so they can be seen as potential assets rather than as threats or merely a drain on resources. The hinge on which this distinction turns is human dignity. Human dignity, as evident in restorative practices, does not arise merely from reflection on abstract definitions of individual existence above all experience—the person as an end in himself or herself (Kant, 1956/1785, p. 95). Dignity as evident in restorative practices arises when the person is included and valued as a member and a contributor to the social whole.

In Sioux Falls, South Dakota, a Habitat for Humanity project brought ten high school students and ten men from the local prison together to renovate three houses in a low-income neighborhood. The men affirmed the dignity of the youth by respectfully teaching them skills with hammers, saws, sanders, and paint; the youth affirmed the dignity of the men by respectfully learning. The dignity of both groups was affirmed by local leaders who treated them as valued members of the community and appreciated their contribution to the neighborhood. In leaving the work site to return to prison, one of the men paused to look at the work they had done and remarked how good it felt to have done something good that he could remember and point to in the future.

Abstract notions of human dignity would be irrelevant—indeed, impossible to conceive—apart from social circumstances that realize the value of persons as meriting respect. The act of respect is a moral duty because of what it creates socially: the possibility for persons to act on behalf of the group. Eglash's criteria for restitution as constructive, creative, and self-determined sanctions acted on as a group reflect this active respect for persons as contributing members.

Community Development and Empowerment

Community justice was proposed by community organizers in the 1970s as part of a larger project of community empowerment and community development. A critical moment in this movement occurred in Pittsburgh in 1973, in a meeting of "Richard Danzig, who was interested in community moots; Michael Lowy, an anthropologist who had recently returned from research on urban moots in Ghana and Paul Wahrhaftig, who was involved in community organizing and bail reform action for the American Friends Service Committee" (Harrington and Merry, 1988, p.718). Experiments in popular justice in Portugal and later in Chile and Cuba supported the notion of criminal justice reform as a way to empower local communities in a process of social transformation (pp. 715-716).

The cross-fertilization of ideas suggested a form of community justice entirely independent of the criminal justice system, organized and governed at the local level by community volunteers (Wright, 1991). Ideally, members of the community would voluntarily bring their disputes to the community's local justice committee or board. The goal of community justice, simply stated, is to "promote [a] just society in which power is more evenly distributed" (Wahrhaftig, 1981, p. 101). Harrington and Merry distinguish three different ways to justify and realize the redistribution: (1) improving access to justice by delivering dispute resolution services in the local community; (2) transforming society by establishing a new basis for justice in the community rather than in the state; and (3) empowering individuals through processes that contribute to their growth and development in community rather than employing processes which merely punish (Harrington and Merry, 1988, pp. 714-16).

Strong theoretical support for this effort appeared in Nils Christie's pivotal article, "Conflicts as Property" (1977). Christie proposes that fear of conflict in communities is motivating the delegation of conflict resolution to outsiders—treatment professionals, lawyers, and criminologists. This constitutes the theft of a valuable resource for individual growth and community development, stealing conflicts that "ought to be used, and become useful, for those originally involved in the conflict" (p. 1). He cites appreciatively the example of community resolution of conflict in Tanzania, where the whole community gathers to witness, assist, and reinforce the resolution of a dispute between members of the village.

This is in contrast to Scandinavian (and typically Western) pattern of relocating criminal justice in administrative capital cities, separate administrative buildings, and courtrooms which are unfamiliar and foreign-feeling to all who enter them—except to the professionals who specialize in this specialized and bewildering administration of justice. The Western system not only segregates conflict spatially and socially from the community where it originates, it also silences the principal figures—the victim and offender. Even when and if they are present, the victim and the offender sit passively while their representatives, who are specialists, speak and carry primary responsibility for their cases. The system isolates offenders from their communities, encourages dependence on professionals rather than community resources and capacities for problem-solving, encourages offenders to perceive and use the system as a game, and results in offenders being recycled through the system indefinitely while costs escalate.

Christie redefines conflict as "*potential for activity, for participation . . . as property that ought to be shared*" (Christie, 1977, pp. 7, 11, emphasis in original). Admittedly, he writes, "conflicts might kill, but too little of them might paralyze" (p. 1). Communities are robbed of opportunities to clarify norms, victims are robbed of opportunities to confront offenders and the satisfaction of seeing remorse and receiving compensation, and offenders are robbed of the responsibility to admit guilt and act to remedy the harm they have done. Offenders may be "perfectly willing to give away their property right to the conflict," Christie notes, but "the question is more: are we willing to let them give it away" (p. 9, emphasis in original). He proposes an outline for neighborhood courts that keep conflict in communities as a valuable form of property in short supply.

The interest in community justice over the last three decades is more a recovery than an innovation, returning to restitution and community justice after four centuries of specialization and centralization in criminal justice. Specialization occurred as royal justice replaced local justice and professional expertise replaced local knowledge. Criminal justice became a scientific endeavor, embodying the Enlightenment's "confidence in the ability of human reason to penetrate to the essential truth of physical and social conditions, thus making them amenable to rational control" (Boyne and Rattansi, 1990, p. 3). This Enlightenment theory of criminal justice assumed that the essential truth of criminal activity could be uncovered and that rationally formulated measures of punishment could be applied in accord with a precise knowledge of the individual offender, directed to his or her repentance and reform (Foucault, 1977, p. 125). Centralization was part of the gradual erosion of the political authority of towns and cities—of communities—to locate authority in the autonomous individual and the impersonal state. Gerald Frug summarizes this process of disenfranchisement:

> Instead of seeking to understand the harmonious working of the whole, emerging political thought separated out from each aspect of life an individual interest as contrasted with a group interest and, at the same time, consolidated all elements of social cohesion into the idea of the nation-state. . . . Modern political philosophy thus undermined the vitality of all groups that had held an intermediate position between what we now think of as the sphere of the individual and that of the state (Frug, 1999, p. 31).

It is important to note the fundamental shift in political understanding that has emerged in restorative practices. By relocating the response to crime from the courts to the community, reformers are tapping into communal sources of authority long underused in Western society. Indeed, this communal authority has been discredited both as a threat to individual rights and as a threat to national sovereignty. Yet, the experience of those involved in restorative justice indicates that the communal perspective in corrective justice is necessary for an adequately rich response to crime. This response is more constructive, less expensive, more educative, and more likely rehabilitative for offenders and reparative for victims. It is not simply that a group of people—a task force, a committee, a project team—can do a better job crafting restitution agreements than the courts can; rather, it is a matter of recognizing the power of belonging and the implications of belonging—the power of accountability and care—in the exercise of justice.

Human beings are not only individuals and citizens of the state. Each is also a member of relational networks and is accountable to other members of the network: giving and receiving support, earning and bestowing trust, loving and being loved, hurting and forgiving, being hurt and being forgiven. These networks may be familial, associational, or commercial, or a mix of all three. They may be geographical or based on interest, or both. They may be as large as a town or band, or as small as a single extended family. Naroll (1983) has designated these networks as "moralnets," the primary group defining moral accountability for individuals and the fundamental building blocks of society. Restorative justice taps into this fundamental human reality and provides a process through which it can take public action and be held publicly accountable—thus, in part, restoring a human social entity that has been in decline politically throughout the modern age. Restorative justice does not only draw on the community to restore individuals who have been hurt; restorative justice restores the community as a political and social entity capable of responsible public work.

Community Justice in Non-European Cultures

The example of nonwestern forms of community-based justice have provided important models for American reformers since the beginning of the restorative justice movement. Three elements from these practices stand out as especially formative for experiments in restorative practices. The first is the process of justice, which employs local leadership and informal settings open to community participation to reduce barriers between offenders and victims and to enable the community as a whole to play a role in settling disputes. The second concerns the purpose of justice, which is to address a harm done by one member of the community to another, or to resolve a dispute among members, in ways that restore the community's ability to work and live together fruitfully and that decrease the likelihood of the offense or dispute recurring. The third is the authority for justice, which depends on customs and traditions accepted by the local community as normative and embodied in its local leaders. This often includes elements of symbolic significance in the process and the authority invoked. The mere fact of holding the offender accountable before the community vindicates the victim, even prior to determining sanctions, and public apologies carry even greater symbolic weight.

It is not possible here to cite a complete record of non-European influences on restorative practices. What follows are the most commonly cited sources of inspiration, reprinted and retold many times in the restorative justice movement.

Wright recounts James Gibbs' description of the traditional village moot of the Kpelle people in Liberia, "one of the articles most often cited in literature on mediation" (Wright, 1991, pp. 50-51). The Kpelle moot exists alongside the criminal courts as an effective alternative for certain kinds of offenses. The complainant chooses a mediator, who convenes the moot and gives the complainant and then the accused an opportunity to state what happened. Anyone from the village is free to attend and take part, including interrupting the opening statements of the victim and offender. "Proceedings are orderly, but informal and even convivial," with considerable give and take among participants. "The 'losing' party apologizes and brings token gifts, and rum and beer for those who heard the case. . . . the 'winning' party gives a smaller token in return, to show good will" (p. 50). Wright cites similarities in Tanzanian moots and Mexican Zapotec courts (p. 51).

Nils Christie describes the Tanzanian court process in more detail, characterizing it as "a happy happening, fast talking, jokes, smiles, eager attention, not a sentence was to be lost. It was circus, it was drama" (Christie, 1977, p. 2). The principal disputants were in the center, surrounded by relatives, friends, and villagers who questioned them, listened carefully to what they said, and commented. Three judges were present and largely inactive, allowing the disputing parties to take responsibility for working out a solution, with support (p. 3).

Japanese practices have held particular interest because of that country's low crime rate, which according to Marshall, is due not to harsh enforcement but to the highly interdependent and communitarian nature of Japanese culture. Their "emphasis on apology and reparation, reinforced by a culture which values family, community and interpersonal respect . . . [is an important] source of ideas for a parallel reform of criminal justice processes in the West" (Marshall, 1992, pp. 16-17). Braithwaite notes that the Japanese justice system is efficient but lenient, prosecuting only "in major cases or more minor cases where the normal process of apology, compensation and forgiveness by the victim breaks down." Only 10 percent of those convicted are incarcerated and two-thirds of these sentences are suspended (Braithwaite, 1989, p. 62).

Even more influential have been the practices of communal accountability and pubic apology among the Maori people of New Zealand, translated worldwide into "family group conferencing." The Maori convene members of the families of both victims and offenders, "to shame the deed and explain the full impact of the crime on the victim and the community while allowing the offender to earn his way back into the good graces of the community" (Quinn, n.d., p. 15). Responsibility for the offender's behavior is shared by his or her family and friends, and the victim takes an active role in resolving the conflict (McDonald, et al., 1994, p. 4). The "sacredness of the public interests involved" is signified by beginning and ending the conference with a prayer (Braithwaite and Mugford, 1994, p. 159).

Native American traditions of conflict resolution have been very influential in Canada and the United States, with growing appreciation for their "emphasis on collective responsibility, on consensus-based decision making, and on healing individuals, relationships and communities" (Stuart, 1996, January 31, part one, p. 5). In the Skokomish Community Peacemaking Panel, implemented in 1983 in western Washington state, tribal peacemakers are selected from among community members. They facilitate the panels, which include family members and people from the community. Or they act as mediators between disputants who will not meet face to face. The Assembly of Manitoba Chiefs asserts in a 1989 inquiry that the "adversarial system is antithetical to the traditional approach of conflict resolution." Traditional ways help victims "regain a sense of harmony and respect as a member of their families and community," require offenders to acknowledge responsibility for their actions and for harming family and community, keep offenders in the community while requiring them to take responsibility for personal reform and restoration of peace, and seek remedies of restitution and healing rather than punishment of offenders (Marshall, 1992, p. 16).

Similarly, the cultural personality of conflict avoidance and overt friendliness in Eskimo villages in Alaska emphasize communal harmony and depend on the informal power of shame for social control. Standards of good conduct are reinforced daily and especially in gatherings of elders and youths in the traditional meeting place, the men's house. "Underlying all this social activity was a recognition that there was no end to a conflict once it began" as an ever-widening circle of community members and relatives were drawn into a cycle of retribution and revenge (Hippler and Conn, 1975, p. 32). Therefore, when disharmony or violence appeared, the elders convened to head off the violence through a process of noncoercive and nonadversarial problem solving, lectures, compromises, and admissions of guilt. The goal was to reestablish harmony rather than to reinforce the rule of law; rules could be flexible to allow community members to retreat from conflict with dignity.

Such indigenous justice is an entirely different paradigm "based on a holistic philosophy of the circle "that connects everyone involved with a problem or conflict on a continuum, with everyone focused on the same center"(Melton, 1995, p. 126). "[C]rime can be viewed as a natural human error that requires corrective intervention by families and elders or tribal leaders. Thus, offenders remain an integral part of the community because of their important role in defining the boundaries of appropriate and inappropriate behavior and the consequences associated with misconduct"(p. 127).

Advocates of restorative justice have recognized the power in the indigenous process to reinforce and restore relationships and local communities. First, the dependence on customary law and tribal traditional law in indigenous justice processes demonstrates how the power of community norms is enhanced when affirmed in a public process of conflict resolution. Customary law is derived from long-established practices that are accepted by the community and passed on informally to new generations; tribal common law is articulated on the basis of values and norms expressed in community practices, rituals, and traditions (Melton, 1995, p. 131). Giving these informal mechanisms the force of law in criminal proceedings affirms the moral authority of parents, elders, and community members in general.

The process of open and informal discussion demonstrates the willingness of people to seek common solutions in an atmosphere of support and trust. By expanding participation to include family, extended family, and community members, the principals in the conflict are reintegrated in the relationships on which they depend. Furthermore, this expanded area for problem solving also can address concerns of distributive justice by revealing the close linkage between crime and community conditions of well being. Investigations or inquiries into a single offense can provide access to larger social problems. Communal commitments to support victims and offenders in healing and responsible participation in the community bring public attention to inadequate public services, unequal economic opportunities, and detrimental social patterns.

What these non-European processes of justice have contributed, through restorative justice, is above all the sense of justice as a whole, concerned with the total welfare of the whole community. The moral health of the community is necessary for justice to be exercised in individual cases, and the exercise of justice in individual cases helps create and maintain the moral health of the community.

Biblical Justice

Biblical traditions of justice are associated both with the doctrine of divine retribution and punishment of evildoers *and* with doctrines of everlasting mercy and forgiveness. Perhaps no passage highlights the inspirations and contradictions of the biblical heritage in the Western European criminal justice system as clearly as this brief passage from the Gospel According to Matthew:

> You have heard it said, "An eye for an eye and a tooth for a
> tooth." But I say to you, do not resist an evildoer. But if any-
> one strikes you on the right cheek, turn the other also; and if
> anyone wants to sue you and take your coat, give your cloak

as well; and if anyone forces you to go one mile, go also the second mile. Give to everyone who begs from you, and do not refuse anyone who wants to borrow from you. (Mt. 5: 38-42, *New Revised Standard Version* (NRSV)).

"An eye for an eye and a tooth for a tooth" is often understood as referring to justice as equivalent and proportionate suffering. The context in the Hebrew scriptures from which the phrase is taken, however, indicates that this is a formula for reparation rather than retribution.

If anyone strikes the eye of his slave, male or female, and destroys the use of it, he will give the slave freedom to compensate for the eye. If he knocks out the tooth of his slave, male or female, he will give the slave his freedom to compensate for the tooth. (Ex. 21: 26-27, NRSV)

As in other ancient societies, justice as reparation was an important element of biblical justice. Yet, the bible goes beyond retribution and reparation to redemption, emphasizing justice as "making right" what is not right. Eglash refers to this redemptive dimension in defining what creative restitution requires, quoting Matthew 5:41, "And whosoever shall compel thee to go a mile, go with him twain" (Eglash, 1958, p. 619). Merely returning like for like, in punishment or in reparation, is acting under compulsion and equivalent to going only the one mile; creative restitution calls upon offenders go further than this and redeem the situation. "Only a second mile is restitution in its broad meaning of a complete restoration of good will and harmony" (p. 620).

The biblical tradition thus presents not one but three dimensions of justice: retribution, reparation, and redemption—all grounded in a communal understanding of religious faith linking divine justice to community well-being in a covenant of mutual loyalty. At the center of biblical justice is God, both source of all life and just judge of the living and dead, acting to restore or fulfill the divine purpose in creation. Violations of the covenant merit terrible punishment, but the last word is always mercy. Indeed, from the Christian perspective, the last word is divine mercy incarnate.

Throughout the biblical tradition, mercy and judgment do not merely ratify the status quo. God acts in pursuit of right relationships—with other members of the community, with the widow and orphan and stranger, and with the earth. Jesus speaks as the merciful judge when he says, "But if anyone strikes you on the right cheek, turn the other also, and if anyone wants to sue you and take your coat, give your cloak as well, and if anyone forces you to go one mile, go also the second mile" (Mt. 5: 39-41, NRSV).

This is justice that goes beyond reparation to redemption. Justice as reparation, which simply replaces what has been damaged, can only return the situation to the status quo in material terms. Reparation does not automatically restore the harmony that has been lost, and it does not involve the extra steps required to heal the victim and reintegrate the offender into the community. Even more, simple reparation does not address unjust conditions that exist prior to the crime and may even contribute to the crime.

Therefore, drawing upon the traditions of the historical peace churches, the Mennonites and the American Friends Service Committee, who launched some of the first victim offender reconciliation programs in the United States, found in the biblical tradition more than theories of justice (Woolpert, 1991; Wahrhaftig, 1981). They found, in biblical justice itself, a theory of social intervention: not satisfied with repaying the debt of crime, not satisfied with a return to the status quo, but an intervention in the cycle of crime and violence. The ultimate aim of this justice is human dignity and relationships of human flourishing, justice as love, and love as justice. The aim of this kind of justice is *shalom*:

> Within ancient Jewish communities, the goal of social arrangements and practices, of which criminal justice was a part, is shalom. Shalom refers to the dynamic peace of the community; that "all-rightness" of things which God intends. It embraces fulfillment, wholeness, right relationships between individuals, the community and God. (Burnside and Schluter, n.d., p. 3)

Biblical justice is always more than corrective and shows true correction to be redemptive. The distinction between a politically and a socially conservative notion of justice as merely restorative and a progressive notion of justice as transformative disappears. The just act cannot ever merely restore to a previous condition. Time—and human experience in time—cannot be reversed. The just act always creates something new. It always changes the circumstances from which future actions can proceed. Justice is an intervention in the dynamics of injustice which set the welfare of one or some against the welfare of others, redeeming those trapped or harmed by this kind of warfare, giving them a new possibility for well-being.

From Retributive Justice to a Restorative Theory of Justice

The preceding review of restorative practices presents a constellation of moral and philosophical foundations: empowerment in constructive, noncoercive, and fair, practices of mediation; human dignity in practices of restitution; community as a social and political entity in community justice; holistic justice in non-European practices of justice; and redemption and social intervention in biblical justice. One implication of this review is that restorative justice, as a reform movement within criminal justice, can be defended and advocated on strong moral and philosophical grounds. A second implication is that restorative practices provide a fundamentally different way to conceive of justice itself.

Naroll has written that "the moral order is a necessary outgrowth of the social network" (Naroll, 1983, p. 131), and a society's social practices shape its moral possibilities. Social practices thus give rise to substantive matters of justice, but this is not the whole story. The exercise of justice also names what is fundamentally at stake in the social practices and thus gives the social practices a more firm political basis. Consequently, restorative practices create possibilities for community action that are characterized by the qualities named above, but the practices also confirm these qualities as characteristic of community welfare. Justice as restoration simply is the life of the community when the community is functioning well.

The Roots of Retribution

The significance of this shift in the meaning of justice is evident when contrasted with the social practices that generated and sustain the conception of retributive justice. Retributive justice is not merely a rational attempt to deter crime by carefully calibrated punishments. Its roots, violence, vengeance, and social order are much more profound and its appeal much more powerful than such modern calculations of utility.

One attempt to explain the power of punishment in cultures across history is the mimetic theory proposed by Rene Girard (1977). The ordinary social mechanisms of mimesis—learning and cooperation arising from mutual interest in the same things—also gives rise to competition and conflict. This basis of conflict, inherent in every society, inevitably results in a terrifying experience of uncontrolled violence and vengeance: harm returned for injury, death repaid by more death, until social existence itself is threatened by a terrifying spiral of ever-worsening violence. There is no escape, no natural braking mechanism.

Every society that survives must discover a way to interrupt the deadly spiral—and the universal discovery, according to Girard, is the scapegoat. By assigning the cause of the conflict to one individual or to some external group, the community is able to unite against the scapegoat and thus recover its original harmony. Even so, the memory of terrifying near-destruction is not entirely forgotten but retained in rituals that repeat the process. In traditional cultures, these are sacrificial rites in which the community unites in killing or banning a human or animal victim. In Western society, where the authority of law has largely replaced the authority of religion, the criminal justice system provides these ceremonial rites. Convicted felons are slain or banned, executed, or incarcerated, in elaborate rituals that aim to reestablish a sense of communal safety without allowing recourse to the dangers of unrestrained vengeance.

Retribution, then, is a convening of the society against the convicted criminal. The punishment of criminals is fundamentally directed not to the reform of those who are convicted but to the reassurance of society: that social order prevails over disorder. The power of the state overcomes the threat to its power posed by the offender, so that in spite of this threat, the members of society are secure in their persons and dwellings and property.

Retribution, even at a distance, has an intensely personal basis in experience, as is evident in the assumptions underlying retributive justice, articulated by John Stuart Mill (1861/1979). First, it entails a deep sympathy on the part of society with the victim. This is more than a compassionate response to the one who has been hurt. It is rather an identification with that person's loss and suffering as though it is one's own, a sense of feeling violated along with the victim, evoking a response of self-defense against the threat.

Second, it entails an assumption that the offense can be located in a single individual—or a discrete few. In light of the profoundly social nature of humanity and the involvement of each in the lives and decisions that others make, the designation of a single guilty individual is always to some extent arbitrary. Yet, the assumption is necessary for retributive justice to proceed. In light of these reflections, retributive justice appears to be much more communal than impersonal, more symbolic than utilitarian. Retribution is revealed as a communal ritual more than as a rational calculation of cause and effect.

Restoration as Justice

Malvina Kaveny writes that justice in a postliberal society cannot be imaged as blind impartiality, but is more akin to painting a detailed picture as if for the blind (Kaveny, 1991, p. 158). Its authority lies in its complexity, in its grasp of the context and situation of crime and the response to crime. This, in fact, is the great strength of restorative justice: to explicitly bring the context of crime and justice into the adjudication process, where the unique details of each case can be appreciated and solutions can be negotiated in an atmosphere and structure that begins to build a new way of relating to supporters, adversaries, and the public. Retribution keeps its distance, to augment its symbolic power as the saving arm of the state; but restoration moves in close and gathers the community around the crime. The circle formed in the victim-offender conference becomes the symbol of the community as confronting, caring, and constructing solutions.

The aim of restorative justice is to repair the harm done in the immediate situation in a way that contributes to the restoration of harmony and wholeness in the wider circle of relationships in family, community, and society. This includes restoring a balance between the victim and the offender, which the offender has upset by injuring the victim. It is done by restoring the victim to the extent possible, but the restoration of the balance extends beyond the immediate situation of two individuals in conflict to address imbalances within families, communities, and society as a whole. In this way, restorative practices approach distributive justice, as the underlying social disparities implicated in the crime are brought to the discussion.

Restorative justice is also substantive justice, since offenders are called upon to recognize concrete goods that they have damaged and to contribute to restoration in concrete ways valued by the victim. It is procedural justice, a process as much as a result, characterized by rules of fair and equal participation. Restoration brings offenders to justice, not only in a realignment with what is morally right but also back into the circle of society, enabling them to participate as responsible members.

The entire process of restoration is a practice in human dignity and respect, and its ends are also dignity and respect. Restorative justice moves beyond merely individual preference through a process of negotiation, to a larger sense of good and right. The aim is not merely rightness but goodness— not merely getting the penalty right but progressing toward the common good. It is thus a form of communal moral discipline, characterized by the unity of means and ends—the universal mark of spiritual and moral disciplines.

As such a discipline, it is more akin to what Aristotle called *complete* justice than an example of what he called *partial* justice. In the *Nicomachean Ethics* (Book V), Aristotle (1962) identifies complete justice as that which embodies the exercise of all the virtues in the just man, whereas partial justice is of several kinds: distributive, transactional, corrective, reciprocal, and political. Each act of partial justice is an attempt to achieve a kind of balance or proportion between interests. However, complete justice refers to the practical wisdom of the just man who is able to recognize the correct proportion and act on it. Restorative justice is analogous to complete justice, not as the just individual but as the just community. It is the communal wisdom to recognize what justice requires, bringing together in good judgment overarching societal norms, local injuries and affections, and individual and communal capacities. Restorative justice encompasses not only just outcomes as a proportion between crime and consequences, but also a process of just deliberation to arrive at a knowledge of this proportion, and furthermore, doing this in a way that increases the capacity of the community to exercise this practical wisdom in the future—a kind of communal growth in virtue.

It may, therefore, be more accurate to speak of a restorative theory of justice rather than a theory of restorative justice. Restorative justice, as it is being practiced and articulated, is more than merely a part of justice or a set of programs within criminal justice. It is fundamental rethinking of the meaning and ground and practice of justice itself.

A restorative theory of justice incorporates the classic liberal assumptions of political power vested in the free and equal participation of citizens, but locates the exercise of this power in the democratic deliberations of those most affected by the crime. In this exercise of justice, the political power vested in the democratic state is complemented by the political power vested in the deliberating community. Both have a profoundly moral foundation, substantively and procedurally. To be recognized as legitimate, the actions of the legislature must embody the civic virtues of mutual respect, toleration of different views, dialog in the pursuit of truth, and a desire for the common good. The laws enacted by the legislature must concur with the moral judgment of the people for their force, for enforcement alone can never be a sufficient motivation outside a totalitarian state. The same is true for restorative practices. The decisions made in restorative justice conferences—on behalf of the community—must appeal to the participants' sense of moral rightness, in the same way that "group rights" appeal to the "necessary structures of existence" upon which the intrinsic good of the group depends (Garet, 1983, p. 1002). The ultimate ground for restorative justice is a sense of the common good.

Community, in a functional sense, occurs naturally when people are brought together in mutual interdependence in relationships of accountability and care, and this is precisely what restorative practices are designed to do. The power of this movement to attract and inspire participants flows from these deep roots in the social nature of humanity. Thus, the moral and philosophical foundations of restorative justice are also the moral and philosophical foundations of democracy—not only as a theory of justice, but as a theory of community.

References

Aristotle. 1962. *Nicomachean Ethics*, M. Ostwald, trans. Englewood Cliffs, New Jersey: Prentice Hall.

Boyne, R. and A. Rattansi. 1990. The Theory and Politics of Postmodernism: By Way of an Introduction. In R. Boyne and A. Rattansi, ed. *Postmodernism and Society*, pp. 1-45. New York: St. Martin's Press.

Braithwaite, J. 1989. *Crime, Shame and Reintegration*. Melbourne, Australia and New York: Cambridge University Press.

Braithwaite, J. and S. Mugford. 1994. Conditions of Successful Reintegration Ceremonies: Dealing with Juvenile Offenders. *British Journal of Criminology*. 34: 139-171.

Burnside, J. and M. Schluter. n.d. Relational Justice: A Reform Dynamic of the Criminal Justice System. Unpublished manuscript.

Christie, N. 1977. Conflicts as Property. *British Journal of Criminology*. 17: 1-15.

Eglash, A. 1958. Creative Restitution: A Broader Meaning for an Old Term. *Journal of Criminal Law, Criminology, and Police Science*. 48: 619-622.

Foucault, M. 1977. *Discipline and Punish: The Birth of the Prison*, A. Sheridan, trans. New York: Vintage Books.

Frug, G. E. 1999. *City Making: Building Communities without Building Walls.* Princeton, New Jersey: Princeton University Press.

Garet, R. R. 1983. Communality and Existence: The Rights of Groups. *Southern California Law Review.* 56: 1001-1075.

Girard, R. 1977. *Violence and the Sacred*, P. Gregory, trans. Baltimore: Johns Hopkins University Press.

Harrington, C. B. and S. E. Merry. 1988. Ideological Production: The Making of Community Mediation. *Law and Society Review.* 22: 709-735.

Hippler, A. and S. Conn. 1975. The Village Council and Its Offspring: A Reform for Bush Justice. *UCLA-Alaska Law Review.* 5: 22-57.

Kant, I. 1956/1785. *Groundwork of the Metaphysic of Morals*, H. J. Paton, trans. New York: Harper and Row.

Kaveny, M. C. 1991. Neutrality about the Good Life v. the Common Good: MacIntyre, the Supreme Court, and Liberalism as a Living Tradition. Unpublished doctoral dissertation, Yale University.

MacIntyre, A. 1984. *After Virtue: A Study in Moral Theory*, 2nd ed. Notre Dame, Indiana: University of Notre Dame Press.

Marshall, T. F. 1992, September. Grassroots Initiatives towards Restorative Justice: The New Paradigm? Paper presented for the Fulbright Colloquium, "Penal Theory and Penal Practice," University of Stirling.

McDonald, J. M., T. A. O'Connell, D. B. Moore, and E. Bansbury. 1994. *Convening Family Conferences Training Manual.* New South Wales Police Academy.

Melton, A. P. 1995. Indigenous Justice Systems and Tribal Society. *Judicature.* 79: 126-133.

Mill, J. S. 1979/1861. *Utilitarianism.* Indianapolis, Indiana: Hackett Publishing Co.

Naroll, R. 1983. *The Moral Order: An Introduction to the Human Situation.* Beverley Hills/London/New Delhi: Sage Publications.

Quinn, T. J. n.d. *Corrections and Restorative Justice.* Washington, D.C.: National Institute of Justice.

"South Korean Leader Apologizes for Scandal." 1997. *Star Tribune.* February 25, p. A7.

Stuart, B. D. 1996, January. Alternative Dispute Resolution in Action in Canada: Part I. Community-Based Justice Initiatives: An Overview. Unpublished manuscript.

Van Ness, D. W. 1989, November 1. Between Punishment and Restoration. Paper presented at the annual conference of the National Community Service Sentencing Association, San Antonio, Texas.

Wahrhaftig, P. 1981. Dispute Resolution Retrospective. *Crime and Delinquency.* 27: 99-105.

Woolpert, S. 1991. Victim-Offender Reconciliation Programs. In K. G. Duffy, J. W. Grosch, and P. V. Olczak, eds. *Community Mediation: A Handbook for Practitioners and Researchers,* pp. 276-297. New York: The Guilford Press.

Wright, M. 1991. *Justice for Victims and Offenders: A Restorative Response to Crime.* Philadelphia: Open University Press.

Vocabulary and Questions

- mediation

- nonviolent conflict resolution

- restitution

- community development

- community justice

- retributive justice

- moots

- communal resolution of conflict

- tribal law

- moral health of the community

- reparation

- shalom

- mimesis

- scapegoat

- circle

- biblical justice

- empowerment

- common good

1. Why does the author contend that the theory of restorative justice is democracy in action?

2. Discuss how mediation can be constructive, noncoercive, and fair.

3. What is the relationship between restitution and human dignity?

4. Explain how the circle in the victim-offender conferences is the symbol of the community that is confronting, caring, and constructing solutions.

5. What aspects of non-European models of justice have helped to guide restorative practices in the United States?

6. How does restitution differ from reparations?

7. How is restorative justice linked to distributive justice?

8. How does restorative justice differ from retributive justice, and in what ways do these two responses to crime serve the same ends?

COMMUNITY IS NOT A PLACE: A NEW LOOK AT
3 COMMUNITY JUSTICE INITIATIVES*

PAUL MCCOLD
DIRECTOR OF RESEARCH
INTERNATIONAL INSTITUTE FOR RESTORATIVE PRACTICES
BETHLEHEM, PENNSYLVANIA

BENJAMIN WACHTEL
MEDIA AND TECHNOLOGY COORDINATOR
COMMUNITY SERVICE FOUNDATION
PIPERSVILLE, PENNSYLVANIA

C ommunity justice initiatives, such as community policing and restorative justice, have tended to define community rather loosely, if at all.
This has led to confusion about and variation in what exactly constitutes
a community justice program. In community policing, community has often
been equated with the neighborhood. In restorative justice literature, community is often indistinguishable from society. These ways of defining community
have significant consequences for these new justice initiatives. Not only do

*Originally published in *Contemporary Justice Review* 1(1): 71-85, 1998. Used with permission.

they affect the way in which these approaches are designed and implemented, but they may cause confusion about the underlying values and may undermine the goals of community justice.

Critics and evaluators of community policing initiatives have noted the variety of forms and goals that these efforts assume (Rosenbaum,1994). There is some consensus that a primary goal is to mobilize communities to be active partners in responding to crime; however, community policing initiatives have largely failed to reach this goal. One of the obstacles seems to be that, in many areas, "genuine" community does not exist.

Advocates for the new justice paradigm known variously as restorative justice, transformative justice, and relational justice, also have differed greatly in their conceptualization of community. There is general agreement, in theory, that community is as central to restorative justice as are the victim and the offender (McCold, 1997). However, the actual involvement of those other than the facilitator, the victim, and the offender varies widely in restorative justice practice.

If community justice is going to have any success, then, it is necessary to take a deeper look at the meaning of community. This paper will discuss the importance of defining exactly what is meant by the term "community" in community justice initiatives, especially community policing and restorative justice. We propose a nongeographic perspective on community, which can be used to focus and define what community justice initiatives should look like and what they should be trying to achieve. This perspective is based on recent developments in restorative justice and community policing, especially the Wagga/Real Justice model of family group conferences which, when used by police, exemplifies an integration of restorative justice and community policing. The implications of this perspective for community justice initiatives in general will be explored.

Defining Community

What is community? Community is a feeling, a perception of a connectedness—personal connectedness both to other individual human beings and to a group. Building community, then, involves building bonds between human beings. Where there is no perception of a connectedness among a group of people, there is no community. Although we may live in the same neighborhood, municipality, county, state or nation, be governed and served by the same institutions, we may have no sense of connection with each other, no sense that we are part of a unified group. As such, we are not of one community.

On the other hand, we may belong to the same bowling league, go to the same place of worship, work in the same office, or go to the same school. We may be relatives or friends. As such, if we perceive a connection between each other and a common interest in the activities and well-being of the group—the sports league, the religious group, the workplace, the school, the family, the circle of friends—then we are, by definition, part of a community.

When we speak about the "sense of community" that is missing from modern society, we are speaking about the absence of meaningful interrelationships between human beings and the absence of a sense of belonging to and common interest in something greater than ourselves. At a societal level, this manifests itself as individualism. Excessive individualism tends to breed selfishness and a lack of empathy, which lays the groundwork for crime (Braithwaite, 1989; Moore, 1997).

We can, of course, simultaneously value both ideals of the individual and of the group. In terms of political philosophy, we might equate this with valuing elements of both libertarianism and communitarianism. In modern society, we have a problem in that we seem to undervalue collective responsibility and overvalue individual rights, thus losing a sense of balance between the two (if such a balance ever actually existed). As such, we have diminished respect for others and have only a limited sense of responsibility to the collective.

Thus, the promise of community justice initiatives to empower and build community has strong popular appeal. Against a tide of individualism and a perceived decline of community life, we long for a sense of connectedness in our lives and a sense of safety in our neighborhoods. Our sense of safety is obstructed when neighbors are strangers. As Kay Pranis, restorative justice planner for the Minnesota Department of Corrections has suggested, neighborhoods are caught up "in a downward spiral where crime leads to greater fear and increased isolation and distrust among community members, which in turn leads to even more crime. As community bonds are weakened by fear and isolation, the power of community disapproval is reduced and crime increases" (Pranis, 1996a:10).

Place, therefore, can play a role in creating a community of interest around a crime in a specific location, but only coincidentally. In and of itself, community is not a place, other than as a mythical reflection of a romanticized past. Geographical units rarely constitute or correspond to communities. The resident population may lack a sense of shared interests and there may be relatively few interpersonal connections between neighbors. Even where genuine community does seem to coincide with place, "the socio-political constructions of that community may differ greatly from one culture to another" (Tyler, 1995). There is most likely not one unified community, but a number of fairly distinct communities, perhaps at odds with one another.

The consequences of crime extend beyond neighborhoods, towns and cities, because our networks of relationships are not confined by geographical boundaries. A theft committed against a family member in another state probably would affect someone more personally than a burglary committed in their own neighborhood. The problem with many community justice initiatives is that they have defined community primarily in terms of geography, ignoring the very vibrant sense of community that exists in personal networks of relationships. In doing so, in reality, they may be indistinguishable from existing justice practices, failing to address collateral harm and the weakening of community caused by crime, and failing to establish meaningful roles for community members in justice interventions.

Retributive justice approaches actually can make matters worse by alienating both offenders and victims. John Braithwaite explains how offenders who have been stigmatized by the justice system often are drawn together to form their own subcultures. These become communities in themselves, unsympathetic to the norms of conduct and morality of the larger society (Braithwaite, 1989). Ironically, members of these "criminal subcultures" may have a greater sense of belonging and connection than members of mainstream society. The influence that any community has on individuals belonging to that community—community as a perception of connectedness to an individual or a group—is an important source of informal social control (Weiss, 1987). It is a powerful motivator in maintaining group norms, whether these norms are positive or negative.

For community justice initiatives to be effective, they must capitalize on the fact that people act in a certain way because they want to avoid experiencing the external shame of disapproval by people they care about and because of the internal shame experienced through conscience. Conscience is largely developed through a maturation process in which the behavioral values of interdependence become internalized. Where conscience is not fully developed, approval of others is the primary motivator, not punishment or fear of punishment (Braithwaite, 1989).

It follows, then, that a primary goal for community justice should be mobilizing informal social control mechanisms by strengthening, creating, or restoring healthy interdependencies and by encouraging the development of mature internalized control, or conscience. In this process, harm can be repaired, offenders and victims can be reintegrated and supported, empathy can be fostered, and relationships can be healed and formed. Fundamentally, community justice is about building and using perceptions of connectedness to individuals and groups as a way to respond to and prevent crime and wrongdoing.

Community in Community Policing

Community policing has tended to define communities as existing in specified locales or neighborhoods. Community policing initiatives often involve the creation of foot patrols, permanent geographic assignment of officers, and ministations serving a particular neighborhood. Attempts to organize and unify neighborhood residents into a "community" are also common practice (Rosenbaum, 1994; Trojanowicz and Moore, 1988). In urban settings, each neighborhood may have its own look, and perhaps residents feel some sense of collective ownership of their area. However, this does not translate into significant interaction or the formation of stable personal relationships. The natural communities that exist are spread out over varying distances, rarely colocating with geographic boundaries.

The Innovative Neighborhood Oriented Policing (INOP) programs, funded by the Bureau of Justice Assistance to implement community policing approaches to drug-demand reduction, are a prime example of the inter-changeability of "community" and "neighborhood." INOP program efforts included increased law enforcement, drug prevention, education, and treat-ment, and the creation of satellite offices and the purchase of motor homes to increase police presence in specific problem neighborhoods. The cumulative results of these efforts were unimpressive. There was a lack of involvement of community residents in program design, citizens were largely unaware of the project goals, and they did not become involved (Sadd and Grinc, 1994).

In general, community policing means many different things to different people (Hunter and Barker, 1993; Bayley, 1994). There is some consensus that its general aims are to prevent crime and create a better quality of life and to change the reactive, control-oriented style of policing to a proactive, problem-solving, service-oriented style. Its specific objectives, however, are varied: to reduce crime and fear of crime. They include calls for service and complaints against police; to increase preventive knowledge, crime clearance rates, pub-lic satisfaction, number of volunteers, police satisfaction, police efficiency, and police effectiveness; and to build police-community partnerships (Normandeau, 1993). The specific methods of achieving these aims may differ very little from previous policing approaches, and despite its popularity, com-munity policing has been characterized as being "more rhetoric than reality" (Mastrofski,1988; Klockars, 1988; Jones, et al., 1994; Bull and Stratta, 1994; Stenson, 1993).

In summarizing how the community has been utilized in community policing, Buerger (1994: 270-271) points out that community participation has largely been limited to four primary roles: 1) "eyes and ears of police;" 2) cheer-leading (political support for police); 3) monetary assistance (for example, taxes supporting foot patrols) and 4) statement-making (threats of opposition, intolerance and sanctions for misconduct, such as "Drug-Free School Zone" or "Neighborhood Watch" signs). In addition, education and training of neighbor-hood residents for their roles in community policing has been virtually nonex-istent (Sadd and Grinc, 1994). For the most part, then, community policing initiatives have failed to involve communities in meaningful and effective ways.

There are, however, promising signs of innovation in policing. Much of this innovation can be traced to the work of Herman Goldstein, considered by many to be "the father of problem-oriented policing." Community policing and problem-oriented policing are often considered one and the same, but

Goldstein is careful to make a distinction between the two. Community policing is "designed to place great emphasis on one great need in policing, which is to engage the community" (1997:8). Problem-oriented policing has a broader focus—to adopt an analytical approach to identify and solve the specific problems that police confront. A key element in this is intensively engaging the community in problem solving (Goldstein,1990, 1997).

The job of social control in society ultimately depends upon networks other than the police, networks that the police can only facilitate and support. The community should become responsible for policing itself. Several arguments can be made for maximum use of informal controls that are already available in the community. First, invoking informal nongovernmental control may truly be the most effective means for dealing with the problem. Second, doing so reinforces the concept of the police as facilitators in getting the community to control itself rather than depending on the police and the criminal justice system for control. Third, it supports the strong preference, when an option exists, for using the least restrictive, least intrusive method of dealing with a problem (Goldstein,1990:121).

Goldstein offers numerous examples of police mobilizing the community and making use of existing forms of informal social controls, such as involving citizens in developing solutions to specific crime problems, promoting interaction among populations of varying age and racial composition to reduce fear, holding meetings to resolve ongoing conflicts among neighborhood residents, and seeking the help of "those who, because they have some power over an individual, may be able to influence his or behavior" (1990:121).

Goldstein claims that, in actuality, individual police also tend to have a clearer definition of community:

> In what I have observed of the practice, as distinct from the rhetoric of community policing, police tend to engage the citizenry in a very pragmatic and more relaxed manner. They use "community" rather deftly to describe those affected in any way by the specific problem they are attempting to address, or the program being launched in response to the problem (1990: 25).

The community that should be involved in community policing processes, then, are those individuals who have been affected by a specific problem, and their roles should be as active participants in developing solutions and as sources of informal social control and support. Drawing on the work of David Moore (1997), we call this the "microcommunity."

Community in Restorative Justice

Central in understanding the new restorative justice paradigm is an understanding of the roles of stakeholders in crime and the response to crime.

The stakeholders in restorative justice include the victim, the offender, and the community (Zehr, 1990). Yet, for the most part, community remains a concept vaguely defined. While restorative justice advocates are less likely to fall prey to the fallacy of community as place, there is a tendency, by some restorative justice advocates, to confuse the role of community with the role of society. The problem begins with an ill-defined concept of the victim. To whom does the offender owe reparation: 1) the victim, 2) the victim and the community, or 3) the victim, the community, and society? All three perspectives are represented in the descriptions of programs calling themselves "restorative."

Since it seems to be a basic principle of restorative justice that crime harms communities and that some sort of action needs to be taken to repair that harm, how we define community becomes crucial to the development of restorative justice practice. The community "wants reassurance that what happened was wrong, that something is being done about it, and that steps are being taken to discourage its recurrence" (Zehr, 1990: 195). These are needs shared by all three categories of crime victims—primary, secondary, and vicarious victims (the public or society; in other words, those who become aware of the crime). A geographic definition of community brings this assertion dangerously close to the traditional justice system view that offenders must pay their debt to society. Restorative justice initiatives in reality may be no different from existing practices and continue to weaken community by stigmatizing offenders and neglecting victims.

A fundamental principle of restorative justice is that society is not the victim, government is not the victim, the victim is the victim (McCold, 1996). Christie's (1977) principle of ownership reminds us of the danger that the conflict is easily "stolen" from the victim by defining the society as the victim. The question for restorative justice is "Can the principle of private ownership coexist with public ownership of crime?" The current solution to this dilemma has been to order the two principles. For example, Ron Claassen's (1995) first principle of restorative justice is that "Crime is primarily an offense against human relationships and secondarily a violation of a law."

Van Ness and Strong (1997) attempt to deal with the community/society dilemma by distinguishing between the role of the community and the role of government. "In promoting justice, the government is responsible for preserving order, and the community is responsible for establishing peace" (Van Ness 1989:20). Thus, there are actually four parties in restorative justice: victim, offender, community, and government. Van Ness and Strong suggest that it is in the balancing of the order function of government with the conflict resolution and peacemaking functions of community that "balanced and restorative" justice is produced. While they distinguish the local geographical community from the community of interests (microcommunities), they fail to distinguish the injuries, needs, and responsibilities of the local community from those of the personal microcommunities.

With the advent of family group conferencing and sentencing circles, the restorative justice movement has recognized the importance of including the personal communities of care of both offenders and victims in resolution of criminal conflict (Umbreit and Zehr 1996). Restorative justice practice is moving from excluding the microcommunity under early victim offender mediation models to including them as a central part of the restorative process (Van Ness and Strong 1997; Wright 1996).

Tony Marshall (1994) suggests that restorative justice seeks to reduce crime by strengthening bonds of interdependency while holding offenders accountable. Marshall defines restorative justice as

> a process whereby all the parties with a stake in a particular offence come together to resolve collectively how to deal with the aftermath of the offence and its implications for the future. Parties with a stake in an offence include, of course, the victim and the offender, but they also include the families of each, and any other members of their respective communities who may be affected, or who may be able to contribute to prevention of a recurrence (Marshall, 1997)[1]

Thus, restorative justice, like problem-oriented policing, is moving toward a more practical perspective of microcommunities. If done correctly, restorative justice programs empower the victim and offender with control over the nature of the reparation, and empower the personal communities to exercise informal social support and control of the process. Not only are the microcommunities important in the restoration process, but they are the means through which healing and reintegration is possible (Wundersitz and Hetzel, 1996).

Restorative Policing

The collaborative processes developed from restorative justice practitioners are natural tools for police interested in engaging communities for crime control and prevention and might be called "restorative policing." While those experienced at mediation tend to be distrustful of the police and stereotype them as authoritarian, the police have tended to distrust "social workers" and stereotype them as naive and permissive. There is some truth in both perceptions, but both are largely incorrect. Conscientious police officers have always used soothing and smoothing techniques in the vast majority of encounters with citizens (Walter and Wagner 1996). Against the background of major work in the development of mediation and other dispute-resolution techniques in both the public and private sectors, relatively little systematic attention has been given to perfecting the methods of responding to disputes by the governmental agency that probably handles the greatest number of them (Goldstein 1990:113).

Research on police-based family group conferencing projects has demonstrated that police officers are quite capable of assuming the nondirective, empowering roles of facilitators (McCold and Wachtel, 1997; Sherman and Strang,1997). Restorative justice and community policing come together in the Wagga/Real Justice model of family group conferencing, which operationalizes the microcommunity perspective. A powerful way of demonstrating the community empowerment and community building potential of conferences is through the following conference story.

In an upper-middle class suburb, a group of youths vandalized a number of ice fishing houses on a local lake. The public prosecutor, because of the difficulty of matching specific damage to specific offenders, decided not to pursue the case. The traditional justice system failed to deal with the crime. The police, however, had implemented a family group conference program for juvenile offenses and offered the victims an alternative response to the wrongdoing they had suffered. One particular victim, whose elaborate two-story ice fishing house had suffered considerable damage, was particularly irate, agreed only begrudgingly to attend the conference and threatened to display his rage at the conference.

The perpetrators, ice fishing house owners, and their respective family and friends gathered for the family group conference. First, the offenders admitted their wrongdoing and described the damage that they had done. Then, each of the victims expressed how they had been affected by the destruction of the ice fishing houses that they had built themselves, over many years, with their families and friends.

The son of the owner of the two-story fishing house spoke for his father and expressed, in rather poignant terms, how he had spent much of his childhood working with his father and the rest of his family building their house for each winter fishing season. He suddenly realized, when faced with the destruction the youths had caused, how much that experience meant to him. His father, instead of expressing his rage as he had threatened, saved his comments for the close of the conference, after the whole group had worked out the terms of reparation.

Then, he spoke with great emotion and thanked the youths for having vandalized his ice fishing house. He explained that until the conference he had never heard his son express how much all those years of shared experience meant to him. The father then invited all of the boys and their fathers, when the damage was repaired, to spend a weekend with his family fishing on the lake.

All of the people who participated in this conference lived in geographic proximity, but until they were grouped into a "microcommunity" through this powerful restorative justice process, they hardly knew each other. After the conference, bonds had been established that did not exist before the conference. Community, for purposes of a family group conference, can be defined identically to Goldstein's description of community that is used by good problem-oriented police officers: "They use 'community' rather deftly to describe those affected in any way by the specific problem they are attempting to address."

Community and Government

There is still a minor problem with this concept of microcommunity and its implications for community justice processes. It could be argued that anyone "affected in any way," as Goldstein puts it, is anyone who becomes aware of the crime; it follows then that they should be included in the intervention, whether they are members of the same neighborhood, the same state, or the same world. Thus, all government agencies are affected because they have the responsibility to enforce the laws of society within specified geographic boundaries. In practical terms, membership in the microcommunity should be limited to those with a strong personal or emotional connection to the victim or offender.

There is great danger in confusing the needs and responsibilities of the personal communities of crime victims and offenders with more abstract notions of community. All of the natural informal social control mechanisms that operate in everyday life involve the personal communities of care of each of us. When we include organizational relationships such as workplace, recreation, and worship relationships as part of the network of personal microcommunities, the social control structures become more apparent.

It is the deeply interpersonal nature of such interrelations that give the collective community its character and strength. The greater the abstraction in defining community, the further it is removed from interdependency and the locus of existing informal social control. That is why it is important for community justice to encourage and create community, as a perception of connectedness to an individual or group, in its efforts to respond to and prevent crime. The microcommunities created by incidents of crime are a useful framework for action.

Place is only relevant where proximity to a crime has generated fear and concern, thereby creating a host of vicarious victims. The most constructive response to these vicarious victims is to provide reassurance that what happened was wrong, that something constructive is being done about it, and that steps are being taken to discourage its recurrence. In this way, microcommunity empowerment meets the main needs of the "broader" community—to know that something constructive is being done about crime locally (McCold, 1996, 2000).

Because some microcommunities may be punitive and stigmatizing, care must be taken in all community justice programs that reparative or reintegrative principles are structured into the process, for example, by providing positive examples of reparative solutions when only punitive ones are suggested. In this way, government ensures that outcomes are fair and legal. As

Kay Pranis advises, "Formal government is the source of legal authority, as contrasted with the moral authority of the community. The government is in a position of broader oversight than the community and the government is the guardian of individual concerns, in contrast to the community responsibility to collective concerns" (1996b:3).

There is a danger in involving "official" community representatives in conferences, because their role as direct stakeholders in the crime may not be legitimate. Such "community" volunteers may represent interests that are anything but restorative or reintegrative. They may display an attitude of moral superiority, which could disrupt the resolution process. These official community representatives may be little more than geographic or governmental representatives, with no real emotional connection to the crime or to those affected by the crime. Ultimately, the best solutions to the problems of crime come not from government or society, but from the individuals directly affected by crime, the microcommunity (Moore, 1997).

The role of government officials, such as police, should be limited to that of facilitators and information providers, not key contributors to the decision-making process. The responsibility of government is to recognize patterns of dysfunction in society and help provide solutions. Since individuals and communities cannot be expected to have the capacity to address these larger concerns, that responsibility falls to the municipal, county, state, and national government. The responsibility of the microcommunity involved in each specific criminal incident is to intervene constructively in repairing the harm. For this, they need effective informal social control mechanisms. Where these are not available, government has the responsibility to provide them.

Government, however, cannot effectively address crime without the moral authority and informal social control provided by community. By continuing to define community in official geographic and governmental terms, our so-called community justice initiatives can only fail. But by recognizing that community defines itself through individual perceptions of common interest, such as those created by a criminal incident, we can successfully engage a wide range of individuals in the resolution of their own problems.

Endnote

[1]The Alliance of Non-Governmental Organizations Committee on Crime Prevention and Criminal Justice's Working Party on Restorative Justice adopted Marshall's definition as its working definition for drafting resolution language to the Tenth United Nations Crime Congress in 2000. The remainder of that definition is as follows:

> "Coming together may occur as one event, as in Family (or Community) Group Conferencing, or it may occur through a series of less all embracing meetings (for example victim-offender mediation and a separate conference between the

offender and his/her family), depending on the complexity of the case and other practicalities. The coming together may also occur just once, or may happen repeatedly over a more or less extended period of time.

In order to effect the coming together and a collective resolution, there is a crucial role for the neutral facilitator (mediator) with the skills to prepare people for the process, ensure that it progresses in a safe and civilized manner, guide parties through difficult phases, and encourage them to enter fully and creatively into the process. The aftermath of the offence includes ensuring the material well-being or satisfaction of the victim, the reaffirmation that they are not to blame, attention to the victim's emotional needs, resolution of any conflict between the victim and the offender (whether because of the offence or existing beforehand), the resolution of similar conflicts between their families or communities, resolving any difficulties between the offender and his/her family and other friends as a result of the offence (for example, being ashamed to know him/her), and giving the offender a chance to absolve his/her own feelings of guilt through apology and reparation.

The implications for the future include tackling the reasons for the offending, producing a plan for rehabilitation, and agreement among the family and community members present on a system of support for the offender to ensure that he/she is able to adhere to the plan" (Marshall, 1996:37-39).

References

Bayley, D. H. 1994. International Difference in Community Policing. In D. P. Rosenbaum, ed. *The Challenge of Community Policing: Testing the Promises*, pp. 278-281. Thousand Oaks, California: Sage Publications.

Braithwaite, J. 1989. *Crime, Shame and Reintegration*. New York: Cambridge University Press.

Buerger, M. E. 1994. The Limits of Community. In D. P. Rosenbaum, ed. *The Challenge of Community Policing: Testing the Promises*, pp. 270-273. Thousand Oaks, California: Sage Publications.

Bull, D. and E. Stratta. 1994. Police Community Consultation: An Examination of its Practice in Selected Constabularies in England and New South Wales, Australia. *Australian and New Zealand Journal of Criminology*. 273: 237-249.

Christie, N. 1977. Conflict as Property. *The British Journal of Criminology*. 171:1-14.

Claassen, R. 1995. Restorative Justice Principles and Evaluation Continuums. Paper presented at National Center for Peacemaking and Conflict Resolution, Fresno Pacific College. May.

Goldstein, H. 1990. *Problem-Oriented Policing*. Philadelphia: Temple University Press.

———. 1997. Interview in *Law Enforcement News*. 23(461):8-11.

Hunter, R. D. and T. Barker. 1993. BS and Buzzwords: The New Police Operational Style. *American Journal of Police*. 123: 157-158.

Jones, T., T. Newburn, and D. J. Smith. 1994. *Democracy and Policing*. London: Policy Studies Institute.

Klockars, C. B. 1988. The Rhetoric of Community Policing. In J. R. Greene and S. D. Mastrofski, eds. *Community Policing: Rhetoric or Reality*, pp. 239-258. New York: Praeger.

Marshall, T. F. 1994. Grassroots Initiatives Towards Restorative Justice: The New Paradigm? In A. Duff, S. Marshall, R. E. Dobash, et. al., eds. *Penal Theory and Practice: Tradition and Innovation in Criminal Justice*, pp. 245-262. Fulbright Papers, volume 15. Manchester, UK: Manchester University Press.

———. 1996. The Evolution of Restorative Justice in Britain. *European Journal for Criminal Policy and Research*. 4(4): 21-43.

Mastrofski, S. D. 1988. Community Policing as Reform: A Cautionary Tale. In J. R. Greene and S. D. Mastrofski, eds. *Community Policing: Rhetoric or Reality*, pp. 47-68. New York: Praeger.

McCold, P. 1996. The Role of Community in Restorative Justice. In B. Galaway and J. Hudson, eds. *Restorative Justice: International Perspectives*, pp. 85-102. Monesy, New York: Criminal Justice Press.

———. 1997. Restorative Justice: Variations on a Theme. Paper presented to the Restorative Justice for Juveniles-Potentialities, Risks and Problems for Research, International Conference in Leuven, Belgium. May 12-14.

McCold, P. and J. Stahr. 1996. Bethlehem Police Family Group Conferencing Project. Paper presented at the American Society of Criminology Conference, Annual Meeting, Chicago. November 20-23.

Moore, D B. 1997. Pride, Shame and Empathy in Peer Relations: New Theory and Practice in Education and Juvenile Justice. In K. Rigby and P. Slee, eds. *Children's Peer Relations*. London: Routledge.

Normandeau, A. 1993. Community Policing in Canada: A Review of Some Recent Studies. *American Journal of Police*. 121: 57-73.

Pranis, K. 1996a. Building Community Support for Restorative Justice: Principles and Strategies. From http://www.quaker.org/fcadp/Community.html.

———. 1996b. Communities and the Justice System: Turning the Relationship Upside Down. Address given to Communities, Crime and Justice: Making Community Partnerships Work, sponsored by Office of Justice Programs, U.S. Department of Justice.

Rosenbaum, D. P., ed. 1994. *The Challenge of Community Policing: Testing the Promises*. Thousand Oaks, California: Sage Publications.

Sadd, S. and R. Grinc. 1994. Innovative Neighborhood Oriented Policing: An Evaluation of Community Policing Programs in Eight Cities. In D. P. Rosenbaum, ed. *The Challenge of Community Policing: Testing the Promises*, pp. 27-52. Thousand Oaks, California: Sage Publications.

Sherman, L. and H. Strang. 1997. The Right Kind of Shame from Crime Prevention. RISE Working Paper #1, April 21. Australia National University and University of Maryland.

Stenson, K. 1993. Community Policing as a Governmental Technology. *Economy and Society*. 223: 373-389.

Trojanowicz, R. C. and M. H. Moore. 1988. *The Meaning of Community in Community Policing*. East Lansing, Michigan: National Neighborhood Foot Patrol Center.

Tyler, W. 1995. Community-based Strategies in Aboriginal Criminal Justice: The Northern Territory Experience. *Australian and New Zealand Journal of Criminology*. 282: 127-142.

Umbreit, M. and H. Zehr. 1996. Family Group Conferences: A Challenge to Victim Offender Mediation? *Victim Offenders Mediation Association Quarterly*. 71: 4-8.

Van Ness, D. 1989. Pursuing a Restorative Vision of Justice. In P. Arthur, ed. *Justice: The Restorative Vision*, pp. 17-30. New Perspectives on Crime and Justice Issue #7. Akron, Pennsylvania: Mennonite Central Committee Office of Criminal Justice.

Van Ness, D. and K. Strong.1997. *Restoring Justice*. Cincinnati, Ohio: Anderson Publishing Company.

Walter, M. and A. Wagner. 1996. How Police Officers Manage Difficult Situations: The Predominance of Soothing and Smoothing Strategies. In B. Galaway and J. Hudson, eds. *Restorative Justice: International Perspectives*, pp. 271-282. Monsey, New York: Criminal Justice Press.

Weiss, R. P. 1987. The Community and Prevention. In E H. Johnson, ed. *Handbook on Crime and Delinquency Prevention*, pp. 113-135. Westport, Connecticut: Greenwood Press.

Wright, M. 1996. *Justice for Victims and Offenders: A Restorative Response to Crime*, 2nd ed. Winchester, England: Waterside Press.

Wundersitz, J. and S. Hetzel. 1996. Family Conferencing for Young Offenders: The South Australian Experience. In G. Maxwell and A Morris, eds. *Family Group Conferences: Perspectives on Policy and Practice*. Monsey, New York: Criminal Justice Press.

Zehr, H. 1990. *Changing Lenses: A New Focus for Crime and Justice*. Scottsdale, Pennsylvania: Herald Press.

Questions

1. Explain why you agree or disagree with the central proposition that community as a place is a myth.

2. Can a community justice system operate effectively in a microcommunity relational framework that does not model the state and judicial geographical structure of our present criminal justice system?

3. Do you agree that the informal control mechanism of community justice is shame, the social approval/disapproval of behavior as the primary motivator?

4. Is the moral authority of the community a sufficient means to control society, even with the support of the legal authority of the government/police? Explain whether it will work at least as well as punishment or fear of punishment.

5. What role should community policing play in family group conferencing?

6. What type of checks and balances can ensure an even playing field when participants are of one overwhelming persuasion or prejudice—including the moderator?

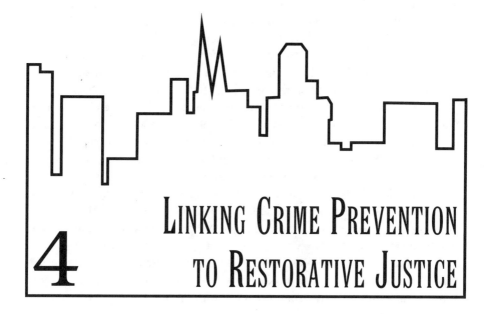

4

LINKING CRIME PREVENTION TO RESTORATIVE JUSTICE

JOHN BRAITHWAITE
MEMBER, CENTER FOR RESTORATIVE JUSTICE
AUSTRALIAN NATIONAL UNIVERSITY[1]
CANBERRA, AUSTRALIA

Restorative justice will never become a mainstream alternative to retributive justice unless long-term research and development programs show that it does have the capacity to reduce crime. Restorative justice theorists, including this author, long have advanced the claim that restorative justice conferences can deliver their benefits without directly attempting to pursue those benefits.[2]

This is true of the concept of reintegrative shaming, which is the community social disapproval of the criminal act combined with activities to foster reintegration of the offender with family and community, for example. The worst way to accomplish reintegrative shaming is to urge conference participants to shame the offender. That is a prescription for minimizing reintegrative shaming and maximizing stigmatization. Instead, reintegrative shaming comes as a by-product of confronting the consequences of the crime and what is to be done to put them right.

There is a similar paradox in procedural justice. Court proceedings are explicitly designed to achieve procedural justice outcomes such as equality before the law. With conferences, in contrast, there is no direct pursuit of equality before the law. Yet, we know from the RISE (Re-Integrative Shaming) experiment that conference participants are more likely to feel that they have experienced equality before the law in conference cases than in court cases (Sherman and Barnes, 1997). Victim-offender mediation studies also have produced encouraging results on procedural justice (Braithwaite, 1999).

There is a temptation to generalize these analyses to the claim that all the benefits of restorative justice are rather like the benefits of being spontaneous, the more directly we try to be spontaneous, the less spontaneous we will be. In some ways, our work may have fallen victim to a generalized tendency to expect the benefits to flow as an indirect outcome of simply pursuing restoration. This paper discuss the linkage between crime prevention interventions and restorative justice. Its argument will be that crime prevention must be directly pursued as an objective of conferences. Crime prevention benefits do not flow inevitably simply as a result of a restorative dialog.

Before moving on to explaining why the best way to make crime prevention work may be to link it to restorative justice, this author will make some remarks about why crime prevention programs that are not linked to restorative justice generally fail.

Why Crime Prevention Programs Mostly Fail

Crime prevention programs tend to be either police-initiated or community-based, or, perhaps most commonly, some mixture of the two. However originated, the author's contention will be that crime prevention programs mostly fail for four reasons:

1. Lack of motivation

2. Lack of resources

3. Insufficiently plural deliberation

4. Lack of follow-through

Now, let us consider each of these reasons for failure and see why linkage to restorative justice conferences might respond to them.

Lack of Motivation

Most of us never attend local Neighborhood Watch meetings. On the other hand, if a next door neighbor asked if we would come along to a restorative justice conference to support him as either an offender or a victim, he would be flattered by the invitation and attend.

Most crime prevention programs are uncoupled from the processing of individual criminal cases. This uncoupling is a lost opportunity in terms of motivating citizens to engage with crime prevention. Every police officer knows that the best time to persuade a householder to invest in security is after a burglary; every business regulator knows that the best time to persuade a company to invest in a corporate compliance system is after something goes wrong and someone gets into trouble. There are some good reasons for this heightened motivation.

In the case of the company that has just been in trouble, it is motivated by the knowledge that the regulator is watching it. In the case of the home-owner who has been burgled, there is worry that someone who knows how to get in will be watching for the arrival of brand-new replacement products. The latter motivation is well placed: one study has shown prospects of another burglary is four times as high as in houses that had not been burgled before (Bridgeman and Hobbs, 1997: 2). A project in Huddersfield that focused resources such as temporary alarms on prior victims reduced domestic burglary by 24 percent, in a Rockdale project by 72 percent (Bridgeman and Hobbs, 1997: 3).

Lack of Resources

Linking crime prevention to existing cases of victimization also mainstreams crime prevention to where the policing resources are—street-level enforcement—rather than leaving it ghettoized in specialist prevention units. Police services are famous for rhetoric about community policing and crime prevention, and then setting up special units for the purpose that attract a minuscule proportion of the police budget. Governments are famous for saying they believe in community crime prevention and then giving more than 90 percent of the crime prevention budget to the police.

As David Bayley and Clifford Shearing (1996) have pointed out, the remedy here may be to abandon the *police* budget in favour of a *policing* budget, so that citizen groups can contest police control over crime prevention resources. In the meantime, however, linking crime prevention to case management by the police may be the way to mainstream crime prevention. A discussion of both household-based and more widely community-based crime prevention options in restorative justice conferences is the path to mainstreaming this author wants to develop.

Plurality of Deliberation

The theory of crime prevention says "involve the community;" the practice says "citizens don't turn up to Neighborhood Watch meetings except in highly organized communities that don't need them." The empirical experience of restorative justice conferences is that citizens are willing to attend, often in large numbers. Indeed, in the design of conferencing, getting a diverse group of citizens affected by the crime to attend is critical to assuring that no one person or perspective dominates the meeting. Hence, if we achieve what is necessary for a well-designed conference, we also lay the foundations for the plurality of deliberation necessary for the design of crime prevention interventions that work. But why do we need this plurality?

The answer is that most crime problems have multiple causes and can be prevented in multiple ways. The burglary is caused by the offender's drug habit, his unemployment, poor security of the targeted house, and by the fact that citizens who saw it happening just walked on by. It follows that what we need is a capacity to read criminal situations from the different angles illuminated by different explanations. Elsewhere this author has argued that plural understandings of a crime problem are needed to stimulate a disparate range of action possibilities that can be integrated into a hedged, mutually reinforcing package of preventive policies (Braithwaite, 1993). Discussion of the problem by a group with local knowledge derived from being affected by the crime in different ways is a good path to a nuanced understanding of the crime.

Courts are not good at the acquisition of this kind of understanding. As Lon Fuller (1964: 33) suggests, only two types of problems are suited to full judicial-legal process: yes-no questions like "Did she do it?" and more-less questions like "How much should be paid?" Polanyi (1951: 174-84) distinguishes polycentric problems from these. They require reconciliation of complex interacting consequences of multidimensional phenomena. Polycentric problems are not well suited to the judicial model. Because most questions about crime beyond the determination of guilt are polycentric, courts are rather ineffective at preventing crime. This analysis can be illustrated with an example of plurality of deliberation coming to grips with preventive solutions to a polycentric problem.

The author was a part-time commissioner on Australia's national anti-trust and consumer protection agency when the most widespread and serious consumer protection frauds ever came before the agency. It involved a number of insurance companies systematically ripping off consumers through misrepresentations about policies that in some cases were totally useless. The worst abuses occurred in twenty-two remote Aboriginal communities and these were tackled first. Top management from the insurance company visited these communities for days on end at meetings with the victims, the local Aboriginal Community Council, the regulators, and local officials of the Department of Social Security in cases where useless policy premiums were being deducted from welfare checks. Some of those executives went back to the city deeply ashamed of what their company had done.

Back in Canberra, meetings were held with insurance regulators and industry associations and even with the prime minister about follow-up regulatory reforms. The plurality of participants led to a plurality of remedies from the first agreement (with Colonial Mutual Life). Colonial Mutual Life voluntarily compensated 2,000 policyholders and also funded an Aboriginal Consumer Education Fund to "harden targets" for future attempts to rip off illiterate people. It conducted an internal investigation to discover failings in the company's compliance program and to identify officers responsible for the crimes. A press conference was then called to reveal the enormity of the problem.

No one realized quite how enormous it was until a police union realized that its own members were being ripped off through the practices of another company (in this case, there were 300,000 victims and a payout of at least $50 million and perhaps $100 million by the company). As a result of the Colonial Mutual Life self-investigation, eighty officers or agents of the company were dismissed, including some senior managers and one large corporate agent, Tri-Global. Colonial Mutual Life also put in place new internal compliance policies. Some procedures relating to welfare checks changed in the Department of Social Security, and there were regulatory and self-regulatory changes concerning the licencing of agents and other matters and changes to the law (Fisse and Braithwaite, 1993, p. 235). This polycentric problem-solving was accomplished without going to court (except with a couple of players who refused to cooperate with the restorative justice process).

The disparate array of preventive measures was grounded in the different kinds of theories that the rich plurality of players involved in this restorative justice process created. They were theories of education, deterrence, incapacitation, rehabilitation, target hardening, moral hazard, adverse publicity, law, regulation, and opportunity theory.

What happens with the best crime prevention practice therefore is the following:

1. Dialog about restoration motivates the engagement of a wide plurality of stakeholders with their analysis of why this crime occurred and how recurrence might be prevented.

2. The polycentric problem is thereby grasped through commonsense versions of a variety of theories, used as metaphors to arrive at a nuanced understanding of the crime by seeing it as many things at once (Braithwaite, 1993).

3. Professionals talk with the stakeholders on their analysis of the advice available from the research literature on what has worked and what has failed in the past with this kind of problem.

4. Prevention professionals design with stakeholders an integrated strategy that is redundantly responsive to the theoretical relevance understood under point two, the research findings in point three, and the contextual differences from the situations in which the research was conducted as revealed by the discussions in point one.

Now, the cynic about restorative justice will say that the Australian insurance cases were unusually sweeping exercises in crime prevention. True, most crime prevention is more banal. Yet, this process was so sweeping in its ramifications precisely because it was restorative. What would have happened if we had prosecuted this case criminally? At best, the company would have been fined a fraction of what it actually paid out and there would have been a handful of follow-up civil claims by victims. At worst, illiterate Aboriginal witnesses would have been humiliated and discredited by uptown lawyers, the case lost, and no further ones taken. The industrywide extensiveness of a pattern of practices would never have been uncovered; that was only accomplished by the communitarian engagement of many locally knowledgeable actors.

To take another extreme example, a court has never convicted 52 adults of child abuse in one town of 600 people, a town in which it is estimated that a majority of the citizens were at some time in their lives victims of sexual abuse.[3] Healing circles in the Manitoba community of Hollow Water have accomplished that (Ross, 1996, p. 29-48; Lajeunesse, 1993). And the crime prevention accomplishments of the preventive measures put in place as a result of the restorative justice process seem creditable too: only two known cases of reoffending in the first few years (Ross, 1996, p. 36).

Restorative justice rituals can be a lever for triggering prevention of the most systemic and difficult-to-solve crimes in contemporary societies, like sexual abuse in families, like the crimes of finance capital. We should take seriously the possibility of family group conferences with leaders of Columbian cocaine cartels. How do we know they are beyond shame? How do we know that they would not like to retire at seventy instead of fear violent usurpation by a rival?[4] How do we know that they might not find very attractive an agreement that allowed them to pass on some of their wealth to set up legitimate businesses for their children so they did not need to bequeath to them the life they had led? How do we know that they do not actually hate killing other human beings in order to survive themselves?

An incipient and only very partially successful model here is the Raskol gang surrenders and gang retreats in Papua, New Guinea, which have involved surrenders of up to 400 alleged gang members (Dinnen, 1996). Political leaders up to the justice minister and prime minister and leaders of the church and other organizations in civil society have participated in these ceremonies receiving apologies, surrendered weapons, ammunition, undertakings to do community work, and work for the rehabilitation of their own members and youth gangs that have been their recruitment base. Dinnen (1996, p. 121) lists just the documented surrenders in a society where little is documented—13 rituals involving 913 alleged gang members.

In fact, one of the few successful antigang programs (Sherman et al., 1997) in one of the few places where the gang problem is worse than New

Guinea, Los Angeles, involved hiring older gang leaders as consultants to assist with the negotiation of truces and the mediation of feuds. Homicides and intergang violence fell among the targeted gangs but not between the targeted gangs and others (Torres, 1981, cited in Klein 1995, p. 149).

With the more banal crimes of screwed-up kids with screwed-up family relationships, plurality of deliberation seems equally relevant. One way of summarizing the literature on the effectiveness of psychotherapy is that in most cases it will do more good than harm and that this is true for most mainstream types of psychotherapeutic interventions in troubled lives. Even though therapy X is no better than therapy Y on average, it seems plausible that if a group of citizens knowledgeable about the problems of a particular individual are given the full facts about how therapies X and Y work, a marrying of those facts with their contextual knowledge of the case should lead to better-than-average selection of the right kind of treatment for their kind of case.

So, the author's hypothesis is that the plurality of deliberation in restorative justice conferences will increase the effectiveness of rehabilitative programs. The contextual wisdom that issues out of plural discussion from various angles is one reason. The other is that programs are more likely to be effective when the offenders and their family freely choose to make a commitment to them and when programs strengthen community support for the offender (Cullen, 1994).

It seems therefore that restorative justice does not involve a rejection of the rehabilitative ideal. It means reframing it. Instead of state professionals in social work or psychotherapy deciding that their pet approach is what is best for the family, the family is empowered with knowledge of a range of rehabilitative options and with the right to choose from among a variety of competing public, private, and charitable providers of rehabilitative services. This disempowering of state therapeutic monopolies is democratically superior—especially for a republican like the author who believes in freedom as nondomination (Braithwaite and Pettit, 1990; Pettit, 1997). The author's hypothesis is that the marriage to conferencing will increase the effectiveness of rehabilitation programs.

Follow-through

One of the things that shocked the author during his decade on the Trade Practices Commission was to learn that offenders often would have fines or community service obligations ordered by courts and then simply not pay them or fail to put in the hours. Mostly nothing would happen to them, even when they were major corporations. Everyone in the Australian criminal justice system seems to believe they have more important things to do than chase offenders who do not comply with court orders.

The hypothesis here is that restorative justice conference agreements attain higher levels of implementation than court orders precisely because they are agreements rather than orders. Collective obligation is brought to bear on securing compliance with agreements. There is little collective obligation when a court orders suspension of a driver's license following a drunk driving offense and implements no targeted follow-through to monitor compliance. So, driving without a licence is pandemic. On the other hand, if the agreement is that Uncle Harry (who lives next door) will make sure the offender always leaves his car in the garage on Friday and Saturday nights— the nights the offender consistently goes out drinking with the boys—collective obligation based on kinship and credible monitoring of compliance are structured into the agreement. The voluntary agreement secures superior compliance to the legally mandated one.

Preliminary evidence shows high compliance with agreements at victim-offender mediations or restorative justice conferences—ranging up from 58 percent in one New Zealand study (Galaway, 1992), and from 64 to 100 percent in various United States, Canadian, and British sites (Haley and Neugebauer, 1992; Dignan, 1992; Pate, 1990), 76 percent in West Germany (Trenczek, 1990), 85 percent in Finland (Iivari, 1987, 1992), and 86 percent (Wundersitz and Hetzel, 1996: 133) and 91 percent (Waters, 1993: 9) in Australian programs.

The RISE (Re-Integrative Shaming Experiment) by Lawrence Sherman and Heather Strang in Canberra will be the first to compare compliance with agreements for cases randomly assigned to restorative justice conferences versus court. The other important part of a follow-through is to learn from evaluations what aspects of restorative justice processes succeed and fail in putting in place credible preventive responses to crime. Evaluation of court processes in these crime prevention terms has been rather lacking. It is hoped that more of an evaluation culture will grow up around restorative justice processes.

Early Disappointments of Restorative Justice Conferences

Not everywhere has an open approach to evaluation and sharing of mistakes been evident among restorative justice practitioners. Many seem sure they have hit upon the right formula without seriously engaging with evaluation research.

In most restorative justice programs of which this author has experience, there is limited linkage of a crime prevention follow-through to the restorative justice process. Time and again in Canberra conferences, we see offenders with serious underlying drug and alcohol problems that are not even discussed, let alone confronted with a dialog about the different treatment programs available. We see problems of unemployment, school dropout, and dim future educational and employment prospects swept under the carpet.

The recently released award-winning Health Canada video, *Widening the Circle: The Family Group Decision Making Experience*, based on the work of

Gale Burford and Joan Pennell with family violence, advances best practices in this regard. The video shows a social worker put up on pieces of butcher paper the range of options available locally for dealing with family violence. The problem in many places is that the range of options genuinely available for the family to choose is not very wide. For all the innovativeness of the New Zealand work on restorative justice, its greatest defect is not to be found in the conferences themselves but in the collapse of the New Zealand welfare state and the paucity of rehabilitative options this leaves available to offenders, victims, and their families, especially in rural areas.

Another disappointment is the rarity of moving beyond individual crime prevention to more structural solutions. Corporate crime conferencing cases such as Colonial Mutual Life, which, as we have seen, does grapple with structural remedies, are very much the exception.

Conclusion

Restorative justice may be able to remove crime prevention from its marginal status in the criminal justice system, mainstreaming it into the enforcement process. It can deliver the motivation and widespread community participation crime prevention needs to work and to protect itself from capture by organized interests (including the crime prevention industry itself). Motivation and participation also improve the follow-through on conference agreements in comparison with the follow-through on court orders. Sometimes, but all too rarely, motivation and participation engendered by the restorative process can deliver the political clout to crime prevention that it needs to tackle systemic problems systemically. Plural participation in conferences fosters a capacity to see a crime as many things at once, caused in context by a variety of different true explanations, each of which suggests preventive options. Deliberation in conferences has the potential to increase the effectiveness of crime prevention by a contextual wisdom that better matches the right preventive options (therapeutic, situational, or structural) to the right case. That potential seems to be rarely realized at the moment.

Endnotes

[1] This paper was originally presented to the Real Justice Conference on Conferencing, Minneapolis, August 5–7, 1998.

[2] This is true in a longer review essay (Braithwaite, 1999) from which some sections of this paper have been taken. One problem, extensively discussed in that paper, is that when criminal justice programs are seen as directly setting out to change people, even by the most benign forms of mandated rehabilitation, they risk psychological reactance on the part of the offender (Brehm and Brehm, 1981). What follows is the virtue of directly pursuing restoration and only indirectly pursuing rehabilitation, deterrence, or remorse.

[3] LaPrairie (1994, p.iii), in a sophisticated study of this problem from a restorative justice perspective in another context, found that 46 percent of inner-city native people in Canada had experienced child abuse.

[4] Even common thieves give up because they find managing a criminal identity takes its toll: "[Y]ou get tired. You get tired trying to be a tough guy all the time. People always expecting this and that" (Shover, 1996, p. 137).

References

Bayley, David and Clifford Shearing. 1996. The Future of Policing. *Law and Society Review.* 30:585-606.

Braithwaite, John. 1993. Beyond Positivism: Learning from Contextual Integrated Strategies. *Journal of Research in Crime and Delinquency.* 30:383-99.

———. 1999. Restorative Justice: Assessing Optimistic and Pessimistic Accounts. In Michael Tonry, ed. *Crime and Justice: A Review of Research, Vol. 25,* pp. 1-121. Chicago: University of Chicago Press.

Braithwaite, J. and P. Pettit. 1990. *Not Just Deserts: A Republican Theory of Criminal Justice.* Oxford: Oxford University Press.

Brehm, Sharon S. and Jack W. Brehm. 1981. *Psychological Reactance: A Theory of Freedom and Control.* New York: Academic Press.

Bridgeman, C. and L. Hobbs. 1997. *Preventing Repeat Victimisation: The Police Officers' Guide.* London: Police Research Group.

Cullen, F. T. 1994. Social Support as an Organizing Concept for Criminology: Presidential Address to the Academy of Criminal Justice Sciences. *Justice Quarterly.* 11: 527-59.

Dignan, J. 1992. Repairing the Damage: Can Reparation Work in the Service of Diversion? *British Journal of Criminology.* 32: 453-72.

Dinnen, Sinclair. 1996. Challenges of Order in a Weak State. Unpublished doctoral dissertation. Australian National University.

Fisse, B. and J. Braithwaite. 1993. *Corporations, Crime and Accountability.* Cambridge: Cambridge University Press.

Fuller, Lon. 1964. *The Morality of Law.* New Haven, Connecticut: Yale University Press.

Galaway, B. 1992. The New Zealand Experience Implementing the Reparation Sentence. In H. Messmer and H. U. Otto, eds. *Restorative Justice on Trial: Pitfalls and Potentials of Victim-Offender Mediation — International Research Perspectives.* Dordrecht/Boston: Kluwer Academic Publishers.

Haley, John, assisted by A. M. Neugebauer. 1992. Victim-Offender Mediations: Japanese and American Comparisons. In H. Messmer and H. U. Otto, eds. *Restorative Justice on Trial: Pitfalls and Potentials of Victim-Offender Mediation — International Research Perspectives.* Dordrecht/Boston: Kluwer Academic Publishers.

Iivari, J. 1987. Mediation as a Conflict Resolution: Some Topic Issues in Mediation Project in Vantaa. Paper presented to International Seminar on Mediation, Finland, September. Cited in T. Marshall and S. Merry, eds. 1990. *Crime and Accountability: Victim Offender Mediation in Practice*. London: Home Office.

————. 1992. The Process of Mediation in Finland: A Special Reference to the Question 'How to Get Cases for Mediation.' In H. Messmer and H. U. Otto, eds. *Restorative Justice on Trial: Pitfalls and Potentials of Victim-Offender Mediation - International Research Perspectives*. Dordrecht/Boston: Kluwer Academic Publishers.

Klein, M. W. 1995. *The American Street Gang: Its Nature, Prevalence and Control*. New York: Oxford University Press.

Lajeunesse, T. 1993. *Community Holistic Circle Healing: Hollow Water First Nation, Aboriginal Peoples Collection*. Canada: Supply and Services.

LaPrairie, C. 1994. *Seen But Not Heard: Native People in the Inner City*. Report 3: Victimization and Domestic Violence. Ottawa: Department of Justice.

Pate, K. 1990. Victim-Offender Restitution Programs in Canada. In B. Galaway and J. Hudson, eds. *Criminal Justice, Restitution and Reconciliation*. New York: Willow Tree Press.

Pettit, Philip. 1997. *Republicanism*. Oxford: Clarendon Press.

Polanyi, Michael. 1951. *The Logic of Liberty*. Chicago: University of Chicago Press.

Ross, Rupert. 1996. *Returning to the Teachings: Exploring Aboriginal Justice*. London: Penguin Books.

Sherman, L. W. and G. Barnes. 1997. Restorative Justice and Offenders' Respect for the Law. Paper 3, RISE Working Paper. Law Program, Australian National University, Canberra.

Shover, Neal. 1996. *Great Pretenders: Pursuits and Careers of Persistent Thieves*. Bolder, Colorado: Westview Press.

Trenczek, T. 1990. A Review and Assessment of Victim-Offender Reconciliation Programming in West Germany. In B. Galaway and J. Hudson, eds. *Criminal Justice, Restitution and Reconciliation*. Monsey, New York: Willow Press.

Waters, Andrew. 1993. The Wagga Wagga Effective Cautioning Program: Reintegrative or Degrading? Bachelor of Arts Thesis, Department of Criminology, University of Melbourne.

Wundersitz, Joy and Sue Hetzel. 1996. Family Conferencing for Young Offenders: The South Australian Experience. In Joe Hudson, Allison Morris, Gabrielle Maxwell, and Burt Galaway, eds. *Family Group Conferences: Perspectives on Policy and Practice*. Sydney: Federation Press and Criminal Justice Press.

Vocabulary and Questions

- reintegrative shaming

- RISE

- polycentric problems

- deterrence

- incapacitation

- rehabilitation

- target hardening

- moral hazard

- adverse publicity

- law

- regulation

- opportunity theory

1. For what four reasons do most crime programs fail? What can be done to reduce the failure rate in each of the areas?

2. What does plurality of deliberation mean in terms of restorative justice conferences?

3. How does restorative justice involve a reframing of the rehabilitative ideal?

4. Why is follow through a vital part of retributive and restorative justice and what can be done to increase its implementation?

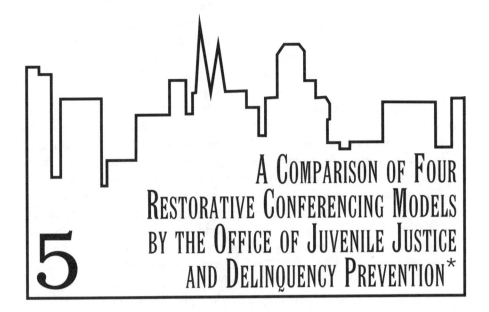

A Comparison of Four Restorative Conferencing Models by the Office of Juvenile Justice and Delinquency Prevention*

Gordon Bazemore, Ph.D.
Professor, Department of Criminology
    and Criminal Justice
Director, Community Justice Institute
Florida Atlantic University
Ft. Lauderdale, Florida

Mark Umbreit, Ph.D.
Director, Center for Restorative Justice
    and Peacemaking
University of Minnesota
St. Paul, Minnesota

Restorative justice is a framework for juvenile justice reform that seeks to engage victims, offenders and their families, other citizens, and community groups both as clients of juvenile justice services and as resources in an effective response to youth crime. Traditionally, when a crime is committed, juvenile justice systems have been primarily concerned with

---

*Originally published by the Office of Juvenile Justice and Delinquency Prevention, Washington, D.C., February, 2001. *Juvenile Justice Bulletin*, NCJ 184738. Reprinted with permission.

---

three questions: Who did it? What laws were broken? What should be done to punish or treat the offender? As noted by Howard Zehr (1990), restorative justice emphasizes three very different questions: What is the nature of the harm resulting from the crime? What needs to be done to "make it right" or repair the harm? Who is responsible for this repair? Restorative justice also suggests that the response to youth crime must strike a balance among the needs of victims, offenders, and communities and that each should be actively involved in the justice process to the greatest extent possible.

The term "restorative conferencing" is used in this chapter to encompass a range of strategies for bringing together victims, offenders, and community members in nonadversarial community-based processes aimed at responding to crime by holding offenders accountable and repairing the harm caused to victims and communities. Such strategies, now being implemented in North America, Australia, New Zealand, and parts of Europe, are one component of a new movement concerned with making criminal and juvenile justice processes less formal, bringing the processes into neighborhoods, and involving community members in planning and implementation (Barajas, 1995; Bazemore and Schiff, 1996; Griffiths and Hamilton, 1996; Travis, 1996).

This chapter focuses on four restorative conferencing models: victim-offender mediation, community reparative boards, family group conferencing, and circle sentencing. Although these four models by no means exhaust the possibilities for community involvement in decisions about how to respond to youth crime, the models do illustrate both the diversity and common themes apparent in what appears to be a new philosophy of citizen participation in sanctioning processes.

The chapter first describes each of the four restorative conferencing models,[1] presenting information on background and concept, procedures and goals, considerations in implementation, lessons learned from research, and sources of additional information. The chapter then compares and contrasts the models on the following dimensions: origins and current applications; administrative and procedural aspects (eligibility, point of referral, staffing, setting, process and protocols, and management of dialog); and community involvement and other dimensions (participants, victim role, gatekeepers, relationship to the formal justice system, preparation, enforcement, monitoring, and primary outcomes sought). Next, the chapter discusses a number of issues and concerns to be addressed in the development and implementation of restorative conferencing approaches. The chapter also offers guidelines for clearly grounding interventions in restorative justice principles and includes a test for determining whether an intervention strengthens the community response to youth crime and creates new roles for citizens and community groups.

In an evolving movement in which innovations are emerging rapidly, it is important to identify common principles that can be replicated by local juvenile courts and communities and that can serve to guide decision makers in choosing models best suited to local community needs. Toward this end, this chapter provides a general framework within which the myriad alternative interventions currently being characterized as restorative justice can be categorized and objectively analyzed and evaluated. Comparative discussions of new approaches at this relatively early stage of development are important because they serve to highlight similarities and differences across emerging models. In considering the four models discussed in the Chapter, however, it is important to avoid confusing the vision of prototypes with the realities of implementation and also to remember that the philosophy and practices of any given restorative conferencing program may deviate substantially from the prototypes presented here.

An Example of a Victim-Offender Mediation Session

The victim was a middle-aged woman. The offender, a fourteen-year-old neighbor of the victim, had broken into the victim's home and stolen a VCR. The mediation session took place in the basement of the victim's church. In the presence of a mediator, the victim and offender talked for two hours. At times, their conversation was heated and emotional. When they finished, the mediator felt that they had heard each other's stories and learned something important about the impact of the crime and about each other.

The participants agreed that the offender would pay $200 in restitution to cover the cost of damages to the victim's home resulting from the break-in and would also reimburse the victim for the cost of the stolen VCR (estimated at $150). They also worked out a payment schedule.

During the session, the offender made several apologies to the victim and agreed to complete community service hours working in a food bank sponsored by the victim's church. The victim said that she felt less angry and fearful after learning more about the offender and the details of the crime. She also thanked the mediator for allowing the session to be held at her church.

Victim-Offender Mediation

Background and Concept

Although still unfamiliar to many mainstream juvenile and criminal justice audiences and marginal to the court process in some jurisdictions where they do operate, victim-offender mediation programs—referred to in some communities as "victim-offender reconciliation programs" and, increasingly, as "victim-offender dialog programs"—have a respectable twenty-year track record in the United States, Canada, and Europe. Currently, there are approximately 320 victim-offender mediation programs in the United States and Canada and more than 700 in Europe. Several programs in North America currently receive nearly 1,000 case referrals annually from local courts. Although the greatest proportion of cases involve less serious property crimes committed by young people, the process is used increasingly in response to serious and violent crimes committed by both juveniles and adults (Umbreit, 1997).

The victim-offender mediation process offers victims an opportunity to meet offenders in a safe, structured setting and engage in a mediated discussion of the crime.[2] With the assistance of a trained mediator, the victim is able to tell the offender about the crime's physical, emotional, and financial impact; receive answers to lingering questions about the crime and the offender; and be directly involved in developing a restitution plan for the offender to pay back any financial debt to the victim. The process is different from mediation as practiced in civil or commercial disputes, because the involved parties are in agreement about their respective roles in the crime. Also, the process should not be primarily focused on reaching a settlement, although most sessions do, in fact, result in a signed restitution agreement.[3] Because of these fundamental differences, the terms "victim-offender meeting," "conferencing," and "dialog" are becoming increasingly popular to describe variations from standard mediation practices (Umbreit, 1997).

Procedures and Goals

Cases may be referred to victim-offender mediation programs by judges, probation officers, victim advocates, prosecutors, defense attorneys, and law enforcement. In some programs, cases are primarily referred as a diversion from prosecution (assuming that any agreement reached during the mediation session is successfully completed). In other programs, cases are usually referred after a formal admission of guilt has been accepted by the court, with mediation being a condition of probation or other disposition (if the victim has volunteered to participate). Some programs receive case referrals at both stages.

During mediation sessions, victims explain how the crime affected them and are given the opportunity to ask questions about the incident and help develop a plan for restoring losses. Offenders are given the opportunity to tell their stories and take direct responsibility through making amends in some form (Umbreit, 1994).

The goals of victim-offender mediation include the following:

- Supporting the healing process of victims by providing a safe, controlled setting for them to meet and speak with offenders on a strictly voluntary basis.

- Allowing offenders to learn about the impact of their crimes on the victims and take direct responsibility for their behavior.

- Providing an opportunity for the victim and offender to develop a mutually acceptable plan that addresses the harm caused by the crime.

Considerations in Implementation

In implementing any victim-offender mediation program, it is critically important to maintain sensitivity to the needs of the victim. First and foremost, the mediator must do everything possible to ensure that the victim will not be harmed in any way. Additionally, the victim's participation must be completely voluntary. The offender's participation should also be voluntary. Offenders are typically given the option of participating in mediation or dialog as one of several dispositional choices. Although offenders almost never have absolute choice (for example, the option of no juvenile justice intervention), they should never be coerced into meetings with victims. The victim should also be given choices, whenever possible, about procedures, such as when and where the mediation session will take place, who will be present, and who will speak first. Cases should be carefully screened regarding the readiness of both victim and offender to participate. The mediator should conduct in-person premediation sessions with both parties to clarify the issues to be resolved. The mediator should also make follow-up contacts and monitor any agreement reached.

Lessons Learned

A large multisite study of victim-offender mediation programs with juvenile offenders (Umbreit, 1994) found the following:

- In cases referred to the four study-site programs during a two-year period, 95 percent of mediation sessions resulted in a successfully negotiated restitution agreement to restore the victim's financial losses.

- Victims who met with offenders in the presence of a trained mediator were more likely to be satisfied with the justice system than were similar victims who went through the standard court process (79 percent versus 57 percent).

- After meeting offenders, victims were significantly less fearful of being revictimized.

- Offenders who met with victims were far more likely to successfully complete their restitution obligation than were similar offenders who did not participate in mediation (81 percent versus 58 percent).

- Recidivism rates were lower among offenders who participated in mediation than among offenders who did not participate (18 percent versus 27 percent); furthermore, participating offenders' subsequent crimes tended to be less serious.[4]

Multisite studies (Coates and Gehm, 1989; Umbreit, 1994) also found that although restitution was an important motivator for victim participation in mediation sessions, victims consistently viewed actual receipt of restitution as secondary to the opportunity to talk about the impact of the crime, meet the offender, and learn the offender's circumstances. The studies also found that offenders appreciated the opportunity to talk to the victim and felt better after doing so.

A recent statewide survey of victim service providers in Minnesota found that 91 percent believed that victim-offender mediation should be available in every judicial district because it represents an important victim service. The American Bar Association recently endorsed victim-offender mediation and recommends its use throughout the United States. As of 1997, victim-offender mediation programs have been identified in nearly every state (Umbreit and Schug, 1997).

For More Information

For more information on victim-offender mediation, contact:

- Dr. Mark Umbreit, Director, Center for Restorative Justice and Peacemaking, University of Minnesota, School of Social Work, 105 Peters Hall, 1404 Gortner Avenue, St. Paul, MN 55108-6160, 612-624-4923 (phone), 612-625-3744 (fax), rjp@tlcmail.che.umn.edu (e-mail), sswche.umn.edu/rjp (Internet).

- Victim Offender Mediation Association (VOMA), c/o Claire Harris, Administrator, Center for Policy, Planning and Performance, 2344 Nicollet Avenue South, Suite 330, Minneapolis, MN 55404, voma@voma.org (e-mail), www.voma.org (Internet).

Community Reparative Boards

Background and Concept

The community reparative board is a recent version of a much older and more widespread community sanctioning response to youth crime, generally known by such terms as youth panels, neighborhood boards, or community diversion boards. These panels or boards have been in use in the United States since the 1920s, and their contemporary counterparts, reparative boards, have been in use since the mid-1990s, principally in Vermont. There, the boards are primarily used with adult offenders convicted of nonviolent and minor offenses; more recently, the boards have also been used with juvenile offenders.[5] Reparative boards typically are composed of a small group of citizens, prepared for their function by intensive training, who conduct public, face-to-face meetings with offenders ordered by the court to participate in the process. The boards develop sanction agreements with offenders, monitor compliance, and submit compliance reports to the court.

Community Reparative Board Session Example

The reparative board convened to consider the case of a seventeen-year-old who had been caught driving with an open can of beer in his father's pickup truck. The youth had been sentenced by a judge to reparative probation, and it was the board's responsibility to decide what form the probation should take. For about thirty minutes, the citizen members of the board asked the youth several simple, straightforward questions. The board members then went to another room to deliberate on an appropriate sanction for the youth. The youth awaited the board's decision nervously, because he did not know whether to expect something tougher or much easier than regular probation.

When the board returned, the chairperson explained the four conditions of the offender's probation contract: (1) begin work to pay off his traffic tickets, (2) complete a state police defensive driving course, (3) undergo an alcohol assessment, and (4) write a three-page paper on how alcohol had negatively affected his life. The youth signed the contract, and the chairperson adjourned the meeting.

Procedures and Goals

During reparative board meetings, board members discuss with the offender the nature of the offense and its negative consequences. Then, board members develop a set of proposed sanctions, which they discuss with the offender until an agreement is reached on the specific actions the offender will take within a given time period to make reparation for the crime. Subsequently, the offender must document his or her progress in fulfilling the terms of the agreement. After the stipulated period of time has passed, the board submits a report to the court on the offender's compliance with the agreed-upon sanctions. At this point, the board's involvement with the offender ends.

The goals of community reparative boards include the following:

- Promoting citizens' ownership of the criminal and juvenile justice systems by involving them directly in the justice process.

- Providing an opportunity for victims and community members to confront offenders in a constructive manner about their behavior.

- Providing opportunities for offenders to take personal responsibility and be held directly accountable for the harm they caused to victims and communities.

- Generating meaningful community-driven consequences for criminal and delinquent actions, thereby reducing costly reliance on formal justice system processing.

Considerations in Implementation

The Vermont Department of Corrections implemented its Reparative Probation Program in 1995, in response to a 1994 public opinion survey (conducted by John Doble and Associates) in which citizens indicated broad support for programs with a reparative emphasis and active community involvement. The program's reparative boards are part of a mandated separation of probation into community corrections service units (designed to provide supervision for more serious cases) and court and reparative service units (which coordinate and provide administrative support to reparative boards).

Based on Vermont's experience, the following factors have been identified by the Vermont Department of Corrections as important in implementing community-driven reparative board programs:

- Marketing the program effectively to the justice system (to judges, prosecutors, and defense attorneys)

- Having a committed, well-trained staff

- Working with victim organizations and ensuring that victims are represented and provided adequate opportunity to participate[6]

- Processing cases expeditiously and in a manner that is easy for community members to understand

- Facilitating a positive experience for the board members

- Providing quality training for the boards

- Supporting the program with adequate resources (for example, space, time, and staff)

- Striving for successful outcomes for offenders, victims, and community participants in the board's initial cases

- Getting support from judges in limiting the time the offender is in the program and on probation

Lessons Learned

Only limited quantitative data have been collected on the effectiveness of community reparative boards. There is growing concern that evaluations of reparative board programs should consider measures beyond the standard offender-focused measure of recidivism. Additional measures should include responsiveness to victim and community needs, victim and community satisfaction, and impact on the community (including physical improvements resulting from board-imposed community work sanctions and indicators of healthy relationships among citizens). At this point, experiential and anecdotal information indicates that reparative boards show much promise as an effective response to nonviolent crime.

For More Information

For more information on reparative boards, contact:

- David Peebles, Director of Restorative Services, Vermont Department of Corrections, 103 South Main Street, Waterbury, VT 05671, 802-241-2261 (phone).

- The National Institute of Corrections Information Center, 1860 Industrial Circle, Suite A, Longmont, CO 80501, 800-877-1461 (phone).

Also, see *Restoring Hope through Community Partnerships* (American Probation and Parole Association, 1996), available from the American Probation and Parole Association, c/o Council of State Governments,. P.O. Box 11910, Lexington, KY 40578-1910, 859-244-8203 (phone); and *Community Reparative Boards: Theory and Practice* (Karp and Walther, 2001).

Family Group Conferencing Session Example

A family conferencing group convened in a local school to consider a case in which a student had injured a teacher and broken the teacher's glasses in an altercation. Group members included the offender, his mother and grandfather, the victim, the police officer who made the arrest, and about ten other interested parties (including two of the offender's teachers and two friends of the victim).

The conferencing process began with comments by the offender, his mother and grandfather, the victim, and the arresting officer. Each spoke about the offense and its impact. The youth justice coordinator next asked for input from the other group members and then asked all participants what they thought the offender should do to pay back the victim and the community for the damage caused by his crime. In the remaining thirty minutes of the hour-long conference, the group suggested that the offender should make restitution to the victim for his medical expenses and the cost of new glasses, and that the offender should also perform community service work on the school grounds.

Family Group Conferencing

Background and Concept

Family group conferencing is based on centuries-old sanctioning and dispute resolution traditions of the Maori of New Zealand. In its modern form, the model was adopted into national legislation in New Zealand in 1989, making it the most systemically institutionalized of any of the four models. In South Australia, family conferencing is now widely used in modified form as a police-initiated diversion approach known as the Wagga Wagga model. Developed by the Wagga Wagga Police Department, this model uses police officers or school officials to set up and facilitate family conferencing meetings. Conferencing is also being used in U.S. cities in Minnesota, Montana, Pennsylvania, Vermont, and several other states and in parts of Canada. (The Wagga Wagga model is the primary approach that has taken hold in North America.) A variety of offenses have been resolved through family group conferencing, including theft, arson, minor assaults, drug offenses, vandalism, and, in a number of states, child maltreatment cases. In New Zealand, conferencing is used in the disposition of all but the most violent and serious delinquency cases (Alder and Wundersitz, 1994; Maxwell and Morris, 1993; McElrea, 1993).

Family group conferencing involves the community of people most affected by the crime—the victim, the offender, and the family, friends, and key supporters of both—in deciding the resolution of a criminal or delinquent incident. The affected parties are brought together by a trained facilitator to discuss how they and others have been harmed by the offense and how that harm might be repaired.

Procedures and Goals

The conference facilitator contacts the victim and offender to explain the process and invite them to the conference. The facilitator also asks the victim and offender to identify key members of their support systems, who also will be invited to participate. The conference typically begins with the offender describing the incident. The other participants then describe the impact of the incident on their lives. Some argue that it is preferable to allow the victim to start the discussion, if he or she wishes to do so (Umbreit and Stacy, 1996). Through these narrations, the offender is faced with the impact of his or her behavior on the victim, on those close to the victim, and on the offender's own family and friends, and the victim has the opportunity to express feelings and ask questions about the incident. After a thorough discussion of impacts, the victim is asked to identify desired outcomes from the conference; in this way, the victim can help to shape the obligations that will be placed on the offender. All participants contribute to the problem-solving process of determining how the offender might best repair the harm he or she has caused. The session ends with participants signing an agreement that outlines their expectations and commitments.

Goals of family group conferencing include the following:

- Providing an opportunity for the victim to be directly involved in the discussion of the offense and in decisions regarding appropriate sanctions to be placed on the offender.

- Increasing the offender's awareness of the human impact of his or her behavior and providing the offender an opportunity to take full responsibility for it.

- Engaging the collective responsibility of the offender's support system for making amends and shaping the offender's future behavior.

- Allowing both offender and victim to reconnect to key community support systems.

Considerations in Implementation

The family group conferencing process has been implemented in schools, police departments, probation offices, residential programs, community mediation programs, and neighborhood groups. Conferencing is most often used as diversion from the court process for juveniles but can also be used after adjudication and disposition to address unresolved issues or determine specific terms of restitution. Conferencing programs have been implemented within single agencies and developed collaboratively among several agencies. After completing a training course, either volunteers or paid employees can serve as conference facilitators.

Participation by all involved in conferences is voluntary. In addition to the victim and offender and their family members, a conference might involve teachers, other relatives, peers, special adult friends, and community resource people.

Lessons Learned

To date, two studies have been conducted to assess the impact of family group conferencing with young offenders. One study (Maxwell and Morris, 1993) assessed the impact of New Zealand's law mandating the widespread use of conferencing. It found that families of offenders in conferencing programs are more frequently and actively involved in the justice process than are families of offenders whose cases are handled by standard procedures. It also found that offenders, victims, and their families described the conference process as helpful. Preliminary evaluations of conferencing programs in the United States also indicate high levels of victim satisfaction with the conference process and high rates of offender compliance with agreements reached during conferences (Fercello and Umbreit, 1999; McCold and Wachtel, 1998).

Practitioners involved in family group conferencing programs observe a reduction in fear for many victims. When used as a diversion from court, conferencing can provide a much speedier and more satisfying resolution of incidents than would otherwise be the case. Family group conferencing also builds community skills in conflict resolution and participatory decision making.

For More Information

For more information about family group conferencing, contact:

- David Hines, Woodbury Police Department, 2100 Radio Drive, Woodbury, MN 55125-9528, 651-714-3600 (phone).

- Kay Pranis or Sue Stacey, Minnesota Department of Corrections, 1450 Energy Park Drive, Suite 200, St. Paul, MN 55108, 651-642-0329 or 651-642-0338 (phone).

- Real Justice, P.O. Box 229, Bethlehem, PA 18016, 610-807-9221 (phone).

Circle Sentencing

Background and Concept

Circle sentencing is an updated version of the traditional sanctioning and healing practices of aboriginal peoples in Canada and American Indians in the United States (Stuart, 1995; Melton, 1995). Sentencing circles—sometimes called peacemaking circles—were resurrected in 1991 by judges and community justice committees in the Yukon Territory and other northern Canadian communities. Circle sentencing has been developed most extensively in Saskatchewan, Manitoba, and the Yukon and has been used occasionally in several other communities. Its use spread to the United States in 1996, when a pilot project was initiated in Minnesota. Circle sentencing has been used for adult and juvenile offenders, for a variety of offenses, and in both rural and urban settings.

Circle sentencing is a holistic reintegrative strategy designed not only to address the criminal and delinquent behavior of offenders but also to consider the needs of victims, families, and communities. Within the "circle," crime victims, offenders, family and friends of both, justice and social service personnel, and interested community residents speak from the heart in a shared search for an understanding of the event. Together they identify the steps necessary to assist in healing all affected parties and to prevent future crimes. The significance of the circle is more than symbolic: all circle members—police officers, lawyers, judges, victims, offenders, and community residents—participate in deliberations to arrive at a consensus for a sentencing plan that addresses the concerns of all interested parties.

Procedures and Goals

Circle sentencing typically involves a multistep procedure that includes (1) application by the offender to participate in the circle process, (2) a healing circle for the victim, (3) a healing circle for the offender, (4) a sentencing circle to develop consensus on the elements of a sentencing plan, and (5) followup circles to monitor the progress of the offender. In addition to commitments by the offender, the sentencing plan may incorporate commitments by the justice system, community, and family members. Specifics of the circle process vary from community to community and are designed locally to fit community needs and culture.

Goals of circle sentencing include the following:

- Promoting healing for all affected parties

- Providing an opportunity for the offender to make amends

- Empowering victims, community members, families, and offenders by giving them a voice and a shared responsibility in finding constructive resolutions

- Addressing the underlying causes of criminal behavior

- Building a sense of community and its capacity for resolving conflict

- Promoting and sharing community values

Considerations in Implementation

The success of the circle sentencing process depends to a large extent on a healthy partnership between the formal juvenile justice system and the community. Participants from both need training and skill building in the circle process and in peacemaking and consensus building. It is critically important that the community's planning process allow sufficient time for strong relationships to develop between justice professionals and community members. Implementation procedures should be highly flexible, because the circle process will evolve over time based on the community's knowledge and experience. As it gains experience, the community can customize the circle process to fit local resources and culture.

In many communities that have implemented the circle sentencing concept, direction and leadership have come from a community justice committee that decides which cases to accept, develops support groups for the victim and offender, and helps to conduct the circles. In most communities, circles are facilitated by a trained community member, who is often called a keeper.

Although circles have been used as a response to serious and violent crimes, circle sentencing is not an appropriate response to all offenses. Key factors in determining whether a case is appropriate for the circle process include the offender's character and personality, sincerity, and connection to the community; the victim's input; and the dedication of the offender's and victim's support groups. Moreover, circles are often labor intensive and require a substantial investment of citizen time and effort; circles should not, therefore, be used extensively as a response to first offenders and minor crime.

The capacity of the circle to advance solutions capable of improving the lives of participants and the overall well-being of the community depends on the effectiveness of the participating volunteers. To ensure a cadre of capable volunteers, the program should support a paid community-based volunteer coordinator to supply logistical support, establish linkages with other agencies and community representatives, and provide appropriate training for all staff.

A Circle Sentencing Session Example

The victim was a middle-aged man whose parked car had been badly damaged when the offender, a sixteen-year-old, crashed into it while joyriding in another vehicle. The offender had also damaged a police vehicle.

In the circle, the victim talked about the emotional shock of seeing what had happened to his car and his costs to repair it (he was uninsured). Then, an elder leader of the First Nations community where the circle sentencing session was being held (and an uncle of the offender) expressed his disappointment and anger with the boy. The elder observed that this incident, along with several prior offenses by the boy, had brought shame to his family. The elder also noted that in the old days, the boy would have been required to pay the victim's family substantial compensation as a result of such behavior. After the elder finished, a feather (the "talking piece") was passed to the next person in the circle, a young man who spoke about the contributions the offender had made to the community, the kindness he had shown toward elders, and his willingness to help others with home repairs.

Having heard all this, the judge asked the Crown Council (Canadian prosecutor) and the public defender, who were also sitting in the circle, to make statements and then asked if anyone else in the circle wanted to speak. The Royal Canadian Mounted Police officer, whose vehicle had also been damaged, then took the feather and spoke on the offender's behalf. The officer proposed to the judge that in lieu of statutorily required jail time for the offense, the offender be allowed to meet with him on a regular basis for counseling and community service. After asking the victim and the prosecutor if either had any objections, the judge accepted this proposal. The judge also ordered restitution to the victim and asked the young adult who had spoken on the offender's behalf to serve as a mentor for the offender. After a prayer in which the entire group held hands, the circle disbanded and everyone retreated to the kitchen area of the community center for refreshments.

Lessons Learned

Very little research has been conducted to date on the effectiveness of circle sentencing. One study conducted by Judge Barry Stuart in Canada in 1996 indicated that recidivism was less likely among offenders who had participated in circles than among offenders who were processed traditionally (Stuart, 1996). Those who have been involved with circles report that circles empower participants to resolve conflict in a manner that promotes sharing of responsibility for outcomes, generates constructive relationships, enhances respect and understanding among all involved, and fosters enduring, innova-

tive solutions.
For More Information

For more information on circle sentencing, see *Building Community Justice Partnerships: Community Peacemaking Circles*, by Barry Stuart. The publication is available from Aboriginal Justice Section, Department of Justice of Canada, Ottawa, Ontario, Canada K1AOH8, Attention: Learning Network, 613-954-0119 (phone), 613-957-4697 (fax).

Comparing and Contrasting the Four Models: Administration and Process

Table 1 (on the next page) describes the origins and current applications of the four restorative conferencing models and summarizes administrative and procedural similarities and differences among them. Although the four models share a nonadversarial, community-based sanctioning focus on cases in which offenders either admit guilt or have been found guilty of crimes or delinquent acts, the models vary along several administrative and procedural dimensions. This discussion highlights selected dimensions in Table 1 that vary significantly from model to model.

The models differ in point of referral and in structural relationship to formal court and correctional systems. The models also differ in eligibility, which ranges from minor first offenders to quite serious repeat offenders (in the case of circle sentencing).

With the exception of most community reparative boards, decision making is by consensus. Specific processes and protocols, however, vary substantially, ranging from circle sentencing's ancient ritual of passing a stick or feather as a "talking piece" (Stuart, 1995) to the more formal deliberation process followed by reparative boards (Dooley, 1995).

The process of managing dialog varies significantly among the four models. In reparative board hearings, a chairperson guides members through their questioning of the offender and their discussions with hearing participants. In family group conferences, a coordinator manages the discussion by encouraging all participants to speak. In victim-offender mediation sessions, the mediator manages the dialog by encouraging the victim and the offender to take primary responsibility for expressing their feelings and concerns directly to each other, by ensuring that each participant respects the other's right to speak, and by occasionally probing to keep the discussion flowing. In circle sentencing, participants rely primarily on the process itself, which requires that only one person speak at a time and only when handed the talking piece. Each circle has a "keeper," but the keeper's role is not to manage the dialog but simply to initiate it, ensure the process is followed, and occasionally summarize progress.

Table 1: Restorative Conferencing Models: Administration and Process

	Victim-Offender Mediation	Reparative Boards	Family Group Conferencing	Circle Sentencing
Origin	Since mid-1970s.	Since 1995 (similar youth panels: since 1920).	New Zealand, 1989; Australia, 1991.	Since approximately 1992.
Current applications	Throughout North America and Europe.	Vermont; selected jurisdictions and neighborhoods in other States.	Australia; New Zealand; United States (since 1990s), in cities and towns in Montana, Minnesota, Pennsylvania, and other States.	Primarily the Yukon, sporadically in other parts of Canada. Minnesota, Colorado, and Massachusetts.
Referral point in system	Mostly diversion and probation option. Some use in residential facilities for more serious cases	One of several probation options (youth panels: almost exclusively diversion).	New Zealand: throughout juvenile justice system. Australian Wagga Wagga model: police diversion. Unite States: mostly diversion, some use in schools and post-adjudication.	Various stages. May be diversion or alternative to formal court hearings and corrections process for indictable offenses.
Eligibility and target group	Varies. Primarily diversion cases and property offenders. In some locations, used with serious and violent offenders (at victim's request).	Target group is non-violent offenders; eligibility limited to offenders given probation and assigned to the boards.	New Zealand: all juvenile offenders eligible except those charged with murder and manslaughter. Australian Wagga Wagga model: determined by police discretion or diversion criteria.	Offenders who admit guilt and express willingness to change. Entire range of offenses and offenders eligible; chronic offenders targeted.
Staffing	Mediator. Other positions vary.	Reparative coordinator (probation staff).	Community justice coordinator.	Community justice coordinator.
Setting	Neutral setting (meeting room in library, church, community center); victim's home (occasionally, if all parties approve).	Public building or community center.	Social welfare office, school, community building, police facility (occasionally)	Community center, school, other public building, church.
Process and Protocols	Victim speaks first. Mediator facilitates but encourages victim and offender to speak, does not adhere to script.	Mostly private deliberation by board after questioning offender and hearing statements. Some variation emerging in local boards (youth panel members generally deliberate).	Australian Wagga Wagga model: coordinator follows script in which offender speaks first, then victim and others. New Zealand: model not scripted, allows consensus decision making after private meeting of family members.	Keeper opens session and allows for comments from judge. Prosecutors and defense present legal facts of case (for more serious crimes). All participants allowed to speak when "talking piece" (feather or stick) is passed to them. Consensus decisionmaking.
Managing Dialogue	Mediator manages.	Board chairperson manages. Participants speak when asked.	Coordinator manages.	After keeper initiates, dialog managed by process of passing talking piece.

Comparing and Contrasting the Four Models: Community Involvement and Other Dimensions

Table 2 (page 86) summarizes aspects of community involvement for each of the four restorative conferencing models. Table 2 also addresses several other dimensions that provide useful points of comparison among the models, including victim role and preparation/followup.

The way "community" is defined and involved in restorative conferencing models is a critical factor affecting the nature and extent of citizen participation in and ownership of the conferencing process. As Table 2 suggests, victim-offender mediation, for example, in effect defines the community as the victim-offender dyad.[7] In circle sentencing, on the other hand, the community is conceptualized much more broadly as all residents of a local neighborhood, village, or aboriginal band; for purposes of implementing the circle process, the community may be defined as anyone with a stake in the resolution of a crime who chooses to participate in the circle.

The remainder of this section focuses on two particularly important additional dimensions of the restorative conferencing models: victim role and preparation/ followup.

Victim's Role

The formal justice system directs its attention primarily toward the offender, first with regard to guilt or innocence and second with regard to appropriate punishment, treatment, or monitoring. The community is often an abstract and distant concern (Barajas, 1995; Clear, 1996). Because victims have been so neglected as stakeholders in both formal and community justice approaches, it is important to give special attention to their role in each restorative conferencing process.

Victim-offender mediation. Mediation programs offer victims an opportunity to tell offenders how the crime has affected them, give victims maximum input into plans for holding offenders responsible, and ensure that victims are compensated for their losses to the greatest extent possible. The programs also provide victims with referrals for needed services and assistance.

Victims frequently are given the opportunity to speak first in mediation sessions, which helps them feel empowered or at least not overwhelmed or abused by the process. Mediation programs give the needs of victims and offenders priority over the needs of other participants in the process (such as parents and other relatives), but victims receive extra attention to ensure that they are not revictimized by the process itself. Victim participation in the mediation process is voluntary. Most programs also are voluntary for offenders and attempt to engage their participation in the least coercive manner possible (Umbreit and Greenwood, 1998). In some jurisdictions, however, offenders are often less-than-willing participants (Belgrave, 1995).

Increasingly, mediation programs seek to offer their services in a victim-sensitive manner (Umbreit, 1994; Umbreit and Greenwood, 1998). In contrast to other models, most research studies report that victim satisfaction with victim-offender mediation has been uniformly high (Belgrave, 1995; Umbreit and Coates, 1993).

Reparative boards. The design of Vermont's reparative boards was shaped to a large extent by restorative justice concepts (Dooley, 1995; and Dooley, Vermont Department of Corrections, personal communication, 1996), and state officials who developed and now monitor the boards strongly encourage an emphasis on victim participation. Nevertheless, in the early months of operation, victim involvement in most local boards was minimal (Dooley, personal communication). Some boards appear to have increased victim involvement, but it remains to be seen to what extent citizen board members will want to take on the demanding task of contacting crime victims and engaging their participation in the justice process (Karp and Walther, 2001). Some boards have demonstrated a strong commitment to making certain that offenders repay victims; ultimately, this commitment might motivate increased involvement of victims as the value of all forms of victim-offender dialog in improving restitution completion rates becomes clearer (Umbreit and Coates, 1993). State administrators have also encouraged boards to refer victims and offenders to victim-offender mediation or family group conferencing programs, if such programs are available in the community and if victims agree to participate (Dooley, 1996).

Family group conferencing. The dimensions of victim protection and empowerment are more complex in models that move beyond the small group or dyad to the larger community. Family group conferencing is perhaps the strongest of all the models in its potential for educating offenders about the harm their behavior causes to others. Concerns have been expressed, however, about the role of victims in this model. Among these concerns are the following:

- Emphasis on offender education may cause victim needs to be overshadowed or trivialized (Belgrave, 1995; Umbreit and Zehr, 1996), as appears to have been the case when conferences have been held with little or no victim input or involvement (Alder and Wundersitz, 1994; Maxwell and Morris, 1993).

- Standard protocol for family group conferences requires that offenders speak first (McDonald et al., 1995), which may affect victims' participation in the discussion.

- Some interpretations of family group conferencing place primary emphasis on getting offenders to experience shame (Alder and Wundersitz, 1994; Strang, 1995). In such interpretations, victim benefits are limited to an apology and perhaps material restitution. Either or both of these benefits may meet the main needs of many victims, but other needs may be neglected. Moreover, if forgiveness is a primary goal, the process may be slanted toward eliciting apologies from offenders, and victims may feel pressured to offer forgiveness and resentful of the implication that they should do so, and resentment may cause some victims to refuse to participate (Umbreit and Stacy, 1996).

- Other criticisms of victim treatment in the family group conferencing model cite a lack of concern with victim empowerment, lack of protection against abuse or retaliation, and use of victims to serve as "props" or to meet offender needs (Umbreit and Zehr, 1996).

Victim participation and satisfaction were indeed significant problems during the early development of family group conferencing in New Zealand (Maxwell and Morris, 1993), but it is wrong to conclude that most advocates of the conferencing model are not concerned with victims' needs (Moore and O'Connell, 1994; Braithwaite and Mugford, 1994). Recent studies of family group conferencing programs in Minnesota (Fercello and Umbreit, 1999; Umbreit and Fercello, 1997), Pennsylvania (McCold and Wachtel, 1998), and South Australia (Daly, 2000) have found higher rates of victim participation and satisfaction than when the model was first introduced in New Zealand (Morris and Maxwell, 2001).

Such criticisms of victim treatment in family group conferencing (or in any alternative model) should have as its context the extent to which the current formal system does or does not provide for victim reparation, empowerment, and support (Stuart, 1996). Nevertheless, as family group conferencing models evolve, it will be important to keep in mind that emphasis on offender shaming and reintegration may limit the model's capacity to meet the needs of crime victims.

Circle sentencing. Proponents of circle sentencing are concerned with protecting victims, providing them with support, and hearing their stories. Circle organizers avoid an unbalanced focus on offenders' issues, which may cause victims to withdraw or react by challenging offenders (Stuart, 1996). Victims' telling of their stories is viewed as important not only for victims, offenders, and their supporters, but also for the community as a whole. If a victim is unwilling to participate in a circle, the organizer may encourage a friend or relative to speak on the victim's behalf; however, organizers emphasize the value of community residents hearing victims' stories firsthand whenever possible (Stuart, 1996).

Because the circle sentencing process is so open and community driven, a potential concern is that the importance given to victims' needs may vary widely. The seriousness of offenders' needs may slant the focus of some circles toward offender rehabilitation, service, and support and away from victims' needs, as also appears to occur in some family group conferences (Maxwell and Morris, 1993; Umbreit and Stacey, 1996). In addition, because

Table 2: Restorative Conferencing Models: Community Involvement and Other Dimensions

	Victim-Offender Mediation	Reparative Boards	Family Group Conferencing	Circle Sentencing
Who participates? (the community)	Mediator, victim, offender are standard participants. Parents often involved. Others occasionally involved.	Reparative coordinator (probation employee), community reparative board, offender and supporters, victim (on a limited basis). Youth panels (a related approach) uses diversion staff.	Coordinator identifies key participants. Close kin of victim and offender invited. Police, social services, or other support persons also invited. Broader community not encouraged to participate.	Judge, prosecutor, defense counsel participate in serious cases. Victim(s), offender(s), service providers, support group present. Open to entire community. Justice committee ensures participation of key residents.
Victim's role	Expresses feelings regarding crime and impact. Has major role in decision regarding offender obligation and content of reparative plan. Has ultimate right of refusal; consent is essential.	Input into plan sought by some boards. Inclusion of victims rare but currently encouraged; more active role being considered.	Expresses feelings about crime, gives input into reparative plan.	Participates in circle and decision making; gives input into eligibility of offender, chooses support group, and may participate in a healing conference.
Gatekeepers	Courts and other entities make referrals.	Judge.	New Zealand: court and community justice coordinator. Australia and United States: police and school officials.	Community justice committee.
Relationship to formal system	Varies on continuum from core process in diversion and disposition to marginal programs with minimal impact on court caseloads.	One of several probation options for eligible low-risk offenders with minimal service needs. Plans to expand. Some impact on case-loads anticipated.	New Zealand: primary process of hearing juvenile cases, required ceding of disposition power, major impact on court caseloads. Australia (Wagga Wagga) and United States: police-driven process, variable impact on caseloads, concern regarding net-widening; in United States, used for very minor cases (most commonly shoplifting).	Judge, prosecution, court officials share power with community, i.e., selection, sanctioning, followup. Presently minimal impact on court caseloads.
Preparation	Typically, face-to-face preparation with victim and offender to explain process. Some programs use phone contact.	Preservice training provided to board members. No advance preparation for individual hearings.	Phone contact with all parties to encourage participation and explain process. New Zealand model requires face-to-face visits with offender, offender's family, and victim.	Extensive work with offender and victim prior to circle. Explain process and rules of circle.

(continued)

Table 2: Restorative Conferencing Models: Community Involvement and Other Dimensions *(continued)*

	Victim-Offender Mediation	Reparative Boards	Family Group Conferencing	Circle Sentencing
Followup (enforcement and monitoring	Varies. Mediator may follow up. Probation and/or other program staff may be responsible.	Condition of probation. Coordinator monitors and brings petition of revocation to board, if necessary	Unclear. Australia (Wagga Wagga): police. New Zealand: coordinator. United States and Canada: others.	Community justice committee. Judge may hold jail sentence as incentive for offender to comply with plan.
Primary outcome(s) sought	Allow victim to relay impact of crime to offender, express feelings and needs; victim satisfied with process; offender has increased awareness of harm, gains empathy with victim; agreement on reparative plan.	Engage and involve citizens in decision-making process; decide appropriate reparative plan for offender; require victim awareness, education, and other activities that address ways to avoid reoffending in future.	Clarify facts of case. Denounce crime while affirming and supporting offender; restore victim loss; encourage offender reintegration. Focus on "deed not need" (i.e., on offense and harm done, not offender's needs). Some emphasis on collective accountability.	Increase community strength and capacity to resolve disputes and prevent crime; develop reparative and rehabilitative plan; address victim concerns and public safety issues; assign victim and offender support group responsibilities and identify resources.

the circle sentencing model requires extensive preparation on the offender's part before the circle convenes (*see* discussion in the following section), some circles become "stacked" with offender supporters who have little relationship to victims.

Initially unique to the circle sentencing model of conferencing is the concept of victim support groups (Stuart, 1996). Support groups are formed by community justice committees, which are responsible for achieving an appropriate balance among victim, offender, and community needs and representation. Usually a support group is formed at the time an offender petitions for admission to the circle, but the group may expand at any time (including during the circle ceremony itself).

Preparation/Followup

The presession preparation stage of any restorative conferencing process offers perhaps the greatest opportunity to engage citizens in the restorative justice process and ensure their meaningful participation (Stuart, 1995; Umbreit, 1994). Followup activities—monitoring and enforcement of sanctioning plans and agreements that result from decision-making sessions—provide critical linkage between court dispositions and correctional intervention. Followup has been particularly at issue among some critics of restorative conferencing models (Alder and Wundersitz, 1994). Thus, the extent to which preparation and followup are viewed as vital to success is one of the most interesting and important differences among the four restorative conferencing models.

Victim-offender mediation. Mediation programs stress the importance of extensive victim and offender preparation prior to the mediation session. The most widely accepted model encourages mediators to hold at least one separate, face-to-face discussion with the offender and the victim. During these discussions, the mediator listens to each person describe how the crime affected him or her, gives an overview of the mediation process, identifies its potential benefits, and invites each person to participate. If the offender and victim agree to participate, the mediator introduces them to the process in a way that minimizes anxiety and maximizes the likelihood that the two parties will engage in direct dialog with minimal intervention by the mediator (Umbreit, 1994,1997). Many practitioners argue that up-front preparation is often more important than the session itself in bringing about a successful result (Umbreit and Stacy, 1996).

Victim-offender mediation programs vary in their approach to monitoring and enforcement. In many programs, mediators usually help session participants devise a reparation schedule and may even ask them to agree to a follow-up meeting to review progress (Umbreit, 1994). In some programs, followup may be the responsibility of probation or diversion staff (depending on the offender's court status), other paid staff, community volunteers, or student interns; in others, victim-offender mediation may be one part of a larger restitution program responsible for development and enforcement of reparation agreements (Belgrave, 1995; Schneider, 1985).

Reparative boards. In Vermont's reparative board programs, case preparation usually is limited to brief intake interviews with offenders to gather information about the offense for the board hearings. Boards can obtain basic information about victim losses from police, court, or probation records. Nevertheless, some board programs increasingly are attempting to contact victims prior to hearings.

Monitoring and enforcement policies and procedures are more formally developed in reparative boards than in other models. Board members themselves have enforcement responsibilities (such as recommending revocation or termination of offender contracts, as necessary), although they do not make final enforcement decisions. A reparative coordinator, who is a state corrections employee, is responsible for monitoring offender contract compliance (Reparative Probation Program, 1995). If offenders do not meet contract conditions, the coordinator may recommend that they be charged with violation of probation or conditions of the diversion agreement and/or that the court take additional corrective action (Dooley, 1996).

Family group conferencing. In New Zealand, preparation is viewed as critical for the success of family group conferences. Preconference face-to-face meetings generally are held with offenders and their families, and victims are contacted by phone (Hakiaha, 1995). The Australian Wagga Wagga model places much less emphasis on preparation, apparently in the belief that spontaneity is important. Some coordinators, for example, argue that hearing victims' and offenders' stories prior to the conference may even diminish the impact and focus of the stories (Umbreit and Stacy, 1996). Recently, however, some proponents of the Wagga Wagga model are placing greater emphasis on the need to ensure accuracy of facts, check with participants, develop plans, and ensure that key participants and their support groups attend conference sessions (McDonald et al., 1995).

Family group conferencing programs generally have often left responsibility for compliance to the offender (Moore and O'Connell, 1994), although the New Zealand model does provide for reconvening conferences in the event of noncompliance (Maxwell and Morris, 1993). Conferencing programs generally do not make monitoring and enforcement responsibilities explicit, although Australia's Wagga Wagga model anticipates that police officers are ultimately responsible for enforcement and that juvenile justice staff may also play a role (Alder and Wundersitz, 1994). In the United States, the enforcement function is evolving and varies from jurisdiction to jurisdiction. Although preferred practice calls for encouraging voluntary compliance and assigning monitoring roles to conference participants, final enforcement authority rests primarily with the police agencies that convene the conferences; however, the extent of actual followup varies.

Circle sentencing. Perhaps because its community empowerment and healing goals are most ambitious, the circle sentencing model demands the most extensive presession preparation. As a condition of admission to a circle, offenders are required to petition the community justice committee, visit an elder or other respected community member for a conference, begin work on a reparative plan that may involve some restitution to the victim and community service, and identify a community support group (Stuart, 1996). This presession process serves as a screening device and an indicator that offenders are serious about personal change. It is not uncommon for circles to be canceled or postponed if offenders fail to complete the preliminary steps (Stuart, 1996). When the screening process works well and offenders meet the presession obligations, however, a circle can actually be less a hearing about disposition requirements than a celebration of the offender's progress and an opportunity for victim and offender to tell their stories.

Follow up should be as intensive as preparation in the circle sentencing model. Circle participants are expected to take responsibility for monitoring and enforcing the conditions of the circle sentence, which often include an extensive list of reparative responsibilities, treatment requirements, and (in aboriginal communities) traditional healing and community-building rituals. Support groups for offenders and victims, which are formed through community justice committees, also monitor offenders and act as victim advocates to ensure that agreements made within the circle are carried out. Sentencing circle agreements are subject to review by a judge, who asks for routine reports from the justice committee and support groups. At the conclusion of a circle, the judge may assign further monitoring responsibilities to members of the community and may withhold a final decision about detention terms or other sanctions pending the offender's completion of obligations as verified at a followup hearing.

Dimensions of Restorative Justice and Decision Making

Efforts to increase community participation in the dispositional decision-making process are nothing new. In the late 1970s, the Law Enforcement Assistance Administration of the U.S. Department of Justice supported neighborhood justice centers (also known as dispute resolution centers) in several cities (Garafalo and Connelly, 1980; McGillis and Mullen, 1977). More recently, a variety of initiatives have placed prosecution and defense services, and even entire courts, in neighborhoods and have adapted services to provide a better fit with the needs of local citizens (National Institute of Justice, 1996b). Federal and State juvenile justice agencies have been especially concerned with promoting a less formal, more accessible neighborhood focus for intervention and in recent years have supported youth courts, juvenile drug courts, and mentoring programs.

These efforts often have been effective in making justice services more geographically accessible to citizens, increasing flexibility of service delivery (for example, more convenient hours, more diversity), and encouraging informality in the decision-making process by relying whenever possible on dispute resolution, negotiation, and mediation practices rather than legal rules and procedures (Harrington and Merry, 1988; Rottman, 1996). However, when facilities and services are merely placed in neighborhoods without the involvement of local residents, the result is an isolated program or process that may be said to be in, but not of, the community (Byrne, 1989; Clear, 1996). Similarly, increasing flexibility and breaking down formal barriers may increase citizens' willingness to seek and receive assistance but will not necessarily increase their involvement as participants in the justice process or even allow them to determine what services they would like in their neighborhoods.

Unfortunately, emphasis on developing programs and increasing accessibility of services has contributed to a one-dimensional definition of restorative justice. Ultimately, neither new programs nor increased access alone will change the role of neighborhood residents from service recipients to decision makers with a stake in (and sense of ownership of) the process for determining what services are provided and how they are delivered. By defining new and distinctive roles for citizens, the four conferencing models examined in this chapter add an important dimension to earlier and ongoing restorative justice initiatives (McGillis and Mullen, 1977; National Institute of Justice, 1996a).

What is the relevance of these apparently esoteric models to juvenile justice professionals, victim advocates, treatment providers, and other intervention professionals? Notably, an increasing number of state departments of juvenile courts, probation departments, parole agencies, and corrections systems are adopting one or more aspects of restorative justice policy (for example, Bazemore and Griffiths, 1997; Dooley, 1995; Pennsylvania Juvenile Court Judges Commission, 1997; Pranis, 1995). What appear on the surface to be simply informal alternatives to courts actually have relevance to the objectives of all components of the juvenile justice system.

The larger promise of the evolving approaches is a new avenue for achieving a wider and deeper level of citizen involvement in the rehabilitative, sanctioning, and public safety missions of juvenile justice than has been possible through offender-focused intervention alone. Prospects for increasing community involvement, the nature of the process of engaging citizens, and the roles assigned to the community (including crime victims) are therefore the most crucial dimensions for comparing and contrasting the four conferencing models that are the focus of this chapter.

Comparing and Contrasting the Four Models: Summary

In comparing these four models, it must be remembered that, as noted earlier, the philosophy and practice of any given restorative conferencing program may deviate substantially from the prototypes presented here. Indeed, the evolution of the restorative justice movement is producing significant changes as practitioners think more carefully about the implications of restorative principles for their practice. For example, reparative boards and victim-offender mediation have been influenced by family group conferencing models, and some family group conferencing programs have recently adopted components of circle sentencing.

The most important conclusion to be drawn from this comparison of the four models is that there is no one best approach for every community or for every case within a community. For example, circle sentencing is perhaps the most holistic of the models. Yet circles also demand the greatest time commitment from participants and thus are not wisely used on minor or less complex cases.

Some have suggested that the future may bring a single hybrid model. More practically, however, jurisdictions can consider developing a "menu" of conferencing alternatives to respond to diverse case needs and to make the most efficient use of scarce resources. For example, a brief encounter with a reparative board may be the most appropriate and cost-effective response to a property offender with few prior incidents and no other complications requiring more intensive intervention, whereas circle sentencing may be more appropriate for serious and chronic offenders involved in dysfunctional relationships.

Each of the four models has its strengths and weaknesses in a variety of dimensions in addition to those considered here. Although much remains to be learned and there is much room for improvement, each model has demonstrated its unique value to juvenile justice systems and communities that are trying to develop more meaningful sanctioning responses to youth crime.

Issues and Concerns

Restorative justice is assuming an ever higher profile, and its new decision-making structures and processes are bound to come under close scrutiny. It is therefore important to address critical issues and concerns related to evaluating the success of new restorative justice approaches, gauging progress in their development, and meeting the challenges of balancing and sharing power.

Evaluating Success and Gauging Progress

Despite the proliferation of restorative justice programs, there is a significant lack of evaluation research to provide an empirical basis for determining whether new initiatives are achieving their stated objectives. The exception is victim-offender mediation, which has been the subject of numerous studies in North America and Europe (Coates and Gehm, 1989; Dignan, 1990; Marshal and Merry, 1990; Umbreit, 1994, 1995; Umbreit and Coates, 1993; Umbreit, Coates, and Roberts, 1997; Umbreit and Roberts, 1997).

Perhaps the most critical concern for evaluators and juvenile justice professionals is that many of the new restorative justice initiatives have objectives that are far more holistic than those of traditional crime control responses. Whereas traditional crime control efforts typically have used recidivism rates as a primary outcome measure, an evaluative framework for these new approaches needs to include criteria for measuring outcomes of community empowerment and solidarity, victim interests, and crime prevention. The framework should also take into account intermediate and process outcomes such as community and victim involvement, reintegrative shaming, reparation to victims, dispute resolution, and healing. As new and more appropriate standards emerge for evaluating restorative justice models, it is essential that the basis for comparison be the reality of the current system rather than an idealized version of its performance. It is also essential that any comparisons between restorative justice models and the current system use similar indicators to measure performance.

Another important consideration for any new restorative justice process is its integrity, that is, its consistency with restorative justice principles. With twenty-five years of experience to draw upon, victim-offender mediation offers the following basic guidelines that can serve to inform any new restorative conferencing initiative and its implementation:

- If public agencies such as police or probation initiate a restorative conferencing process, actual sessions should be cofacilitated by trained community volunteers. This increases citizen participation and reduces the likelihood of an imbalance of power among parties involved in the sessions. Community involvement and volunteer participation are essential to the success of restorative conferencing but do not preclude the need for public support (such as funding to cover the costs of systems development, referrals, training, and so forth) to sustain high-quality programs.

- If a local victim-offender mediation or dialog program already exists, other restorative conferencing initiatives should be developed in collaboration with the existing program. For example, volunteer mediators could also serve as cofacilitators.

- Session facilitators should be trained in mediation and conflict resolution skills, approaches to understanding the experiences and needs of crime victims and young offenders, and cultural and ethical issues that are likely to affect the process and participants.

- Victims should be able to make informed decisions about their participation. They should be told about potential benefits and risks and should never be pressured to participate or told to "just trust" the facilitator's judgment. Victims should also be allowed to choose when and where the session is held and should have the opportunity to present their story first if they wish.

- In-person preparation of primary participants (victims, offenders, and their immediate families) should take place whenever possible. It is important for facilitators to connect with the parties, provide information, encourage participation, and build rapport, trust, and a sense of safety.

Regardless of what model or combination of models a local community or juvenile court might choose, ongoing monitoring and evaluation will be needed to ensure that conferencing processes adhere to restorative justice principles. No model or process is perfect. In practice, therefore, adherence to these principles may be viewed as a continuum within which new approaches can be assessed and continuously improved (Table 3, page 94).

Sharing and Balancing Power

The restorative justice processes discussed in this chapter are often proposed as alternatives to the legal-procedural approach to dispositional decision making by the juvenile court. Concerns have been raised, however, about the mechanisms of accountability in restorative justice decision making.

In considering the development of justice programs in aboriginal communities in Canada, Griffiths and Hamilton (1996) have raised concerns that are just as relevant in urban U.S. communities:

> Care must be taken to ensure that family and kinship networks and the community power hierarchy do not compromise the administration of justice. As in any community, there is a danger of a tyranny of community in which certain individuals and groups of residents, particularly those who are members of vulnerable groups, find themselves at the mercy of those in positions of power and influence. (Griffiths and Hamilton, 1996:187-188)

Table 3: Restorative Community Justice: Least- to Most-Restorative Impact

Least-Restorative Impact	Most-Restorative Impact
Entire focus is on determining the amount of financial restitution to be paid, with no opportunity to talk directly about the full impact of the crime on the victim and the community, and also on the offender.	Primary focus is on providing an opportunity for victims and offenders to talk directly to each other, to allow victims to describe the impact of the crime on their lives and receive answers to questions, and to allow offenders to appreciate the human impact of their behavior and take responsibility for making things right.
No separate preparation meetings with the victim and offender prior to bringing the parties together.	Separate preparation meetings with the victim and offender, with emphasis on listening to how the crime has affected them, identifying needs, and answering questions about the mediation process.
Victims not given choice of meeting place (where they would feel most comfortable) or participants; given only written notice to appear for mediation session at preset time, with no preparation.	Victims continually given choices throughout the process: where to meet, whom they would like to be present, etc.
Mediator or facilitator describes offense and offender then speaks, with the victim simply asking a few questions or responding to questions from the mediator.	Victims given choice to speak first and encouraged to describe offense and participate actively.
Highly directive styles of mediation or facilitation, with the mediator talking most of the time, little if any direct dialog between the involved parties.	Nondirective style of mediation or facilitation with minimal mediator interference, and use of a humanistic or transformative mediation model.
Low tolerance for moments of silence or expression of feelings.	High tolerance for silence, expression of feelings, and discussion of the full impact of the crime.
Voluntary for victim but required of offender regardless of whether he or she takes responsibility.	Voluntary for victim and offender.
Settlement-driven and very brief (10-15 minutes).	Dialog-driven and typically lasts about an hour (or longer).
Paid attorneys or other professionals serve as mediators.	Trained community volunteers serve as mediators or facilitators, along with agency staff.

The often dramatic and dysfunctional power differentials within communities may make true participatory justice difficult to achieve and, in some settings, may instead produce harmful side effects (Griffiths and Corrado, 1998). Ironically, those communities most in need of holistic restorative justice programs that encourage residents to become involved in the disposition process are often precisely those communities that are the most dysfunctional. Also, residents of such communities may have only limited interest in and/or capacity for involvement, in part because they have never had the opportunity to develop meaningful partnerships with the juvenile justice system. If these communities are ever to benefit from a restorative approach to the problem of youth crime, proponents of restorative justice must direct specific attention to developing strategies for building a sense of community among residents and for recruiting and retaining resident volunteers.

A critical issue surrounding the development and implementation of restorative justice models is: "Who controls the agenda?" Traditionally, the formal justice system has maintained a tight rein on initiatives designed as alternatives to criminal and juvenile justice processes. This is evident in the origins and evolution of diversion programs, which in many jurisdictions appear to have become appendages to the formal justice process. In this context, the inability or unwillingness of decision makers in the formal juvenile justice system to share discretion and power with communities is likely to result in "net-widening" (expanding the number and types of youth brought under the supervision of the juvenile justice system) rather than the development of more effective alternative decision-making processes (Blomberg, 1983; Polk, 1994).

If the new restorative justice models follow the pattern of development of earlier neighborhood dispute resolution models (and to a lesser extent of victim-offender mediation, as the oldest of the new models), one would anticipate significant additions to the richness and diversity possible in alternative sanctioning but little impact on the formal system. Both victim-offender mediation and family group conferencing (except as practiced in New Zealand) ultimately depend on system decision makers for referrals; the potential for true sharing of power is minimal. If new models are to avoid net-widening, marginalization, and irrelevance, community advocates should begin to work with sympathetic justice professionals who are also committed to community-driven systemic reform.

Although a primary objective of proponents of restorative justice is to have new concepts institutionalized as part of the justice process, the danger is that system control will lead to top-down development of generic models. Hence, both promise and risk are implied in the degree of institutionalization that some new approaches have achieved in a relatively short time and in the rather dramatic system-community collaboration that appears to be possible with these approaches.

Clearly, the high profile given to restorative justice initiatives may result in grant funding for research and new programs. Yet, such support is no guarantee of long-term impact of the type envisioned in the restorative justice literature. Moreover, in the absence of substantive community input (including input from crime victims) at the design and implementation phases of specific initiatives, an administrative focus (that is, one concerned primarily with grant-funding processes) may even result in the coopting or watering down of new approaches in ways that ultimately function to undermine the philosophy and objectives of restorative justice (Van Ness, 1993).

For example, from a restorative justice perspective, perhaps the biggest challenge to Vermont's reparative boards is the fact that they have been implemented within the state's formal justice system itself. On one hand, the boards may have the greatest potential for significant impact on the response of the formal system to nonviolent crimes. Moreover, the commitment of administrators to local control may also result in communities assuming and demanding a broader mandate. On the other hand, as a creation of the state corrections bureaucracy, the reparative boards may find themselves at the center of an ongoing struggle between efforts to give greater power and autonomy to citizens and needs of administrators to maintain control and ensure system accountability. Indeed, citizen board members may ultimately be challenged to decide the extent to which their primary client is the community or the probation and court system.

Of the four models considered in this chapter, circle sentencing appears to be the most advanced in terms of primacy of the community's decision-making role. In its placement of neighborhood residents in the gatekeeper role (see Table 2), this model provides the most complete example of power sharing. Acting through the community justice committees, communities are clearly the "drivers" in determining which offenders will be admitted to the circle and what should be done in the collective effort to heal the community. Eligibility for circles is limited only by the ability of offenders to demonstrate to community justice committees their sincerity and willingness to change. Surprisingly, the most promising lesson of circle sentencing has been that, when given decision-making power, neighborhood residents often choose to include the most, rather than the least, serious offenders in restorative justice processes (Griffiths and Corrado, 1998; Stuart, 1996). As a result, however, certain tensions have developed within courts and other agencies in Canadian communities that are experimenting with circle sentencing. The tensions concern the extent to which power sharing with the community should be limited and the issue of whether statutes are being violated.

Building Community through Restorative Conferencing

The true test of restorative conferencing. The ultimate measure of success for any approach that claims to advance restorative justice should be its ability to strengthen the capacity of communities to respond effectively to crime (Bazemore, 2000). In restorative justice, crime is viewed as both a cause and result of broken or weakened relationships. As Pranis (1998, p. 10) suggests: "The fabric of community is the weaving of relationships. Crime harms relationships and thus weakens community. Our response to crime needs to attend to these relationships to rebuild or strengthen the community fabric."

If restorative conferencing models are to be more than another programmatic add-on, advocates of the models should be challenged to ask whether the models meet the test of building community. Do these models:

- create positive new relationships or strengthen existing relationships?

- increase community skills in problem solving and constructive conflict resolution?

- increase the community sense of capacity and efficacy in addressing problems?

- increase individual awareness of and commitment to the common good?

- create informal support systems or safety nets for victims and offenders?

Potential roles for the community. Experience has shown that given the chance, citizens and community groups can play significant roles in restorative justice. Such roles may include service on advisory boards at local, county, and state levels; policy input through public forums and community surveys; prevention policy development; a variety of victim and offender support activities, including church- and community-based programs, police chaplaincy programs, healing circles, and neighborhood outreach programs; and volunteer service as victim advocates, mediators for victim-offender mediation programs, and reparative board members.

New functions for juvenile justice professionals. Despite emphasis on the community role, restorative justice should never be viewed as something independent of the formal justice system. Juvenile courts and juvenile justice professionals must play key leadership roles in partnerships with community groups to develop and sustain a credible community response to youth crime. Because current job descriptions for juvenile justice professionals usually do not include functions associated with restorative justice, another test for efforts to engage the community in decision making must be whether new professional roles are being developed. Such new roles are emerging in several communities where restorative justice is now actively practiced. For example, in Deschutes County, Oregon, probation officers are now called community justice officers, and their responsibilities include developing and supporting community service projects, developing restorative conferencing, coordinating services to crime victims, and performing a variety of community-building and restorative functions.

The process of engaging the community. The process followed by juvenile justice professionals in engaging the community may be the most important aspect of creating a new collaborative relationship between the justice system and the community. Such a process is illustrated in the following steps suggested by the Minnesota Department of Corrections:

- Gather information about restorative justice and possible models in the community.

- Educate yourself about the community you will be working with.

- Identify credible leaders in the community or neighborhood, attend community gatherings, read local papers, and ask local residents about issues and leaders.

- Educate yourself about victim services in the community and establish contact with those services.

- Clarify your own goals and values in approaching the community. (What are you trying to achieve? What is important to you about what you are doing and how you do it?)

- Assess potential support in the criminal and juvenile justice systems and educate key leaders about restorative justice.

- Working with community leaders, plan informational sessions to explore community interest. Invite participation by victims' representatives.

- At each session, recruit volunteers who would like to be involved in creating a new approach in the community based on restorative values.

Implications and Conclusions

The perpetual absence of the "community" in "community corrections," either as a target of intervention or as a participant in the justice process (Byrne, 1989; Clear, 1996), may be due in part to an inability to identify meaningful roles for citizens. This chapter has described four nonadversarial decision-making models and compared and contrasted the ways in which they define and make operational the role of citizens in responding to youth crime. As illustrated by a growing number of restorative justice initiatives (Pranis, 1995), such citizen involvement may have important implications for juvenile justice. The models discussed here offer significant potential for changing the current dynamic in which the community is largely a passive observer of juvenile justice processes. When juvenile justice professionals identify citizens willing to participate in a community sanctioning process, they may also have identified a small support group willing to assist with offender reintegration and victim support.

This chapter has also attempted to provide a general framework for describing the dimensions of restorative conferencing processes. One purpose has been to avoid indiscriminate, arbitrary, and all-inclusive groupings of programs and practices under ill-defined terms such as community justice or restorative justice. As noted at the beginning of this chapter, comparative discussions of new approaches at this relatively early stage of development are important because they serve to highlight similarities and differences across emerging models. Such discussions may prevent, or at least minimize, what some have referred to as the "community-policing syndrome": the widespread application (and misapplication) of a generic term to a broad range of initiatives without a clear understanding of the differences between interventions or benchmark criteria that can be used to assess consistency with fundamental principles and objectives (Mastrofsky and Ritti, 1995). Unless proponents of restorative justice distinguish what should and should not be included under that umbrella and unless they refine definitions of success for interventions, they will miss a unique and valuable opportunity to develop more effective methods for enhancing citizen involvement in the response to youth crime and misconduct. A useful context for refining definitions is to view restorative justice as a way of thinking about and responding to crime that emphasizes one basic fact: crime damages people, communities, and relationships. If crime is about harm, a justice process should therefore emphasize repairing the harm.

Systemic reform toward restorative justice must not begin and end with new programs and staff positions. It must encompass new values that articulate new roles for victims, offenders, and communities as key stakeholders in the justice process. Accordingly, such reform should create and perpetuate new decision-making models that meet stakeholder needs for meaningful involvement. The capacity of these models to influence, and even transform, juvenile justice decision making and intervention seems to lie in the potential power of these new stakeholders. If victims, offenders, and other citizens are to be fully engaged in meaningful decision-making processes, however, a dramatic change must also occur in the role of juvenile justice professionals. That role must shift from sole decisionmaker to facilitator of community involvement and resource to the community (Bazemore and Schiff, 1996).

Endnotes

[1] Information on the four models is adapted from *Regional Symposium Training Manual*, U.S. Department of Justice, Office of Justice Programs, 1997.

[2] In some programs, parents of the offender are also often part of the mediation session.

[3] Not all mediation sessions lead to financial restitution.

[4] In the absence of pure control groups, selection bias cannot be ruled out for the comparisons drawn in this study.

[5] Reparative boards are highly localized models, and information on them is sketchy. This chapter uses the Vermont reparative boards as a prototype and case study. As noted above, Vermont has used the boards primarily with adult offenders but more recently has begun to use them with juvenile offenders too. Substantial information is available on the operating procedures of the Vermont boards, and the Vermont model can serve as a new prototype for the board/panel-based approach to youth crime.

[6] As noted earlier, reparative boards are intended to provide an opportunity for victims and community members to confront offenders in a constructive manner. In practice thus far, however, these opportunities have proved better suited to community input than victim involvement. Because of this relatively weak involvement of victims, some suggest that reparative boards are not pure examples of restorative justice. *See* additional discussion under "Comparing and Contrasting the Four Models: Community Involvement and Other Dimensions."

[7] Some feel that the community (volunteer) mediator also is part of the community definition.

References

Alder, C. and J. Wundersitz, eds. 1994. *Family Group Conferencing and Juvenile Justice: The Way Forward or Misplaced Optimism?* Canberra, Australia: Australian Institute of Criminology.

American Probation and Parole Association. 1996. *Restoring Hope through Community Partnerships: The Real Deal in Crime Control.* Lexington, Kentucky: American Probation and Parole Association.

Barajas, E., Jr. 1995. *Moving Toward Community Justice.* Topics in Community Corrections. Washington, D.C.: U.S. Department of Justice, Federal Bureau of Prisons, National Institute of Corrections, Community Division.

Bazemore, G. 2000. Community Justice and a Vision of Collective Efficacy: The Case of Restorative Conferencing. In *Criminal Justice 2000*, Volume 3. Washington D.C.: U.S. Department of Justice, Office of Justice Programs, National Institute of Justice, pp 228-297.

Bazemore, G. and C. Griffiths. 1997. Conferences, Circles, Boards, and Mediations: The "New Wave" of Community Justice Decisionmaking. *Federal Probation.* 61(2): 25-37.

Bazemore, G. and M. Schiff. 1996. Community Justice/Restorative Justice: Prospects for a New Social Ecology for Community Corrections. *International Journal of Comparative and Applied Criminal Justice.* 20(2): 311-334.

Belgrave, J. 1995. Restorative Justice. Discussion paper. Wellington, New Zealand: New Zealand Ministry of Justice.

Blomberg, T. 1983. Diversion's Disparate Results and Unresolved Questions: An Integrative Evaluation Perspective. *Journal of Research in Crime and Delinquency.* 20(1): 24-38.

Braithwaite, J. and S. Mugford. 1994. Conditions of Successful Reintegration Ceremonies. *British Journal of Criminology*. 34(2): 139-171.

Byrne, J. M. 1989. Reintegrating the Concept of Community into Community-based Correction. *Crime and Delinquency*. 35: 471-479.

Clear, T. R. 1996. Toward a Corrections of "Place": The Challenge of "Community" in Corrections. *NIJ Journal*. (August):52-56.

Coates, R. and J. Gehm. 1989. An Empirical Assessment. In M. Wright and B. Galaway, eds. *Mediation and Criminal Justice*. London: Sage Publications, Ltd.

Daly, K. 2000. Ideals Meet Reality: Research Results on Youth Justice Conferences in South Australia. Paper prepared for the Fourth International Conference on Restorative Justice for Juveniles, Tuebingen, Germany, October 2000.

Dignan, J. 1990. *An Evaluation of an Experimental Adult Reparation Scheme in Lettering, Northamptonshire*. Sheffield, UK: Centre for Criminological and Legal Research, University of Sheffield.

Dooley, M. J. 1995. *Reparative Probation Program*. Waterbury, Vermont: Vermont Department of Corrections.

————. 1996. *Restoring Hope Through Community Partnerships: The Real Deal in Crime Control*. Lexington, Kentucky: American Probation and Parole Association.

Fercello, C. and M. Umbreit. 1999. *Client Evaluation of Family Group Conferencing*. St. Paul, Minnesota: Center for Restorative Justice and Mediation, University of Minnesota.

Garafalo, J. and K. Connelly. 1980. Dispute Resolution Centers, Part 1: Major Features and Processes. *Criminal Justice Abstracts*. 12(3): 416-439.

Griffiths, C. T. and R. Corrado. 1998. Implementing Restorative Youth Justice: A Case Study in Community Justice and the Dynamics of Reform. In G. Bazemore and L. Walgrave, eds. *Restorative Juvenile Justice: Repairing the Harm of Youth Crime*, pp. 237-263. Monsey, New York: Criminal Justice Press.

Griffiths, C. T. and R. Hamilton. 1996. Spiritual Renewal, Community Revitalization and Healing: Experience in Traditional Aboriginal Justice in Canada. *International Journal of Comparative and Applied Criminal Justice*. 20(2): 289-311.

Hakiaha, M. 1995. New Zealand Youth Family Conference Coordinator. Presentation in Whitehorse, Canada.

Harrington, C. and S. Merry. 1988. Ideological Production: The Making of Community Mediation. *Law and Society Review*. 22(4): 709-733.

Karp, D. and L. Walther. 2001. Community Reparative Boards: Theory and Practice. In G. Bazemore and M. Schiff, eds. *Restorative Community Justice: Cultivating Common Ground for Victims, Communities and Offenders*. Cincinnati: Anderson.

Marshall, T. and S. Merry. 1990. *Crime and Accountability*. London: Home Office.

Mastrofsky, S. and R. Ritti. 1995. Making Sense of Community Policing: A Theory-based Analysis. Paper presented at the annual meeting of the American Society of Criminology, Boston, November 1995.

Maxwell, G. and A. Morris. 1993. *Family Participation, Cultural Diversity and Victim Involvement in Youth Justice: A New Zealand Experiment.* Wellington, New Zealand: Victoria University.

McCold, P. and B. Wachtel. 1998. *Restorative Policing Experiment: The Bethlehem, Pennsylvania, Police Family Group Conferencing Project.* Pipersville, Pennsylvania: Community Service Foundation.

McDonald, J., M. Thorsborne, D. Moore, M. Hyndman, and T. O'Connell. 1995. *Real Justice Training Manual: Coordinating Family Group Conferences.* Pipersville, Pennsylvania: Piper's Press.

McElrea, F. W. M. 1993. A New Model of Justice. In B. J. Brown, ed. *The Youth Court in New Zealand: A New Model of Justice.* Auckland, New Zealand: Legal Research Foundation.

McGillis, D. and J. Mullen. 1977. *Neighborhood Justice Centers: An Analysis of Potential Models.* Washington, D.C.: U.S. Department of Justice, Law Enforcement Assistance Administration, National Institute of Law Enforcement and Criminal Justice.

Melton, A. 1995. Indigenous Justice Systems and Tribal Society. *Judicature.* 70(3): 126-133.

Moore, D. B. and T. O'Connell. 1994. Family Conferencing in Wagga-Wagga: A Communitarian Model of Justice. In C. Adler and J. Wundersitz, eds. *Family Conferencing and Juvenile Justice: The Way Forward or Misplaced Optimism?* Canberra, Australia: Australian Institute of Criminology.

Morris, A. and G. Maxwell. 2001. Restorative Conferencing. In G. Bazemore and M. Schiff, eds. *Restorative and Community Justice: Cultivating Common Ground for Victims, Communities and Offenders.* Cincinnati: Anderson.

National Institute of Justice. 1996a. *National Symposium on Restorative Justice Proceedings*, Spring. Washington, D.C.: U.S. Department of Justice, Office of Justice Programs, National Institute of Justice.

————. 1996b. *Communities: Mobilizing Against Crime: Making Partnerships Work.* Washington, D.C.: U.S. Department of Justice, Office of Justice Programs, National Institute of Justice.

Pennsylvania Juvenile Court Judges Commission. 1997. *Balanced and Restorative Justice in Pennsylvania: A New Mission and Changing Roles Within the Juvenile Justice System.* Harrisburg, Pennsylvania: Juvenile Court Judges Commission.

Polk, K. 1994. Family Conferencing: Theoretical and Evaluative Questions. In C. Adler and J. Wundersitz, eds. *Family Conferencing and Juvenile Justice: The Way*

Forward or Misplaced Optimism? Canberra, Australia: Australian Institute of Criminology.

Pranis, K. 1995. Building Community Support for Restorative Justice: Principles and Strategies. Unpublished paper. St. Paul, Minnesota: Minnesota Department of Corrections.

————. 1998. *Restorative Justice: Principles, Practices and Implementation, Section 6, Building Community.* National Institute of Corrections Curriculum. Washington, D.C.: U.S. Department of Justice, Federal Bureau of Prisons, National Institute of Corrections.

Rottman, D. 1996. Community Courts: Prospects and Limits in Community Justice. *NIJ Journal.* (August): 50-51.

Schneider, A., ed. 1985. *Guide to Juvenile Restitution.* Washington, D.C.: U.S. Department of Justice, Office of Justice Programs, Office of Juvenile Justice and Delinquency Prevention.

Strang, A. 1995. Family Group Conferencing: The victims' Perspective. Paper presented at the annual meeting of the American Society of Criminology, Boston, November 1995.

Stuart, B. 1995. Sentencing Circles Making "Real" Differences. Unpublished paper. Whitehorse, Canada: Territorial Court of the Yukon.

Stuart, B. 1996. Circle Sentencing: Turning Swords into Ploughshares. In B. Galaway and J. Hudson, eds. *Restorative Justice: International Perspectives*, pp.193-206. Monsey, New York: Criminal Justice Press.

Travis, J. 1996. Lessons for the Criminal Justice System from Twenty Years of Policing Reform. Keynote address at the First Annual Conference of the New York Campaign for Effective Crime Policy, New York.

Umbreit, M. 1994. *Victim Meets Offender: The Impact of Restorative Justice in Mediation.* Monsey, New York: Criminal Justice Press.

————. 1995. Holding Juvenile Offenders Accountable: A Restorative *Justice Perspective. Juvenile and Family Court Journal.* (Spring): 33-41.

————. 1997. Humanistic Mediation: A Transformation Journey of Peacemaking. *Mediation Quarterly.* 14(3): 201-213.

Umbreit, M. and R. Coates. 1993. Impact of Mediating Victim-Offender Conflict: An Analysis of Programs in Three States. *Juvenile and Family Court Journal.* 43(1): 21-28.

Umbreit, M., R. Coates, and A. Roberts. 1997. Cross-national Impact of Restorative Justice Through Mediation and Dialogue. *ICCA Journal on Community Corrections.* 8(2): 46-50.

Umbreit, M. and C. Fercello. 1997. Family Group Conferencing Program Results in Client Satisfaction. *Juvenile Justice Update Journal.* 3(6): 3-13.

Umbreit, M. and J. Greenwood. 1998. *Victim Sensitive Guidelines for Victim Offender Mediation*. Washington, D.C.: U.S. Department of Justice, Office of Justice Programs, Office for Victims of Crime.

Umbreit, M. and A. W. Roberts. 1997. Victim Offender Mediation in England: An Assessment of Two Programs. In G. Pisapia and D. Antonucci, eds. *The Promise of Mediation*, pp. 63-83. Milan, Italy: CEDAM.

Umbreit, M. and B. A. Schug. 1997. *Directory of Victim Offender Mediation Programs in the US*. St. Paul, Minnesota: Center for Restorative Justice and Mediation, University of Minnesota.

Umbreit, M. and S. Stacy. 1996. Family Group Conferencing Comes to the U.S.: A Comparison with Victim Offender Mediation. *Juvenile and Family Court Journal.* 47(2): 29-39.

Umbreit, M. and H. Zehr. 1996. Restorative Family Group Conferences: Differing Models and Guidelines for Practice. *Federal Probation.* 60(3): 24-29.

Van Ness, D. 1993. New Wine and Old Wineskins: Four Challenges of Restorative Justice. *Criminal Law Forum.* 4(2): 251-276.

Vermont Department of Corrections Reparative Probation Program. 1995. *Program Design.* Waterbury, Vermont: Vermont Department of Corrections.

Zehr, H. 1990. *Changing Lenses: A New Focus for Crime and Justice.* Scottsdale, Pennsylvania: Herald Press.

Bibliography

Bazemore, G. 1997. What's New about the Balanced Approach. *Juvenile and Family Court Journal.* 48(1): 1-23.

Bazemore, G. and M. Umbreit. 1995. Rethinking the Sanctioning Function in Juvenile Court: Retributive or Restorative Responses to Youth Crime. *Crime and Delinquency.* 41(3): 296-316.

Depew, R. C. 1994. *Popular Justice and Aboriginal Communities: Some Preliminary Considerations.* Ottawa, Canada: Department of Justice of Canada.

Goldstein, H. 1987. Toward Community-oriented Policing: Potential, Basic Requirements and Threshold Questions. *Crime and Delinquency.* 33: 6-30.

Hudson, J., O. Galaway, A. Morris, and G. Maxwell. 1996. Research on Family Group Conferencing in Child Welfare in New Zealand. In *Family Group Conferences: Perspectives on Policy and Practice.* Monsey, New York: Criminal Justice Press.

Klien, A. 1995. *Community Probation: Acknowledging Probation's Multiple Clients.* Topics in Community Corrections. Washington, D.C.: U.S. Department of Justice, Federal Bureau of Prisons, National Institute of Corrections, Community Division.

LaPrairie, C. 1994. Community Justice or Just Communities? Aboriginal Communities in Search of Justice. Unpublished paper. Ottawa, Canada: Department of Justice of Canada.

Office of Juvenile Justice and Delinquency Prevention. 1998. *Guide for Implementing the Balanced and Restorative Justice Model.* Washington, D.C.: U.S. Department of Justice, Office of Justice Programs, Office of Juvenile Justice and Delinquency Prevention.

Robinson, J. 1996. Research on Family Group Conferencing in Child Welfare in New Zealand. In J. Hudson et al., eds. *Family Group Conferences: Perspectives on Policy and Practice*, pp. 49- 64. Monsey, New York: Criminal Justice Press.

Young, M. 1995. *Restorative Community Justice: A Call to Action.* Washington, D.C.: National Organization for Victim Assistance.

Vocabulary and Questions

- victim-offender mediation

- community reparative boards

- family group conferencing

- circle sentencing

1. What are the goals of victim-offender mediation?

2. What are the goals of community reparative boards?

3. What are the goals of family group conferencing?

4. What are the goals of circle sentencing?

5. How does each of the four models of restorative conferencing handle community involvement?

6. Discuss the role of the victim in the four models of restorative conferencing.

COMMUNITY CONFERENCING
6 AS CONFLICT TRANSFORMATION

JOHN M. MCDONALD AND DAVID B. MOORE
DIRECTORS
TRANSFORMATIVE JUSTICE AUSTRALIA
SYDNEY, AUSTRALIA

This essay is a contribution toward the theory and practice of transformative justice and conflict transformation. It is based on the authors' experience as principals of Transformative Justice Australia. In this capacity, they have applied a theory of conflict transformation in the state and national justice systems of several countries, in a wide range of workplaces, and in other communities bound by faith, geography, or some common not-for-profit goal. As Transformative Justice Australia sees it, conferencing remains the major reactive intervention based on a theory of transformative justice and conflict transformation. This chapter focuses on applications of conferencing in justice systems where the process is used as an alternative or as an adjunct to the use of court and corrections.

Community Conferencing

Conferencing, in all its variants, involves most or all of the people affected by a specific conflict. In most justice system applications of conferencing, conflict is the result of one or more incidents of undisputed harm. Participants are brought together by a conference facilitator who leads them through three stages, determining what happened, how people have been affected, and how their situation might now be made better. The facilitator's role is to referee these stages, not to become a player in the conference.

To referee fairly, the facilitator must judge whether participants are playing by agreed rules, informed by a set of guiding principles. As guiding principles of the conferencing process, we use the precepts of deliberative democracy: participation, deliberation, equity, and nontyranny (Fishkin, 1995). Thus, a facilitator determines who has been affected, to determine who should attend the conference, to satisfy the precept of *participation*. (The time required for preparation depends on the nature of each case and the nature of the conferencing program.) The precepts of *deliberation* and *equity* are satisfied if participants speak in an appropriate sequence, are prompted with open questions, and are allowed adequate time to speak and be heard. Finally, a facilitator may need to use subtle intervention techniques should one or more participants breach the precept of nontyranny by using their position, personality, or political ideology to exercise excessive power over other participants. In short, a conference facilitator must ensure:

- everyone affected is encouraged to attend

- everyone in attendance is given the opportunity to speak and be listened to

- each issue is given adequate consideration

To fulfill these precepts, a conference facilitator:

- identifies sources of conflict in a system of relationships

- brings the people in that system together in a circle

- asks questions of participants in a scripted sequence

- begins with open questions about incidents that contributed to the conflict

- moves to questions that foster acknowledgment and greater understanding of the conflict

- concludes by overseeing and recording an agreement on ways to repair damage and minimize repetition of harmful behaviors

Early theory

The origins of the conferencing movement are routinely traced to New Zealand, where highly significant 1989 legislation introduced an indigenous process into a national common law justice system. Conferencing was introduced for both matters of care and protection and for youth justice. The next stages in the story involve attempts to adopt conferencing in broader movements for justice reform (Hudson et al., 1996).

In Australia, the first structured pilot program of conferencing began in the rural New South Wales city of Wagga Wagga in 1991, using a conferencing process that continued to evolve during the pilot (McDonald and Moore, 1995). The first major article analyzing the program and process appeared in the New York-based journal *Criminal Justice Ethics* in 1993 (Moore, 1996a).The title of the article, "Shame, Forgiveness, and Juvenile Justice," carried deliberate echoes of John Braithwaite's influential *Crime, Shame and Reintegration*, which provided a theoretical starting point for the debate about conferencing in Australia. The title also highlighted what we considered to be the key psychological and sociological elements of a juvenile justice system built around conferencing. As we saw it, shame was the key psychological element. Forgiveness was the crucial sociological element. Ten years of experimentation and experience has qualified those judgments.

We still feel that shame is expressed at a turning point in the conference. We still feel that the offer of forgiveness can be very important. But, we now emphasize that the most significant experience of shame seems to be collective. We emphasize that emotional transformation is more significant in the emotional dynamic of a conference than is the experience and expression of any specific emotion. We describe forgiveness more as a process of transformation than of reintegration.

These changes seem subtle, but they are highly significant criminologically, psychologically, philosophically, and politically. These were the four overlapping disciplinary frameworks within which "Shame, Forgiveness, and Juvenile Justice" analyzed the conferencing process and the two programs then extant.

The *political* impetus for Australian and New Zealand conferencing programs was clear enough. Critics had identified and denounced various injustices of the justice system. Collectively, their constructive critiques called for a system that could:

- increase diversion from courts

- reduce recidivism

- increase participant satisfaction with the official response to the incident

- foster collective solutions to harm minimization

- engage the emotions which guide the moral values linked to justice

Conferencing promised to do all this. A key political question in the Australian program of conferencing concerned strategy: how to introduce conferencing into the criminal justice system. We distinguished between central and local implementation strategies, between a model of the "scientifically guided society" and a model of the "self-guiding society." In the former, solutions are imposed by a central technical elite. In the latter, the opinions of experts are consulted and considered, but the aim is to reach mutually satisfactory arrangements through broader political debate (Lindblom, 1990). We favored the model of the self-guiding society as a strategy for introducing conferencing into the justice system.

This model of a self-guiding society was entirely consistent with the principles guiding the conferencing process. At the same time, these principles offered a profound challenge to the principles traditionally guiding our welfare and justice systems. Instead of state officials asking "who is our subject and what do we do to them?" conferencing allows those most affected to paint as full a picture of their circumstances as possible, and then to decide what they might do for themselves.

In the Australian pilot program, a rural city police patrol used conferencing within existing administrative guidelines. Hence the formal program title "Effective Cautioning Using Family Group Conferencing." This program had the imprimatur of the local (civilian) police consultative committee; it was administered by a community policing unit; and it was evaluated by the local university campus. Thus, the program devolved administrative responsibility for dealing with crime to the lowest appropriate levels.

Within the framework of *criminology*, conferencing seemed to:

- move beyond retributive and rehabilitative models

- offer more than situational prevention and opportunity reduction

- accommodate reintegrative shaming practices without undermining the hard-won rights protected by the legal system

Our initial hypothesis saw conferencing as the most prominent practical example of the theory of reintegrative shaming. That practice required more than a criminological explanation; it also required justification. The task seemed best suited to moral *psychology* and *philosophy*, disciplines concerned with values such as respect, civility, and reciprocity.

We were least confident about these psychological and philosophical aspects of our account. The theory of reintegrative shaming, derived from points of agreement in key schools of criminology, predicted what the experience of shame could do but said little about what shame is. And questions about the nature of shame soon became politically important in Australian justice systems because of the close connection between the theory of reintegrative shaming and the practice of conferencing. Accordingly, a great deal of effort was devoted to seeking an adequate understanding of the emotion of shame.

Emotions and the Conferencing Sequence

The literature on emotions called shame and pride "emotions of self-assessment," which were both inward and outward-looking, could be generated by internal and external sources, and influenced behavior to maintain equilibrium between perceptions of the self and perceptions of others.

This regulatory function was evident at both the individual level and at the broader cultural level. External sources of shame and pride were said to be learned, to change over time, and to perform a social regulatory role (Elias, 1978/1982). Clearly, these emotions of self-assessment were complex. It seemed inadequate to analyze them as purely physiological, purely psychological, or exclusively as sociocultural phenomena. But many studies had oversimplified the idea in just this way. Furthermore, some of the literature adopted the simple dualism of cognition and emotion common to much psychological theory (*see* Damasio, 1994; Ramachandran and Blakeslee, 1998). The significance of emotions as regulators of social conduct had been downplayed. Insufficient attention had been paid to mechanisms for learning, practicing, and strengthening social or moral responsibility.

There was a similar dualism in the literature. Some accounts understood moral motivation as coming from within; others understood social conformity to be imposed from without. There were some promising attempts to synthesize these accounts, dealing with specific phenomena such as apology (Tavuchis, 1991). But even the more insightful works focused primarily on *what* was happening between parties in an exchange of apology and forgiveness, not *on why* this was happening.

Writers dealing specifically with shame tended to distinguish shame from guilt. Guilt was said to be felt in anonymity; shame to require an audience. Guilt was said to be felt only by the transgressor; shame could be felt vicariously. Guilt distinguished act and actor; shame did not. Guilt protected the self because it allowed persons to distance themselves from their unworthy actions (Taylor, 1985). But again, the *mechanisms* by which emotions were generated remained unexplained.

An exception was the "microsociology" of Thomas Scheff and Suzanne Retzinger (1991), which came closer to explaining how these emotions were generated and why people were motivated to engage in apologetic exchanges. Retzinger suggested that guilt was a cognitive rationalization of the basic emotion of shame. Moore (1996a; 1996b) took this argument a step further, distinguishing guilt as *legal culpability* from guilt as *feeling*. Once these two manifestations of guilt are distinguished, guilt as feeling can indeed be identified as one manifestation of the basic emotion of shame (*see also* Hepworth and Turner, 1982).

Modern Western legal systems have separated guilt as legal culpability from guilt as a feeling. The state makes technical judgments about culpability; communities make judgments about morality. This institutional separation may have a psychological counterpart. A person's acceptance of technical guilt for their actions might be separated from possible feelings of guilt about their moral status in a community. A rationalized legal system may make possible "rationalization" in the psychological sense of "self-absolving justification." Classic literature in developmental psychology contained similar arguments (Miller and Swanson, 1960). Guilt could correlate with inner conflict, constricting anxiety, or empathy.

Empathic guilt could be a healthy phenomenon. It could foster criticism of one's own actions in the service of interpersonal relations. Empathic guilt was the obverse of a guilt that "rationalizes" behavior to protect the self, but magnifies the indignation felt by others. On the other hand, if the shame of empathic guilt is consciously acknowledged, indignation can be transformed into something positive. In short, the expression of shame, followed by the ritual of apology and forgiveness, might present the clearest path beyond the anger of moral indignation.

How could this path be mapped out? The sequence in which conference participants speak proved to be of crucial importance. As we discovered early, the sequence of a conference determines the ease with which participants begin to move beyond anger and fear, emotions which limit their interactions to destructive engagement or to disengagement.

In justice system applications of conferencing, offenders speak first. This arrangement minimizes defensiveness, while removing from victims the burden of initiating a conference with accusations. The offender's account is followed by the primary victim's account. Initially, we still thought it appropriate that the offender's supporters should then be next to speak. Thus, the sequence in which conference participants told their story and explored the consequences was first the offender(s), then the victim(s), followed by the offender's supporters, and then the victim's supporters.

Our reasoning from that time still sounds plausible. We argued that offenders are encouraged by the vicarious shame of their supporters to feel and acknowledge shame and then to express remorse. Victims are encouraged by their supporters to regain some sense of self-respect and then to be more readily forgiving. Remorse is followed by forgiveness, so the offender's (ashamed) supporters should speak first, and the victim's (encouraging) supporters should follow.

And yet, in practice, this arrangement did not prove as satisfactory as having the victim's supporters speak before the offender(s)' supporters. The latter sequence provided the most direct path to constructive engagement. By the middle of 1993, on the basis of observation and intuition, we had switched to this alternative sequence: first offender(s), next victim(s), then victim's supporters, followed by offender's supporters.

Turning from Conflict to Cooperation

We could not clearly explain the greater efficacy of this sequence until 1995, following extensive discussions with colleagues in North America. Yet, a personality theory based on the system of human affects (or "basic emotions") should have alerted us earlier to the reasons why this sequence worked so well. Briefly, the reasons are as follows.

Offenders generally express a sense of shame most strongly when everyone has spoken, and the extent of the harm has been most thoroughly illustrated. Offenders, as the primary cause of that harm, are now at their most vulnerable. Precisely at this moment, a common relationship becomes tangible. There may be an echo of everyone's original indignation, but there is also a shared sense of relief at having spoken. Above all, there is a sense of what a Canadian colleague has called "collective vulnerability." Its physiological manifestation is perhaps best described as "deflation." All participants feel as if they have had "the wind knocked out of their sails."

At this moment, for the first time, all participants have explained how they have been harmed. Collectively, they have "painted a picture" of what happened, and what has happened since. There is shared reflection on the harm that has been caused to relationships, on "how things got worse." Participants sense that they are a community of people all harmed by the incident, and are "all in the same boat."

This is the point just before the coordinator marks the transition to the final stage of the conference by asking the victim(s) what they would like to see come out of the conference. In short, this is the turning point of the conference, and, in retrospect, the 1993 article spelled out clear reasons why.

Offenders feel on the verge of rejection or acceptance and strongly need support. Their supporters are best placed to provide that support. They are generally closest to the offender and most aware of injustices and mitigating circumstances within the private sphere of family and friends. So, they are best able to strike a balance between the partiality of love and the impartiality of justice.

In contrast, the supporters of the victim tend still to display indignation at the offense, their indignation strengthened by concern for the victim. They are not in a position to offer forgiveness. So, it is appropriate for them to speak for the first time immediately after the primary victim has first spoken, but then not to be formally prompted to speak again until the final stage of the conference.

When the victim's supporters do speak, they often demand material reparation on behalf of the victim. In contrast to this claim for *material* reparation, victims themselves tend to place more value on *symbolic* reparation. An apology and other symbolic reparative gestures from offenders are generally seen as crucial.

This is a purely *rational* account of why forgiveness works in the victim's self-interest. Yet, our early observations consistently were that conference participants responded intuitively or emotionally. People's intuitive responses appeared to work both in their own best interests and in the interests of the whole group. This particular configuration and format prompted individual and collective intuition in each conference. The empathy generated through the process seemed to benefit all participants, laying the basis for the restoration of trust within this community.

Indeed, the most striking general impression left after watching, audio-recording, and analyzing dozens of conferences was that the power of each conference seemed to derive from the collective emotional transformation of participants. Some of us involved in the operation and/or evaluation of the Wagga pilot conferencing program became increasingly sensitized over time to this phenomenon, as an early publicity exercise illustrates.

In 1992, two commercial television film crews filmed drama students from Charles Sturt University role-playing a typical conferencing scenario. On first viewing, the students' acting seemed highly realistic. Viewed again six months later, however, the role plays seemed far less realistic, and for one clear reason: the actors' individual emotional expressions were not synchronized. In real conferences, in contrast, emotional expression becomes increasingly synchronized in the course of the conference.

The students were working with an overly cognitive model of psychology, one which seemed logical in terms of what their individual characters had experienced and how they ought to feel. But cognitive theories of psychology did not match the collective experience of participants in real conferences. In conferences of various sizes, dealing with a range of offenses, and with participants from a host of different cultural and ethnic backgrounds, very similar patterns of collective emotional transformation had been observed. So, what was clearly needed was a model of emotionality that explained:

- emotional "contagion"

- the consistency of emotional sequence in each conference

- the power of feelings to influence thinking

- the apparent universality of basic emotional experience and expression

The model of personality offered by Silvan Tomkins and other theorists of personality subsequently helped to answer many of our questions (Moore 1996c; Nathanson 1992; Demos 1994). Conversations in 1995 with Lauren Abramson of Johns Hopkins University (*see* her chapter in this volume) helped to articulate this emerging model of connected emotional transformation. The model identifies the underlying emotional dynamic of the generic conference, which involves three general stages:

1. a stage marked by contempt, anger and fear, directed at individuals (on the basis of their actions in the past)

2. a stage marked by disgust, distress, and surprise, evoked by revelations in the present about those actions, and associated emotions and motivations

3. a stage marked by interest and then by relief, as plans for the future are developed

The collective sense of vulnerability, the collective experience of shame or deflation, marks the transition from the second to the third of these three general emotional stages. Importantly, this transitional collective experience is not simply a negative experience.

Shame is essentially a brake on the positive affects of interest and enjoyment (or relief), so there is a neutral aspect to the experience; shame is an absence of the positive, rather than something negative in its own right. And there is even a positive aspect to this collective experience. Shame, the brake on the positive affects, is a visceral reminder that participants can experience positive emotions in each other's company. The experience of shame sets the stage for reaching, then implementing, a constructive agreement.

In short, this account suggests the crucial dynamic of a conference is not that one conference participant expresses shame, after which social reintegration can occur. Rather, the crucial dynamic is that *everyone* experiences a sense of shame, which marks the transition from a generally negative emotional climate to a generally positive emotional climate. A collective sense of shame marks the transition from conflict to cooperation.

This psychosocial account of conference dynamics has political consequences. The origins of the theory of reintegrative shaming are in theoretical criminology. But the language of "reintegrative shaming" has been open to misinterpretation as theory has been put into practice. Most obviously, the meaning of reintegrative shaming has tended to change when the phrase is interpreted within the frameworks of legalist and welfarist ideology. To reiterate an earlier point, justice and welfare systems traditionally ask "who is our subject and what do we do to them?" Not surprisingly, then, the concept of "reintegrative shaming" has frequently come to be (mis)understood in these systems as:

- *punishment* imposed on an individual by the *state* or

- *therapeutic treatment* imposed on an individual by the *state* or

- punishment or therapy imposed on an individual, by a *collectivity*, on behalf of the state

Our alternative understanding is that the conferencing process is a means by which a group of people, harmed by behavior that has generated conflict, may begin to understand themselves as a community with a common concern. The collective experience of shame marks the transition from a focus on past and present conflict, to a focus on future cooperation. Reaching this understanding-that-runs-deeper-than-cognition involves individual and collective emotional transformation. Personal emotional transformation is interwoven with the interpersonal transformation of relationships.

Refining Practice

The implications of this evolving body of theory have since been worked into the practice of Transformative Justice Australia. We moved from explaining conferencing primarily as an example of reintegrative shaming to understanding conferencing as a process by which the negative emotions associated with conflict can be transformed into the positive emotions associated with cooperation.

This may seem a very simple reformulation, but it has broadened significantly the applications of conferencing. We have summarized some of the philosophical and psychological reasoning. The reformulation has also been prompted by our recognition that:

- The language of "victims," "offenders," and "bullying" is inadequate or inappropriate in many cases that are otherwise suitable for conferencing.

- Situations where all conference participants have known each other for some time are generally far more complex than situations where those who have caused harm were not previously known to those who have been harmed.

- In these more complex situations, conflict has often been caused by the cumulative effect of many minor disputes, rather than by any single incident.

- Particularly in more complex situations, design principles for conferencing programs need to be derived more obviously from politics and systems theory than from criminology and welfare theory.

- Much "family group conferencing," as currently practiced in North America, seems to be informed respectively by a theory of reintegrative shaming in justice systems, and by family systems theory in welfare systems, where the term "family group decision making" is increasingly used. In short, traditional justice and welfare philosophies have reasserted themselves within the conferencing process.

- Conferencing is being compared with victim-offender mediation, circle sentencing, and other processes with related origins and/or goals and/or a categorization as "restorative."

All these developments suggest that, unless practitioners consider very carefully the first principles guiding the conference process, the reforming potential of conferencing will be diluted within traditional programs. To this end, we have found it essential to:

- distinguish specific *disputes* from general *conflicts*
- refer to conference participants in the morally neutral language of "people in conflict"
- distinguish the task of mediating disputes from the task of facilitating a conference for people in conflict
- distinguish three categories of possible outcome from processes that deal with situations of conflict: conflict maximization, conflict minimization, and conflict transformation

We distinguish conferencing from other "restorative justice" or conflict resolution processes. Many of these processes minimize conflict. They do so as an alternative to adversarial court, which maximizes conflict as a side effect of emphasizing differences between disputing parties. But where conflict is the primary problem facing people—as it is after a crime, or after many poorly resolved disputes in one community—minimizing conflict will not solve the problem. What is required is a process that acknowledges the sources of conflict, seeking understanding before seeking to make things better. Conferencing exemplifies this approach, which we now articulate less as transformative justice and more as "conflict transformation" (especially outside the formal justice system).

As a summary of our current thinking, then: we suggest that community conferencing in justice systems is a prime example of conflict transformation. Conferencing is appropriate in those situations where conflict has been caused by one or more acts defined as criminally harmful. Accordingly, we suggest a change in the formula that represented our original hypothesis in this area. The phrase *crime, shame and reintegration* might be usefully reformulated as: *conflict, acknowledgment, and transformation.*

Crime causes anger, fear, and contempt within a community of people. Until the causes and consequences of the crime are acknowledged, these emotions remain, fuelling further conflict. But when a conference allows conflict to be acknowledged, it can be transformed into cooperation.

Programs

This reformulation of conferencing as a process for conflict transformation provides programs with very clear guidelines on process dynamics. With hindsight, we can see that one of the most significant outcomes of the Australian pilot program of conferencing was to distinguish program and process. Acting within existing administrative guidelines, we were able to experiment with the format of the process, to distill first principles from careful observations of the process, and to draft a training manual which then evolved as the training workshop was tried out in different jurisdictions, first in Australia, then in North America, more recently in Europe. We were also able to engage in dialog about the most appropriate program structures to deliver this process.

By the mid-1990s, it was becoming clear that the short-term strengths of the pilot program might eventually become weaknesses. To institutionalize the process on a large scale would require a different program structure. The authors chose to leave the debate about program structure to others, founding Transformative Justice Australia in Sydney in 1995, and focusing on two aspects of the conferencing process: applying conferencing in workplaces, and continuously improving a facilitators' training workshop, particularly for community and government sector applications of conferencing.

By 1997, legislation for conferencing had emerged in our home state of New South Wales. Arising from constructive debate among several government departments, the new conferencing program was part of a revised young offenders act. The program designers learned lessons from previous conferencing legislation in New Zealand and South Australia, recommending a structure that is not only proving resilient, but also inspiring conferencing programs under the aegis of other government departments.

The "youth justice conferencing" program in New South Wales allows for referrals from the police or the court. Each administrative district of the state has one youth justice coordinator from the Department of Juvenile Justice. These coordinators accept referrals from police or courts, and assign each referred case to a convenor, a local resident trained in the conferencing process developed by Transformative Justice Australia, and in the legislated program requirements. Importantly, convenors are not employees of the Department of Juvenile Justice. Rather, they "subcontract" to the department (and are paid per session rates) for each case they facilitate.

This arrangement meets the demands of coordination and quality control on one hand, and community involvement in justice on the other. The program has generated impressive results since its inception in 1998. Participant satisfaction rates were judged "truly remarkable" by the director of the Bureau of Crime Statistics and Research. (Trimboli, 2000). Rates of reoffending have been reduced at the same time as rates of court appearance and detention for young people have been nearly halved around the state.

The success of this model makes it easier for other government departments to experiment with conferencing. The New South Wales Department of Education and Training in 1998 began to use conferencing for cases that would otherwise have resulted in suspension or exclusion.

Then, in 1999, the Department of Corrections began a fascinating experiment. A Restorative Justice Unit was established within the department. Transformative Justice Australia ran a facilitators' workshop for a group of clinical psychologists within the department, and also convened the first conference under the aegis of the Restorative Justice Unit conferencing program: a meeting between the families involved in a case of culpable driving causing death.

After further carefully prepared and well-run conferences, the Restorative Justice Unit began publicizing more broadly the opportunity to attend a conference for anyone involved in a case that had received a (custodial or probationary) sentence from a court. This program was publicized both through corrective services networks, and through victims' advocacy groups. The Minister for Corrective Services announced in 2001 that the program was to be made statewide and permanent.

This program is not diversionary. The harm that has been done cannot, in most cases, be undone in any obvious way. Yet, people affected by crime are lining up to attend a conference, with referrals coming from victims and offenders. Those involved report that the conference offers the chance to achieve some sort of shared understanding of what has happened, and to move beyond the crushing sense of conflict that punishes everyone affected by serious crime. Appropriately, the use of conferencing in correctional settings has now been included in a major randomized controlled experiment of conferencing in various justice settings, which began in the United Kingdom in 2001.

Thus, the use of conferencing is spreading well beyond its initial applications in cases involving young people. Broader applications have been made possible by broader theoretical underpinnings. And these broader theoretical underpinnings have also created a link to broader social debate about conferencing. In 1998, Transformative Justice Australia entered into discussions with Australia's preeminent playwright David Williamson (Williamson, 2001).Williamson's professional qualifications include psychology, so he was fascinated not only by the raw drama of conferences, but also by the theory that underpins conference design. He decided to base a series of plays on the work of Transformative Justice Australia. *Face to Face* premiered in Sydney in 1999 (Williamson, 1999), followed, in 2001, by *Charitable Intent*, and *A Conversation*. The plays are set, respectively, in a privately owned building company, a charitable foundation, and a correctional setting. Reviewers have consistently judged all three plays as among the most powerful dramas they have experienced.

A clearly articulated and evaluated process, working program structures, and broader cultural debate about the theory and practice of conferencing are now together promoting a transformative approach to conflict. We remain confident that the right mix of centralization and decentralization will be found, with the right mix of standardization and experimentation, according to the general principle of a self-guiding society. The practical application of this philosophy is, after all, a good part of the reason why conferences are effective: the facilitator only guarantees the process; participants generate the outcome. And in many cases, it seems, the more significant the conflict, the more "the process is the outcome." When people in conflict are provided with a structure to revisit what happened and how they have been affected, they have already gone a long way to making things better. They have begun to transform conflict into cooperation.

References

Braithwaite, J. 1989 *Crime, Shame and Reintegration*. Cambridge, Massachusetts: Cambridge University Press.

Braithwaite, J. and P. Pettit. 1990. *Not Just Deserts, A Republican Theory of Criminal Justice*. Oxford: Oxford University Press.

Damasio, A. R. 1994. *Descartes' Error: Emotion, Reason, and the Human Brain*. New York: Avon Books.

Demos, E. V., ed.1994 *Exploring Affect: The Selected Writings of Silvan S. Tomkins*. Cambridge, Massachusetts: Cambridge University Press.

Elias, N. [1939] 1978/1982. *The Civilising Process: I. The History of Manners; II. State Formation and Civilisation*. Oxford: Basil Blackwell.

Fishkin, J. S. 1995. *The Voice of the People: Public Opinion and Democracy*. New Haven, Connecticut: Yale University Press

Hepworth, M. and B. S. Turner. 1982. *Confession: Studies in Deviance and Religion*. London: Routledge and Kegan Paul

Hudson, J., A. Morris, G. Maxwell, and B. Galaway, eds. 1996. *Family Group Conferences: Perspectives on Policy and Practice*. Sydney: The Federation Press.

Lindblom, C. 1990. *Inquiry and Change: The Troubled Attempt to Understand and Shape Society*. New Haven, Connecticut: Yale University Press.

McDonald, J. M. and D. B. Moore. 1995. Achieving the Good Community: A Local Police Initiative and its Wider Ramifications. In K. Hazlehurst, ed. *Justice and Reform, Vol. 2: Regenerating Communities Through Crime Prevention*. Aldershot: Avebury.

Miller, D. and G. Swanson. 1960. *Inner Conflict and Defense*. New York: Norton.

Moore, D. B. 1996a. Shame, Forgiveness, and Juvenile Justice. In M. C. Braswell, B. R. McCarthy, and B. J. McCarthy, eds. *Justice, Crime and Ethics*, 2nd

Edition. Cincinnati, Ohio: Anderson Publishing [Originally published in *Criminal Justice Ethics* 12, 1993. Also available at www.lib.jjay.cuny.edu/cje/html/sample2.html.

————— . 1996b. Shame: Human Universal or Cultural Construct? In R. Dalziell, D. Parker and I. Wright, eds. *Shame and the Modern Self*. Melbourne: Australian Scholarly Publishers.

—————. 1996c. Criminal Action, Official Reaction: Affect Theory, Criminology, and Criminal Justice. In D. L. Nathanson, ed. *Knowing Feeling*. New York: W. W. Norton.

Moore, D. B. and J. M. McDonald. 2000. *Transforming Conflict in Workplaces and Other Communities*. Sydney: Transformative Justice Australia. Also available at www.tja.com.au.

Nathanson, D. L. 1992. *Shame and Pride: Affect, Sex, and the Birth of the Self*. New York: W.W. Norton.

Ramachandran, V. S and S. Blakeslee. 1998. *Phantoms in the Brain: Probing the Mysteries of the Mind*. New York: William Morrow.

Scheff, T. J. and S. M. Retzinger.1991 *Emotions and Violence: Shame and Rage in Destructive Conflicts*. Lexington, Massachusetts: Lexington Books.

Tavuchis, N. 1991. *Mea Culpa: A Sociology of Apology and Reconciliation*. Stanford, California: Stanford University Press.

Taylor, G. 1985. *Pride, Shame and Guilt: Emotions of Self-assessment*. Oxford: Clarendon Press.

Trimboli, L. 2000. *An Evaluation of the NSW Youth Justice Conferencing Scheme*. NSW Bureau of Crime Statistics and Research, Sydney (available through: www.lawlink.nsw.gov.au).

Williamson, D. 1999. *Two Plays: Corporate Vibes and Face to Face*. Sydney: Currency Press.

—————. 2001. Beyond Hatred. *Spectrum, Sydney Morning Herald*, October 27-28.

Further information is available at the Web site of Transformative Justice Australia, www.tja.com.au.

Questions

1. What four precepts serve as the guiding principles of conferencing?

2. What are some of the differences between guilt and shame as discussed in this chapter?

3. Describe the three stages that are involved in Silvan Tomkins' model of personality which identifies the underlying emotional dynamic of a generic conference.

4. Why do the authors believe that minimizing conflict does not solve the problem of conflict?

THE PSYCHOLOGY OF
COMMUNITY CONFERENCING

7

LAUREN ABRAMSON
ASSISTANT PROFESSOR, DEPARTMENT OF PSYCHIATRY
    AND BEHAVIORAL SCIENCES
JOHNS HOPKINS UNIVERSITY
AND DIRECTOR, COMMUNITY CONFERENCING CENTER
BALTIMORE, MARYLAND

DAVID B. MOORE, PH.D.
DIRECTOR
TRANSFORMATIVE JUSTICE AUSTRALIA
SYDNEY, AUSTRALIA

C ommunity conferencing is a process for transforming conflict. A com-
        munity conference assists a community of people to experience a col-
        lective emotional transition. Together, they move from the negative
emotions associated with conflict to the positive emotions associated with
cooperation.

   This chapter provides a case study that illustrates this transition from
conflict to cooperation. We begin by examining how conflict transformation

differs from other approaches to conflict. Conflict transformation is the appropriate class of response in cases where the negative feelings associated with general conflict are far more significant to those affected than are the facts of any particular dispute. This is true when:

- A community of people has been affected by a single incident of undisputed harm.

- One or more disputes have been inadequately managed, leaving enduring ill-feeling in the affected community.

- Individuals may have no specific dispute with each other, but belong to different groups which are in conflict (McDonald and Moore, 2000).

In all such cases, in our experience, a dispute resolution process is not the required medicine. In such cases, there is either no dispute, or specific disputes are symptoms of the general conflict. Either way, destructive conflict is the primary problem. The community of people affected requires a process by which they can acknowledge and then transform that conflict.

We distinguish this approach from approaches that maximize or minimize conflict (Moore and McDonald, 2000). An example of conflict maximization is an adversarial court process. One side claims: "You did it!" The other counters: "No, I didn't!" The court is faced with a clear dispute, but no apparent common ground. To settle the dispute, an adjudicator arranges for both sides to gather their supporters and their evidence and to attack the supporters and evidence and to emphasize the differences between themselves and the other side. The conflict between the two sides is maximized as a side effect of seeking the best apparent outcome to the dispute: a win-lose outcome. This approach is considered a fundamental guarantee of the liberty when people are falsely accused, and the side effect of conflict maximization simply has to be endured.

An example of conflict minimization is negotiation assisted by a third party. In cases where a win- win outcome is still considered possible, the third party or mediator can help clarify issues and identify common ground, assisting the disputants to "get to yes" without getting overly heated. In this way, the disputants can resolve their dispute without destructive conflict developing between them.

Conflict minimization is the right approach when there is no deep conflict between disputants. When people are deep in conflict, however, conflict minimization is not the optimal approach. It may bring people together, but it fails to address the main problem that affects them. To focus on "clarifying the facts" under these circumstances is likely to make matters worse. It will produce stronger fuel for the existing fire of conflict, while the feelings associated with the conflict remain. A community of people who have been affected by a single incident of undisputed harm is certainly a community in conflict. So is a community beset by resentments because one or more disputes have been inadequately resolved. These communities require a process of conflict transformation.

Community conferencing is emerging as the most appropriate intervention for such cases. Through the 1990s, the process was introduced in programs in education, justice, welfare, workplaces, and the governance of local neighborhoods. In some of these programs, the most common cases involved incidents of undisputed harm. In other programs, many poorly resolved disputes in the past and present were the more common cause and consequence of conflict.

A facilitator's preparation is generally more complex in those cases where many disputes have fueled and been fueled by conflict. Nevertheless, the fundamental dynamics of the community conference itself are essentially the same, regardless of whether the conflict is associated with many disputes, undisputed harm, or perceptions of fundamental differences between groups.

We examine the community conference here as an intervention in a program that is improving the governance of local neighborhoods. Some of the behavior in our case study could be defined as criminal. It is in such cases that community conferencing contrasts most strikingly with other current approaches. Unlike other approaches, a community conference does not ask: "who has done it? and what is to be done to them?"

A conference is only appropriate in cases where those who were involved actually acknowledge their involvement. In such cases, a community conference does not need to ask "who has done it? " Then, instead of asking "what is to be done to them?", it asks:

- What happened?

- What has happened since? Who has been affected?

- What do we need to do now?

In this way, community conferencing shifts the focus from an individual to a network of relationships. It does not focus simply on the individual who has most caused harm, nor does it just focus additionally on people who have been directly harmed.

Community conferencing also avoids the other extreme of focusing on society at large. Instead, it works with a specific community, all the members of which, by definition, have been affected by a specific conflict. Thus, they have a common interest in improving the situation that faces them.

It should be clear from this definition that community conferencing, as we understand and practice it, is decidedly not a process whereby: punishment is imposed by public officials on an individual; or therapeutic treatment is imposed by public officials on an individual; or punishment or therapy is imposed on an individual, by a group, on behalf of public officials (McDonald and Moore, 2000).

It should follow that the psychological dynamic of a community conference is decidedly not one in which individuals, confronted with the anger of those they have harmed, experience and express a cluster of shame-based emotions, such as remorse and guilt, and then design their own punishment. Nor is the psychological dynamic one in which individuals, confronted with the unquestioning support of those present, contribute to the design of their own therapy. Various versions of conferencing have been understood this way in theory and applied this way in practice. They, however, are not examples of conflict transformation and are not part of this discussion.

We have suggested what the associated psychological dynamic is not. To examine in some detail what the psychological dynamic is, we consider the experience of participants in one particular community conference—what they may have learned about themselves and others. Lauren Abramson facilitated this conference in a Baltimore inner-city community during the fall of 1999. It is similar to many conferences run by the Baltimore Community Conferencing Center in recent years.

The two-square block neighborhood where the conflict was occurring is filled with row houses. For decades, these housed families of European descent. In the past several years, many African-American families moved into the area. Most recently, the neighborhood has received refugee and immigrant families from Central America and Eastern Europe. The cultural transition in the neighborhood has not been easy. However, this particular conflict was not about clashing cultures or racism. The families primarily involved in this situation were African American. The most evident conflict involved some residents who were very angry at people living in a house around the corner and wanted them evicted from their subsidized housing. But was it this simple? What were they really angry and upset about? The answers to such questions tend to be more complex than they first appear—and so it was in this case.

Manifestation

A community organization wanted to provide some angry residents with resources to handle their ongoing conflict with the residents of one particular house. They said the mother, Mrs. Gray, did not have control of her two children, a boy age fifteen and girl age thirteen. The youths' friends would come and hang out in groups of thirty or more. They would cuss, make noise at all hours, vandalize, shoot, and make the block unsafe and unlivable. Three families were ready to move. The police were not helping either. Several calls had been made to no avail, according to the residents.

The community organization, to their credit, brought together a number of "providers" who might have something to offer the residents regarding the conflict. They would let the residents decide how they wanted to proceed. Mediation, parenting workshops, a listening project, and community conferencing were available. Everyone sat one day to listen to three women talk about their rage at the situation. Mrs. Blue, the most angry and vocal resident, had a teenage son and mother for whose safety she feared. As she heatedly told her story, we learned that her oldest son and her nephew had been killed right by her house. "Something in her died" when she lost her son. Though she was no longer afraid for herself, she still lived in fear of something happening on the street to her mother or her surviving son.

Mrs. Blue had been speaking for more than twenty minutes when the mediation representative offered to mediate between Mrs. Blue and Mrs. Gray and her children. Mrs. Blue thought this was a good idea. Then, she heard about community conferencing and decided that having more people there would make it easier for her and probably better for the neighborhood. By the end of the meeting, they all agreed that a community conference should be their first step to deal with the situation.

Lauren told the residents that this "meeting" would be for anyone who is affected by this situation and for their supporters. We would hear what had been happening, and how people had been affected. Then, the group would decide how they could make things better. Mrs. Blue then turned to Lauren and pointed to a teenager walking outside by the window of the office and said, "There! There's one of the kids who is causing the trouble." Lauren left the office to talk to this young man about the conference, and so began the preparation. [Later, she learned that this spontaneous action had put the residents and community workers very much at ease. They were thrilled that she would "hit the street" to talk to conference participants.]

Preparation

Over the next week, Lauren knocked on doors and made phone calls to see who would attend the conference. At the identified "problem residence," she first spoke with a sixteen-year-old boy who was at home in the middle of the day on a Tuesday. When asked why he was not in school, he said he was trying to get into a GED class but they did not have the $108 he needed for tuition. When Lauren finally spoke with his mother, Mrs. Gray, she turned out to be a very hard-working single parent. Not only was she supporting her son, she was also supporting two others whom she took in due to extreme circumstances in their original homes. Mrs. Gray was fed up with people harassing her children. She loved them, and felt they were good kids. She agreed to attend the conference with her son and the other two in her home.

The more Lauren knocked on doors, the more neighbors stepped forward and expressed interest in attending the conference. Two long-standing residents, older women of European descent, agreed to participate as they were also concerned about the kids hanging out. One of these women, in fact, would walk two blocks out of her way to avoid having any contact with the teens. A mother, Mrs. Green, agreed to come, as did her teen daughter, who was in constant conflict with the teen daughter Gray.

After visiting the problem corner twice, Lauren still found no teens hanging out. Teen Green, however, knew most of the boys who hung out, so Lauren asked how she could invite them to the conference. Teen Green did not know their numbers, but agreed to get the word out. Three of the police officers who had been involved in this conflict also came: a lieutenant, a sergeant, and a community officer. They all knew the situation well. Fifteen people had agreed to come. By the time everyone sat down for the conference, word had indeed gotten out to the teens about this "meeting." Five minutes before the conference was to begin, twelve African-American male teenagers showed up because they "heard there was a meeting where they could have a voice." A city councilman showed up. All told, twenty-five participants sat down to hear about this problem residence.

Deliberation

The scripted community conference sequence (McDonald and Moore, 1998) is designed to encourage participants to paint a collective picture of what has happened and how people have been affected. Mrs. Gray was the first to speak. Nearly in tears, she told the group that she works hard at two jobs, had just earned her degree, and just wants to raise her children and provide for them. She stays to herself and wishes that her neighbors would stop harassing her children. If they had something to say about their behavior, she would like them to come to her, not call the police or yell at the children. Then, we went to find out how others had been affected.

Mrs. Blue spoke. Everyone was waiting to hear the litany against the Gray family. But not one word for the rest of the conference was about Mrs. Gray and her children. As it turned out, the conflict was not about this house, or that mother, or her children. Not at all. Instead, Mrs. Blue glared at the fifteen teenagers sitting across from her in the circle and yelled about how fed up she was with all these gangs of kids hanging out at the corner by her house. She was especially angry about one teen who had come to the conference, because he lived in another neighborhood. She shook her finger at him as she spoke. She told the group assembled how much noise and bother the kids are to her and her family. She told them she lost a son at that very corner. She complained bitterly about how the kids jumped all over cars when they played football, and screamed and used foul language.

At this point the young people chimed in. "Listen to what you're saying, Mrs. Blue! We were playing football! We just fell on your car going to catch a ball! We weren't climbing all over it or destroying it! We just have no place else to play. The lights go off in the park, and we get kicked out of the rec center at six! Where do you want us to go?" This was the primary source of the conflict: a group of fifteen (not thirty) teenagers who had no other place to play.

Twenty minutes of back and forth ensued between the teens and Mrs. Blue. The young men were very articulate. They even acknowledged to Mrs.

Blue, "We know you might want to make a memorial out of that corner, but we have nowhere else to go. The rec center closes at six and the lights go off in the park." Everyone was impressed. The city councilman told the youngsters that the rec centers are supposed to be open until nine. Several young men then told him how they are kicked out at six because there is another program that comes in, leaving them with no adult supervision. The councilman immediately got on his phone and left a message for the head of the city Department of Parks and Recreation, telling him that he had fifteen teenagers right in front of him with some issues about their recreation opportunities, and he needed to set up a meeting with them to work things out.

Several other related conflicts unfolded. Teen-girl Gray spoke with an air of defiance. It turned out that she was intimidated by teenage-girl Green and that they had some scuffles in the past. Girl Gray said that she "doesn't need anybody, so I just stay inside my house and mind my own business." The two teens and their mothers exchanged some words about their frustrations as well as their mutual desire to just stay out of trouble. But what this has come to mean for many young people in the city is that they keep to themselves and trust none of their peers.

Mrs. Gray and others spoke up about the nuisance that the vacant house next to her posed. Rats get in there because it is not properly boarded up. Mrs. Blue added that the graffiti on the house was an eyesore.

Everyone got a chance to speak. Most everyone talked about being kept awake at night due to noise, or being afraid of what the kids might do. But now that they heard these young people speak, they wanted to help them out. Everyone also talked about how angry and lousy they feel when others cuss at them. The adults do not like the young people cussing. And the teenagers were also angry that the adults cuss at them.

At one point when participants were discussing these issues, Mrs. Red, who came in late, began screaming at the male teenagers. The teens listened with looks of great disdain on their faces, but said nothing. Finally, the female police lieutenant chimed in to let the angry woman know that she would have her turn to speak, but that to interrupt in such a domineering way was not acceptable.

Decision

The police sergeant agreed that the vacant house was both a danger and an eyesore. He knew that a complaint had been made to the owner once before. He agreed to take this matter to the next level and put the process in motion to have the house properly boarded up. All of the residents expressed their thanks and said they would be even happier when it was done.

Then came the issue of how people would agree to speak to one another. Clearly, the use of offensive language was an issue for the participants. The proposed agreement was that the adults would agree not to cuss at the teens, and the teens would agree not to cuss at the adults. The teens immediately agreed. To the surprise of many, two of the adults shouted forth with protests. "We don't swear at the kids!" "I'm not going to agree to something I don't take part in anyway!" The councilman spoke up. "Who are the adults here?" he asked. Both he and the lieutenant implored the adults to set an example for the young people; to be role models that can help them find their way. After ten minutes of discussion, the adults consented to an agreement stating that they would not cuss at the young people.

Several stories were shared by the adults about their own childhoods. They tried to convey to the young people that they knew some of the hardships that the children faced. They also said they wanted to help them in any way they could. The young people nodded with serious looks on their faces. Some adults said they would volunteer at the rec center, which was later detailed in the agreement. The councilman began to plan a meeting between the teens and the young people, when the community organizer piped in with, "Well, if this meeting is for the young people, why don't we see if one of them will volunteer to organize it?" A few moments of silence in the room ended when one fourteen-year-old young man raised his hand and quietly said, "I'll do it."

Refreshments

All community conferences end with some refreshments. This is an important time for participants to come together and talk to each other informally once the circle is dissolved. This conference was no exception. As pretzels, cookies, and chips were being devoured by hungry people (especially the teens!), the police lieutenant helped the new youth organizer get everyone's name and number so that he could contact them for their next meeting. Miss Mauve, an elderly white resident, made it a point to introduce herself to each of the young people present. There was a festive atmosphere as everyone ate and talked about what had just transpired and what they hoped might happen in the future.

Aftermath

There is simply not enough space in this chapter to describe in detail all that unfolded as a result of this conference. What follows is a simple list of some of the outcomes.

In addition, something very interesting happened two days after the conference. Mrs. Gray called the community organization in distress. Apparently Mrs. Red, the resident who had spoken so harshly at the teens during the conference, had called Mrs. Gray to tell her that the "real" reason for the conference was to get Mrs. Gray and her family evicted. Mrs. Gray was furious. Lauren immediately contacted Mrs. Gray. "You were there, Mrs. Gray. Is that what you think the meeting was about?" "No. I guess she really just wants to get attention, huh?" The two talked for several minutes about her choices on this matter. She could follow through with the plans of the agreement and the spirit of the meeting which was to try to help each other. Or she could fuel the path of conflict and negativity and give this woman negative attention that might lead to another fight. Mrs. Gray laughed.

The following list summarizes the outcomes of the conference in the month that followed:

- The teen organized a series of meetings with young people and the recreation department/teen center.

- The youth organizer invited Mrs. Blue in person. Mrs. Blue agreed to volunteer to work with the teens.

- Several adults also agreed to help out the young people (including the associate director of Parks and Recreation, the councilman, the recreation center director, a police lieutenant, and the sergeant).

- Mrs. Gray and her daughter attended the young peoples' meetings.

- Mrs. Blue identified one teen who comes from another neighborhood as being "the problem."

- The police lieutenant told the young people how proud she was of them.

- The adults soon learned that no one comes to dances because they are held too early. The "problem teen" was assigned to work on organizing better dances.

- Teens met for a second meeting soon after the first. They discussed their desire for mentors, and decided to become mentors for younger children. Arrangements were made for this.

- Teens and adults planned a field trip to a local nature center that could offer summer activities.

- Two days after the conference, Mrs. Mauve, the older white resident who attended the conference, stopped by the neighborhood organization.

- She was ecstatic, because a group of the teens said hello to her by name and stopped to talk.

- The police sergeant checked on the vacant house. A registered letter had already been returned unclaimed. Actions were taken to get it properly boarded up.

- Free GED classes were located by the neighborhood organization, and two of the young people living in the original "problem residence" have enrolled. A third was offered information about Job Corps, and an on-site visit was arranged.

- Regarding the recreation center:
  - The director is now more accessible.
  - Adult volunteers have stepped forward.
  - Miss Mauve now offers a sewing class for girls to make their own prom dresses.
  - The director now offers a cooking class.
  - An inter-rec basketball league team was established.
  - Jerseys were donated by a community worker's husband's store.
  - Two coaches volunteered, making a total of four teams.
- An adult who volunteered to coordinate youth activities for six months will be given space.
- The community organizer at the conference developed a new, positive view of teens.
- Regarding the establishment of new relationships:
  - Mrs. Gray and Mrs. Red (after Mrs. Red's "wedge" about the conference being about eviction) are now friends.
  - Mrs. Blue and the young people converse regularly.
  - Miss Pink and young people are now on friendly speaking terms.
  - The two teenage girls are now friends. A mediation had been offered, but they worked it out on their own.
- The city councilman brought twelve Orioles (professional baseball) tickets over to the corner the weekend after the conference. He was going to give them to the teens but they were not there. They had heeded the plea to not hang out on the corner.
- Mrs. Blue will be coordinator for the "Stoop Reading" Project.
- Teen mediators are being recruited from among the newly empowered group of teens.
- The police lieutenant met with the refugee center to look into ways to handle the conflicts related to the number of refugees who are being placed in this neighborhood.
- Teens have been asked to consult on a park development project in an adjacent community. The developer heard about the initiative of these young people and has enlisted them to help with the project.

All agreed, as one resident said to the lieutenant, they "can't arrest the problem away."

That is a profound insight. Yet, litigation is a common course of action for community organizations faced with these sorts of problems. One organizer told Lauren that, had it not been for the community conference, they would have proceeded with legal sanctions. Since the Grays live in subsidized housing, the community organization would have, upon the neighbors' request, approached the community board with the list of complaints and police calls about teen gangs. They would then have requested that this family be evicted. Yet, that family, in the end, proved not really to be part of the problem. To the contrary, the dialog of the community conference enabled them to play a significant part in the search for a practical solution.

The "Identified Conflict" and its Role in a System of Relationships

In family therapy, there is a common phenomenon that brings families into treatment. One family member, usually a child, is identified as needing the help; the rest of the family comes along to help this troubled family member. Therapists call this person the emissary or identified patient and sees them as the symptom. The actual client is the family system itself.

In much the same way, this community conflict had its emissary, its identified patient: the one house with a mother and her two children. In actuality, however, there were many interlocking relationships, all of which played a part in the conflict. Mrs. Gray and her children got the ball rolling. Once it began, the conflicts between several different groups of individuals emerged: Mrs. Blue and the teens; Mrs. Red and Mrs. Gray; the teens and the recreation center; the two teenage girls; the community and the police, and so forth.

Similarly, when a family begins to change patterns of maladaptive behavior, other members will react to try to maintain the status quo. In a sense, they benefit from the dysfunction. In the same way, Mrs. Red called Mrs. Gray in an attempt to keep the neighborhood in conflict. Mrs. Gray did not "take the bait." And then, without the currency of an ongoing conflict, Mrs. Red finally joined in the effort to build more positive relationships with her neighbors.

The Expression of Emotion as a Necessary Condition for Conflict Transformation

Our understanding of the emotional dynamic at work here is informed by a theory, which understands emotions to be the primary source of human motivation. This theory of personality was articulated most extensively by psychologist and philosopher Silvan Tomkins (1962, 1963, 1991, 1992; Demos,

1994). Tomkins extended the work of Darwin, who identified a set of innate emotional programs, or affects, which are part of our inherited physiology. The inherited affects include joy, interest, surprise, shame, distress, fear, anger, disgust, and "dissmell." Each of these "comes with" a facial expression that is universally recognized by all humans. However, these innate affects not only help us communicate with one another; their primary purpose is actually to motivate us.

As is elaborated by Tomkins (1962), the affect system is an amplifier. It draws our attention to whatever signal is being amplified at any given moment. And it is an abstract amplifier. Any similar signal will produce the same output from the amplifier, regardless of the source of the signal. For example, the affect level of distress is produced by any steady signal that produces an above optimal level of neural stimulation. A baby will experience and express distress in response to "too much." It makes no difference whether the signal "too much" is from the system of pain receptors (too much physical pain), from the thwarted drive system (too much hunger, too much thirst), from the five senses (too bright a light, too loud a noise, too much separation from touch, and so on).

These specific signal sources all produce the same general or abstract response. They all trigger the program for the affect of distress: the closed eyes, the clenched mouth, the tensed muscles throughout the body, and so on. So, it is with the other affect programs: anger, interest, fear, surprise, and enjoyment. Each responds to a particular type of signal triggered with a general response.

The system of six affects is supplemented or complicated by three additional programs. The negative response to taste (disgust) and the negative response to smell ("dissmell") are technically components of the drive system (emergency attenuators of the drives to breathe, drink, and eat). But they also function as elements of our emotional repertoire when they are used symbolically (to motivate and communicate about things that "make us sick" or "stink").

If disgust and "dissmell" are emergency attenuators of the drive system, shame can be understood as an emergency attenuator of the affect system. When we are having a good time and it suddenly stops, we feel ashamed. The shame program is triggered by any sudden and incomplete cessation of either of the positive affects: interest or enjoyment.

To be sure, socialization in the family, the community, and the society shape our emotional responses and our personalities. But the physiological programs of the affect system remain our most fundamental source of motivation and communication throughout our lives. Without emotions, our capacity for adaptation would be nominal. We need this system of motivation and communication to survive. Anger motivates us to attack. Fear makes flight possible. Interest prompts us to engage with the world. Sadness engenders care and comfort from others but what does this have to do with conferencing?

People in conflict come to the circle feeling strong negative affects. The experience is toxic, difficult, and distancing. Contempt, fear, and rage all keep us from getting along with one another. And our society provides few opportunities to cope with and/or transform these feelings. Therapists in this country can tell stories about the countless clients they see who suffer from high blood pressure, nightmares, panic attacks, and phobias as a result of being a victim of a crime in a highly charged conflict with others. Our institutional responses offer victims very little to address these matters, which deeply affect the quality of people's lives.

Conferencing, however, offers people in conflict a safe place in which they can literally give voice to these feelings. As they do so, they can begin to find ways to interpret their situation in a way that is healthier for themselves and ultimately for others as well. The conferencing process makes possible the transformation of conflict at several levels: within individuals, b e t w e e n individuals/within groups, and between groups.

In the generic community conference this transformation is, at its heart, a process dealing with emotion. Though many conferencing proponents have focused on the offenders' shame as being the cornerstone of this process, we feel this to be only one possible part of a successful conference. We assert that the sequences of emotions throughout a conference are critical to understanding the source of the efficacy and the power of the process. These affective sequences were first identified by Lauren Abramson (Abramson, 1998) and have since been characterized as taking place in four stages (McDonald and Moore, 2000). Again, this pattern tends to be particularly clear in cases where there has been a single incident of undisputed harm. In such cases, a conference will tend to begin with the following stages.

Stage I is marked by contempt, anger and fear, directed at individuals (on the basis of their actions in the past). However, as soon as people begin to describe what happened, and particularly when others respond with how they have been affected, the facilitator will notice the first major affective transition. The focus shifts from people to actions and incidents. This shift of focus is colored by a shift in affective tone. The conference moves to the next stage.

Stage II is marked by disgust, distress, and surprise that is evoked by revelations in the present about those actions and associated emotions and motivations. When everyone has had an opportunity to speak about what happened, and what has happened since, there is a powerful silence in the room. The sense that "we are all in this together" is tangible. Indeed, although it is only a brief interregnum in the process, we classify this short period as a stage in its own right.

Stage III is marked by a sense of collective vulnerability, a collective experience of the physiology of shame, as the community reflects on how things got worse. This moment is the fulcrum of the conference, the point at which the general tone is poised to shift from negative to positive. By asking those most directly affected what they would like to see come from the conference, the facilitator initiates the next stage.

Stage IV is marked by interest and then by relief, as plans for the future are developed.

Collective painting of the picture generates an experience of connected feeling and results in connected learning. We would argue that learning takes place on many levels: the most powerful of which is neither individual nor collective, but connected. Connected means that there is an understanding-beyond-cognition which can happen only when feelings are shared, thereby allowing individuals to be open to relating to themselves and others in a way that was not possible before. It is not initially an easy process in which to engage. Each participant takes a risk when sharing and when connecting, since these strategies leave us vulnerable. But our experience across classes, genders, and cultures suggests that this process, with remarkable consistency, brings about a sense of satisfaction, excitement, and a sense of renewal in those who participate.

Once together, participants feel the community become more than the sum of its parts. The motivational transition underlying this process goes a long way to explain this phenomenon. Participants typically move from the more distancing and toxic negative emotions (contempt/anger/fear), through the less distancing negative emotions (sadness and shame), and finally to positive feelings (joy and interest) about oneself and others.

For example, participants often arrive at a conference full of contempt, rage and/or terror. The associated motivations are those of distance. The contemptuous person wants to keep the offensive other as far away as possible. The terrified person withdraws so as to avoid the dangerous other. As these feelings are given a safe room for expression, however, the transformation of affect begins.

The feelings of the conference often then move to disgust, surprise, or tears of sadness. Participants are often surprised at hearing how others have been affected. After the initial bursts of hard feelings, tears begin to flow. Already we are feeling the possibility of cooperation.

At this point, those who have caused the harm may feel the weight of what they have done and realize the consequences of their actions. Shame arises from a genuine inner sense that others have been harmed. Many others have been harmed. And sometimes there is also the sense that one's self-respect has been damaged. Tomkins (1962/1963) asserted that shame is triggered in the context of a positive bond; and there has been a perceived barrier to that bond. A person feeling shame will seek to restore that bond. Thus, the emergence of shame during a conference signals an openness to repair, to reconnection, and to healing. It is also at this point that others in the conference may realize that they, too, all share responsibility in all aspects of this event. This shift in the conference has been elegantly characterized by a

Canadian colleague, Marie Fitzgerald, as being a state of "collective vulnerability." Participants all feel a sense of responsibility in making things right with each other and in their community.

The final phase is marked with feelings of relief, joy, and interest, as participants move toward one another, psychologically and literally, as they dissolve the circle and share food and conversation with one another.

This theoretical model helps explain the empirical evidence that, when used in education, justice, and neighborhood settings, community conferencing:

- minimizes the likelihood of harmful behavior being repeated

- maximizes the sense among all participants that justice was done

- maximizes the number of relationships either created or strengthened as a result of the intervention (Moore with Forsythe 1995; Sherman and Strang 1996-1999; Chatterjee 1998).

This is a process that appears to truly build social capital—in that networks of relationships are created, repaired, and brought to bear on building a better community. Much of the discussion in restorative justice as well as many of the now-popular school curriculums teaching nonviolence is based on teaching people skills for how to treat each other "more nicely." We have collectively recognized the need to learn how to build healthy relationships. For instance, one popular and well-researched intervention (Greenberg et al., 1995) has five conceptual domains: self-control, emotional understanding, positive self-esteem, relationships, and interpersonal problem-solving skills. The experience of community conferences address all these issues making them a real and experiential means of building these skills. Learning by doing is effective; learning by doing and feeling is optimal.

The forces behind the power of the conferencing process are at once biological, emotional, social, political, cultural, and spiritual. Emotional attachments and a sense of belonging are vital to our survival. Without an understanding that we depend on each other for our safety, growth, and advancement, we will be destined to harm each other with our greed, anger, and isolation. The skills needed to get along with each other used to be woven into the fabric of daily life in villages, communities, and families. This is no longer so evident. Our society tends to teach our children less about getting along with each other than it teaches about how to compete with or to "safely" avoid each other. Conferencing offers a powerful way to bring us back to the teaching of cooperation. And the beauty of it is that the process accommodates novices and elders alike. The only requirement is that people show up.

When they do show up, they find themselves moving from the negative emotions associated with conflict to the positive emotions associated with cooperation. One more community is transformed for the better.

References

Abramson, L. 1998. Keeping it Restorative: Focusing on All Emotions and not Just Shame. *Correctional Psychologist*. 30:2-3, p. 1-3.

Chatterjee, J. 1998. Evaluation of the RCMP Restorative Justice Initiative, Ottawa: RCMP Community, Contract and Aboriginal Policing Services.

Demos, E. V., ed. 1994. *Exploring Affect: The Selected Writings of Silvan S. Tomkins*. Cambridge, Massachusetts: Cambridge University Press.

Greenberg, M. T., C. A Kusche, E. T. Cook, and J. P. Quamma. 1995. Promoting Social Capital in School-aged Children: The effects of the PATHS Curriculum. *Development and Psychopathology*. 7, 117-136.

McDonald, J. M. and D. B Moore. 1998. Community Conference Facilitator's Kit. Sydney: Transformative Justice Australia.

——————. 2001. Community Conferencing as a Special Case of Conflict Transformation. In J. Braithwaite and H. Strang, eds. *Restorative Justice and Civil Society*. Cambridge, Massachusetts: Cambridge University Press.

Moore, D. B. with L. Forsythe. 1995. *A New Approach to Juvenile Justice: Family Conferencing in Wagga Wagga* (Report to the Criminology Research Council). Wagga Wagga, Australia: Centre for Rural Social Research.

Moore, D. B and J. M. McDonald. 2000a. Guiding Principles of the Conferencing Process. In G. Burford and J. Hudson, eds. *Family Group Conferences: Perspectives on Policy, Practice and Research*. Monsey, New York: Willow Tree Press.

——————. 2000. Transforming Workplace Conflict: A Guide to Preparing and Convening Workplace Conferences. Sydney: Transformative Justice Australia. Available at <www.tja.com.au>

Sherman, L. and H. Strang. 1996-1999 RISE Papers, Canberra, Australia: Australian National University. Available at <www.aic.gov.au/rjustice/progress/index.html#contents>

Tomkins, S. S. 1962. *Affect/Imagery/Consciousness, Vol. 1: The Positive Affects*. New York: Springer.

——————. 1963. *Affect/Imagery/Consciousness, Vol. 2: The Negative Affects*. New York: Springer.

——————. 1991. *Affect/Imagery/Consciousness, Vol. 3: The Negative Affects - Anger and Fear*. New York: Springer.

——————. 1992. *Affect/Imagery/Consciousness, Vol. 4: Cognition - Duplication and Transmission of Information*. New York: Springer.

Questions

1. What advantage does community conferencing have over litigation?

2. Does conflict transformation actually solve problems or just bypass them?

3. Conflict transformation can be described as: "First getting to peace, then getting to yes." What might be the ramifications of trying to get to "yes" before you get to "peace"? In what instances would you want to make sure you get to "peace" before you try to get to "yes"?

4. Does the re-identification of the conflict from an individual to a specific community change the focus of responsibility?

5. How would the acceptance of Tomkins' theory of emotions as the primary source of human motivation impact our current criminal justice system?

6. Explain that if emotions are a necessary part of our biology, a person can be held accountable for his or her behavior.

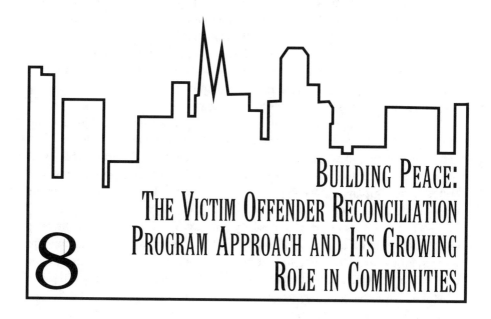

BUILDING PEACE:
THE VICTIM OFFENDER RECONCILIATION PROGRAM APPROACH AND ITS GROWING ROLE IN COMMUNITIES

8

RON CLAASSEN
CODIRECTOR, CENTER FOR PEACEMAKING
   AND CONFLICT STUDIES
FRESNO PACIFIC UNIVERSITY
FRESNO, CALIFORNIA

When a crime occurs, those people who have been impacted are at a crossroads; there are dangers and opportunities. The community response will determine whether movement is in the direction of danger or opportunity. The danger is that the primary offender(s) and victim(s) emerge from the response feeling disrespected, disempowered, alienated, and less inclined to cooperate with the community. The opportunity is for the response to leave them feeling safe, cared for, respected, empowered, restored, and more inclined to cooperate with the community.

The Victim Offender Reconciliation Program (VORP) provides a structure and trained facilitators or mediators to assist the most impacted parties in deciding how they want to respond. For those who are interested in searching for the opportunity, the Victim Offender Reconciliation Program provides people and processes to assist them.

The Victim Offender Reconciliation Program Approach

Reconciliation, trust, respect, restoration, good, and hope are some of the key words in the victim offender reconciliation program as it is practiced in the Victim Offender Reconciliation Program in Fresno.

Reconciliation is the heart of the Victim Offender Reconciliation Program. When crime occurs, much more has happened than a violation of law. The violation of law is primarily an indicator that there has been a violation of people and possibly property. This means that there has been a breach in the community, that has caused some people to experience an injustice and to trust each other less, at least temporarily. Depending on the many factors, including the individual personalities and the severity of the crime, this experience of injustice and this movement toward less trust may be greater or less and the accompanying feelings range from slight irritation to extremely intense anger and hate.

These feelings are not necessarily directly proportional to the severity of the crime. Even a relatively "minor" offense may cause very significant movement toward less trust and intensify feelings. For example, when someone who is regarded as a trusted friend steals something, the resulting distrust and accompanying feelings are often very significant and intense.

If healing and movement toward reconciliation does not happen, the distrust and distance intensifies. Time usually reduces the intensity of the feeling, but time alone does not repair the damage. Victims report that when nothing is done to recognize the injustice and repair the damage, while time reduces the intensity, if something brings it back up, the intense feelings come right back. Offenders report that when they have done nothing to repair the damage, although with time they think about it less, if they drive by the location or see the victim, the feelings reemerge. Both report that the result is at least a more stressful, less productive, and less joyful life. For some, this leads to depression or aggression that result in a downward spiral that is hard to reverse.

If we as a community ignore this very predictable consequence of crime, we bear significant responsibility for creating a less safe, more stressful, less productive, less peaceful, and less joyful community. This is especially true when we know that there are better alternatives.

Reconciliation is movement along a continuum from increasing hate and distance toward increasing caring and closeness. More than 90 percent of those who participate in a Victim Offender Reconciliation Program meeting report movement toward reconciliation. When we do nothing as a community to help repair the breach, our neglect is contributing to the movement in the opposite direction.

Reconciliation is a voluntary and cooperative process so the most the community can do is to encourage and assist. Some community members and some criminal justice officials are hesitant to even talk about reconciliation with victims or offenders for fear of imposing or making things worse for either the victim or the offender. Yet, our experience is that victims and offenders welcome discussion about the topic when it is done in a way that recognizes and is sensitive to their concerns and empowers them to make more informed choices.

It is not uncommon for a victim or offender to ask a question such as: do you think there is any hope for something good to come out of meeting? Sometimes it is said in a very serious tone and sometimes in a very cynical tone. In either case, it is very significant. This wonderful question provides some significant insight. The victims and offenders who ask this question are looking for hope and valuing good. Hope is at the heart of good mental and spiritual health. People doing good are what makes it possible for us to live in a civil society. Both hope and good are violated when a crime occurs, and without some positive action to restore both of these, each crime leaves the community a little less civil and in poorer mental and spiritual health.

A symptom of less civility and poor mental and spiritual health is a lack of respect. It may be difficult to relate this directly to our response to crime, since there are many contributing factors. Nevertheless, if we look at a classroom as a microcosm of our community, the relationship becomes clearer.

My wife, Roxanne, an eighth grade teacher, and I have been thinking about this and observing it for twelve years. Most of our schools operate their discipline systems in a very similar way to our criminal justice system. Rules are established and those who violate the rules are punished. Often those who are punished are forced to be separated from their community for a period of time. Within a school, rather than dealing with the problem and working for reconciliation and restoration between teacher and student, the student or the teacher is transferred to another classroom. Or, if two students cannot get along, they are both punished or one is punished, and then they are usually separated, rather than asking them or helping them to find a way to modify their behavior so they can live civilly together. These sound a lot like the way we deal with those who violate the law and their victims.

Roxanne has viewed her classroom as a community. She has developed a method for establishing an agreement for how they will be a community. She starts by asking each student to write what they think it would mean for each person to respect his or her peers, to respect their teacher, for their teacher to respect them, and for all of them to respect the property of the school and others. After they each write about this, she compiles these statements on a large sheet of butcher paper and posts them for everyone to examine. (She has observed that all students know a lot about respect, even if they often do not show it.) She asks each student to examine each statement and to point out any of these that are not fair, respectful, or reasonable. If they identify some that meet these criteria, they are discussed and negotiated and by consensus they decide if they should be taken off. The remaining items are written on a large piece of butcher paper for everyone to see.

Then, the whole class, including the teacher, are invited over the next week to consider signing this as their class agreement. They are asked to sign it if this is the kind of class in which they want to participate. Most want that kind of classroom. A few are reluctant to sign because it would mean taking more responsibility for acting more civilly. However, even these usually decide to sign.

When conflicts or violations occur, people are reminded of the agreement and this usually takes care of the problem. If problems are reoccurring or more serious, a meeting (like a Victim Offender Reconciliation Program meeting) is held. Those who are impacted by the offensive behavior are invited to consider if they would like to work it out together or if they would like a mediator to help them. Almost all problems are worked out and agreements are made. Meetings are scheduled for follow-up and if agreements have been kept, they celebrate.

If they have not been kept, they again decide if they are willing to work it out. If a student refuses to cooperate, the authority makes decisions about consequences and next steps. These decisions, the way they are communicated, and the consequences if any, are jointly evaluated to determine if they are reasonable, respectful, and encourage and invite restoration and reintegration. As soon as the student is ready to search for a way to restore a respectful and just way of being together, a Victim Offender Reconciliation Program type meeting is held, agreements are made, and follow-up is scheduled. In some cases, the meeting involves parents, extended family members, and other school or community members.

The Victim Offender Reconciliation Program type meetings are a way of restoring respect. Yet, it is not possible to restore respect without recognizing the injustices (from all perspectives), making things as right as possible, and creating a plan for the future that will prevent reoccurrence of the injustice. When this process has been completed in the meeting, there are agreements. Then, follow-up and accountability are essential. If agreements are made and kept, trust grows. If individuals are unwilling to make agreements or if the agreements are not kept, trust goes down (Claassen, 1991).

Punishment is not accountability. Accountability is when people agree to something and then are open to others who monitor, encourage, and support the people in keeping the agreements. It is rare that people do not keep any part of the agreement and if the agreement calls for significant change, it is also rare that on the first try they will keep all of the agreement. Accountability is the process of keeping in touch with those aspects of the agreement that are being kept and noting what is not being kept. Accountability is celebrating those parts that are kept and bringing into the light those parts that are not kept so that they can be discussed, examined, reevaluated, and new commitments made. Accountability is hard work and not an easy or quick fix.

While this Victim Offender Reconciliation Program type approach is not a quick fix, Roxanne finds it to be more effective and more efficient. The other discipline alternatives that rely on punishment and external control often look easier or quicker on the surface. But as time passes and an increasing number of conflicts are not resolved, they get bigger and end up requiring even more significant time and resources. Using this Victim Offender Reconciliation Program type approach saves time, resources, and creates not only a more peaceful community but also a more efficient and effective learning community.

Just as the Victim Offender Reconciliation Program approach works in the school and classroom, it builds trust and respect in the larger community. Trust grows when agreements are made and kept. Trust goes down when we are unwilling to make agreements or make agreements and do not keep them (Claassen, 1991). The Victim Offender Reconciliation Program provides a structure and process to encourage and assist in making of agreements and keeping them. The more agreements that are made and kept, the higher the trust will be in our communities. If we refuse to allow or encourage the victim and offender to make agreements, we are contributing to developing a community in which trust is low.

The Victim Offender Reconciliation Program process is built on a Peacemaking Model (Claassen, 1986). The Peacemaking Model has evolved by observing the Victim Offender Reconciliation Program meetings and looking for patterns where the result was significant reconciliation (movement along the continuum from hate and distance toward caring and closeness). It also has been influenced by listening to many stories about what it was that made it possible for people who were upset with each other and somewhat distant to move to being okay and closer. It also reflects how the Bible says one moves beyond violation and injustice toward right relations.

The Peacemaking Model says that the starting point is for someone to make a commitment to be constructive, even if it is not clear if the others are committed to being constructive. This unconditional commitment to be constructive includes respecting, valuing, and caring for all people. It is the opposite of eliminating the opponent. Peacemaking starts when one is willing to make this commitment. Making this commitment involves risk because the others might not reciprocate. This commitment does not mean giving up on what is right or saying that violations or injustice are okay. This commitment is not a proposal on how to resolve the injustice or violation. Rather, it is a commitment to enter a process. It includes an offer for a fair and just process to recognize the violations and injustices from each person's perspective, to recognize injustices, to search for ways to make things as right as possible (restore equity) and to develop a plan that will create a safe, fair, and just future (future intentions). What we have observed is that when all of these are completed, forgiveness happens. Trust begins to grow with the making of the agreement and continues to grow as the agreements are kept.

The Fresno Victim Offender Reconciliation Program Process

Most victim offender reconciliation program cases start with a referral from police, probation, or the court. The case is then assigned to a trained volunteer mediator. The mediator makes a commitment to be constructive in all of their meetings with victims and offenders.

The mediator arranges an individual meeting with the victim and his or her family or support persons and with the offender and his or her family or support persons. At each of these meetings, the mediator does several things.

1. The mediator listens to their experience, trying to understand it and trying to put themselves in the other person's shoes as much as possible.

2. The mediator informs them what a victim offender reconciliation program joint meeting process usually includes by:

   - listening to each person's perspective on what happened and what its impact was/is and summarizing for each other to be sure that each is heard and understood.

   - deciding on how to repair the damage (physical and relational) as much as possible.

   - deciding on how to move forward in ways that create a more safe, just, civil, and even joyful future.

   - deciding on how accountability will be handled (usually with a specific trusted person and with follow-up meetings).

3. They discuss the ground rules that will guide the meeting.

   - Allow the mediator to lead the process.

   - Tell the mediator if the process seems like it is not fair or is not covering what you thought you agreed to.

   - Agree to no name-calling or profanity.

   - Be willing to summarize when requested by the mediator.

4. They discuss the purpose for meeting: to listen to each other and search for ways to repair the damage and make things as right as possible.

5. They discuss any questions they might have about the process and purpose.

6. They invite them to consider who should be at the meeting.

7. They discuss the need for voluntary participation for a cooperative process like this to be constructive.

8. An invitation is offered to participate in a Victim Offender Reconciliation Program meeting.

9. If they decide to participate in a Victim Offender Reconciliation Program meeting, they discuss future convenient dates, times, and places.

10. If they are unsure or if they do not want to participate, they discuss alternatives.

Generally, the first meeting is with the offender and then if the offender agrees to participate, the next meeting is with the victim. This is the process when the referral is from the criminal justice system. The order of contact intends to avoid revictimizing the victim since the meetings are voluntary and an offender may choose not to participate. The victim initiates some cases and then the first meeting is with the victim. Our Victim Offender Reconciliation Program experience is that approximately 80 percent of offenders and 80 percent of victims will voluntarily agree to participate.

Our program only works with cases where both the victim and the offender voluntarily agree to participate. It is not a victim-offender process unless they both voluntarily agree. There might be value in some situations that force offenders to meet with victims who would like to tell the offenders about their pain or ask them some questions. It is very helpful for offenders to listen to the experiences of many victims to gain more understanding of the impact of what they have done.

Our Victim Offender Reconciliation Program is open about who should be at the meetings when victims and offenders come together. We require a parent or guardian to be with a juvenile offender or victim. Our experience is that the victim and offender usually choose to have just one or two people with them but there have been meetings when they have chosen to have a much larger group. In one pipe bomb case at a school in 1986, we had a group of twenty people. This was the exception. The usual meeting has four to seven people.

Preparation for most of our cases is one meeting in which the major items are covered. However, in some cases, the preparation is much longer, sometimes several meetings and sometimes several years.

The Victim Offender Reconciliation Program usually takes one meeting but sometimes they want or need several meetings. The process of this meeting is for the victim and offender to each describe their experience of the offense and its impact. They might also add some history leading up to the offense. We aim for understanding and do this by asking each to summarize what the other has said. This is something that is negotiated in the individual meeting and if the victim does not want to, someone else does the summary for the victim. Usually the victim prefers to do it himself or herself. We always ask the offender to summarize the victim's experience because victims report significant satisfaction in knowing that the offender listened and understood enough to repeat it. Of course, the tone and nonverbal communication during this time also are very significant. Offenders report gaining substantial insight and empathy while doing this. Tears are not uncommon.

We know it is time to move on when everyone present agrees that the violations and injustice have been recognized or that each person has had an opportunity to describe their experience and knows that the person they needed to hear it has listened, and even summarized it. We then move on to the next two agenda items. One is to decide together what it is that could be done to restore equity as much as possible. We say as much as possible because we understand from victims that restitution and apologies and other things can restore some or even in some cases most of the equity, but there is always some that simply needs to be let go. The readiness for this letting go part (grace) varies from victim to victim. Some are ready much sooner than others. Most report that it is helpful when the offender has made a serious effort at all three parts of the agenda. The other agenda is to discuss what it would take to create a safer, more respectful and civil future for everyone.

When the injustices are recognized and agreements made on restoring the equity as much as possible and creating a more peaceful and just future for everyone, as these agreements are kept, trust grows and forgiveness happens. Then, reconciliation, movement along a continuum from hating toward caring, also happens.

The follow-up stages are critical. If the agreements are made but not kept, the trust that grew in the meetings is quickly dissipated. Thus, we devote at least equal staff time to follow-up as to the preparation and meeting. We prefer that someone in the family serves as the primary support and accountability person and that our staff stays in touch.

When we do work directly with the offender, if they are late on completing an agreement, our starting point is, "you made an agreement with the victim, do you still intend to keep it?" Almost always they say yes. In thousands of cases over the last seventeen years, only a few have said no. Some say yes hoping that now that they said the right thing, we will go away. Often it is a new experience for them to have someone say that they will not go away, that they will keep on asking, until they either complete the agreement or they say no. Many complete their agreements as made or very close to the time they agreed. Some complete them very late. Some come back in after five years and complete their agreement. They always feel good when they complete their agreements. Trust grows most when all agreements are kept on time. It also seems to grow even when offenders are late but are making some effort to complete them.

In 1995 Judge Fred McElrea and Matt Hawkiaha from New Zealand visited our program and explained their experience with Family Group Conferencing. As a result of their visit and some restorative justice training and planning, our community developed a Community Justice Conference process. It was developed by the Juvenile Court, District Attorney, Public Defender, Probation, and the Victim Offender Reconciliation Program. We decided to use the Victim Offender Reconciliation Program Conferencing process as an alternative for some of the court processes. We wanted to be sure that we were really working with cases that would have gone to court so we chose to work with nonviolent felony cases. We used this process with six cases per month where the offender accepted responsibility.

More than 80 percent of the cases in 1998 and 1999 came to a Victim Offender Reconciliation Program meeting and almost all arrived at agreements that were then submitted to the court and made the order of the court. Because this process is not something in addition to or just a part of the court sentence, the considerations are broader than when the Victim Offender Reconciliation Program is just asked to work with restitution and the victim/offender relationship. We have found that they often want additional time or meetings to deal with the offender/family relationship. While this occasionally became a part of our other Victim Offender Reconciliation Program meetings, this experience has heightened our awareness to this need.

Early information indicates an equally high victim and offender satisfaction with this process when compared to other Victim Offender Reconciliation Program meetings. Preliminary numbers indicate that recidivism is about 17 percent, and what is very interesting is that those who have been arrested again have been arrested for offenses that are less serious. This would correspond with Roxanne's experience in her classroom. It also corresponds with research that indicates that most offenders who quit offending often do less serious crime before they quit. This would mean that this process is working and needs to be used again and again until the criminal behavior is extinguished. If we do this, we would truly be tough on crime.

Growing Use of the Peacemaking Process in the Community

The Fresno Victim Offender Reconciliation Program started with five experimental cases in 1983 and grew to 595 case referrals in 1995. As this numerical growth occurred, the number of referral points also increased. The Fresno Victim Offender Reconciliation Program now receives referrals as a diversion, postadjudication and presentence, postsentence, and from institutions as a part of the transition back into the community. In addition, the Victim Offender Reconciliation Program receives occasional referrals from inmates in state prison and from victims of a wide range of offenses. Whether our process looks more like the traditional victim and offender plus mediator or a conference with more people depends on the case. There is not just one effective process.

In addition to this growth in cases and referral points at the Victim Offender Reconciliation Program, others in the community have begun to incorporate these processes into their way of responding to conflicts. Schools are increasingly using peer mediation for student conflicts and teachers, like

Roxanne, are beginning to use the process as an integral part of their discipline structure. When this approach becomes the culture as it has at Roxanne's school, we also see teachers using it to resolve conflicts between teachers and with parents.

The Victim Offender Reconciliation Program approach is also being used in the workplace. One manager, after participating with his son in a Victim Offender Reconciliation Program case, decided that this would be a very good approach for him and his employees. They asked for training and added a Victim Offender Reconciliation Program type meeting as a standard part of the early intervention when dealing with grievances.

Even churches, whose foundational guide teaches this approach, are encouraged to use this Victim Offender Reconciliation Program approach when members are trained and become aware and skillful. Over the last seventeen years, the Fresno Victim Offender Reconciliation Program has trained more than 1,500 volunteer mediators. Mediators tell us that they use the Victim Offender Reconciliation Program approach in their work and home environment much more than at the Victim Offender Reconciliation Program. This is very exciting news.

So, why isn't the Victim Offender Reconciliation Program approach in more communities? This author believes there are four reasons why we do not use this approach more.

1. We simply do not have the skills and strategies to do it successfully. Frequently people say they want to resolve something cooperatively, but when they open the topic of conflict up for discussion, it turns quickly into an argument. This is usually because they simply have not done the necessary preparation work and do not know how to deal effectively with the problem or injustice in a cooperative way. The good news is that if we were not lucky enough to grow up in a home and school in which we learned how to cooperative effectively, it is never too late to learn. There are specific skills and strategies that can be learned that will very significantly increase the likelihood that when we try, we will be able to resolve a conflict cooperatively.

2. We think that when someone violates a rule or a law, even an informal one, they must be punished. It is a fundamental question: Do we respond to hurts and violation through revenge and distance or by aiming for "making things right" and reintegration? We will only give the Victim Offender Reconciliation Program approach a chance when, because we value all people, our preference is for "making things as right as possible."

3. We often miss the opportunity to invite others to work out the problem in a constructive way. The Victim Offender Reconciliation Program approach always requires someone to do this. Someone has to initiate the idea that it might be possible to work the issue out in some constructive way.

4. Our structures sometimes are designed in ways that prevent the Victim Offender Reconciliation Program approach or at least do not encourage

it. Our structures are not valueless. Some structures are designed in a way that they help people make peace between them and others drive people apart. We need to examine our structures.

The New Zealand model is a good example of a very large structure that changed its approach. The structure at Roxanne's school has been changed. The manager who changed the process in his business is another example of how a structure can be changed. When we really examine our families, we have a structure for handling conflict. Some of those structures bring people together and others drive people apart. We need to examine our structures and if they do not include the Victim Offender Reconciliation Program approach, they can be modified.

Peacemaking in the community builds one relationship at a time. Each time a relationship in our community is violated, if we neglect the relationship, we are contributing to increased long-term stress and increased potential for violence. Each time we follow the Victim Offender Reconciliation Program peacemaking approach, we are encouraging responsibility, accountability, and reintegration. While the Victim Offender Reconciliation Program peacemaking approach takes time and seems stressful while we are working it out, the long-term benefits are clearly worth the efforts. Retribution leads to more retribution. The cycle is changed when justice, mercy, forgiveness, responsibility, accountability, and peace all meet. This wonderful meeting leads to reconciliation. This is one of the central components of restorative justice.

Vocabulary and Questions

- reconciliation

- trust

- respect

- restoration

- good

- hope

- healing

- accountability

1. What occurs in a Victim Offender Reconciliation Program meeting?

2. Most Victim Offender Reconciliation Program cases start with a referral from police, probation, or the court. How are they different from traditional resolutions of such cases?

3. What limits the Victim Offender Reconciliation Program approach from being more widely used?

4. What are the three basic components of the Peacemaking Model?

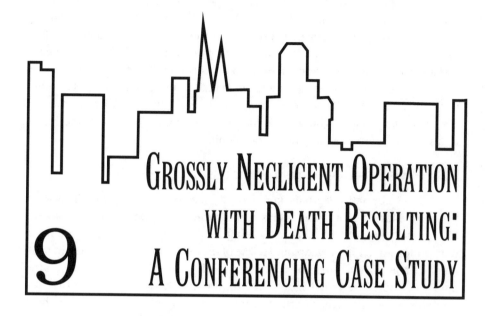

GROSSLY NEGLIGENT OPERATION WITH DEATH RESULTING: A CONFERENCING CASE STUDY

CHRIS DINNAN
COMMUNITY RESOURCE COORDINATOR
VERMONT DEPARTMENT OF CORRECTIONS
RUTLAND, VERMONT

The Incident

At approximately 7:00 AM on January 24, 2000, Jane Jones* attempted to pass a northbound vehicle on a state highway in rural Vermont. In attempting to overtake the pickup truck operated by Bob Daily, Ms. Jones crossed double yellow painted lines and entered the southbound lane at a point where a crest in the highway obstructed her view. This location is clearly posted with warning signs indicating the location is unsafe to pass. Although she did not overtake the pickup truck, Ms. Jones remained in the southbound lane of travel to the hill crest at which time she collided with the vehicle of Mary Johnson, resulting in a severe collision. Apparently, there was no time for braking by either operator.

---

*Note: All names in this case, other than those of professionals employed by the State of Vermont in the criminal justice system, have been changed.

Immediately following the crash, Bob Daily braked, stopped, and backed up, placing his pickup truck across the roadway on the north side of the vehicles that had collided. After exiting his vehicle, he walked up to Jane Jones' van and observed her sitting in the driver's seat. The airbag had deployed. He moved Ms. Jones' head back slightly, out of the air bag. Her mouth and face were bleeding and she was in and out of consciousness. She was, however, managing to breathe on her own. He then proceeded to the car driven by Mary Johnson. She appeared deceased and when Mr. Daily checked for a pulse at her neck, he found none. Mary Johnson, age thirty-eight, was pronounced dead at the scene. Jane Jones, who was six months pregnant at the time of the crash, was severely injured, as was her unborn child.

The Presentence Court Process

The information and affidavit in this case were filed in Rutland District Court on May 1, 2000. Jane Jones was charged with one count of Grossly Negligent Operation with Death Resulting, a felony that could result in imprisonment for up to fifteen years and a fine of up to $15,000. At the initial arraignment on May 15, she pled not guilty on the advice of her counsel. Also on the advice of counsel, she had not contacted the family of the deceased victim, though she had strongly desired to do so. Four status conferences were held prior to a status conference held on October 2, at which point it became clear that the state and the defense were nowhere near reaching a plea agreement. The parties agreed to and Judge Theresa DiMauro ordered a pre-plea investigation to be completed by the Department of Corrections by November 11. Corrections Services Specialist John Alexander was assigned to the case.

During a final status conference on January 8, 2001, they arrived at a plea agreement. It was also determined that final sentencing would be held on February 22. While Jane Jones agreed to plead "no contest" to the original charge, there was no agreement as to a sentence. The state would recommend a split sentence: four to twelve years with all but one year suspended, the balance on probation. In other words, the state was recommending one year in jail with an additional three to eleven years on probation. The state would also recommend special conditions of probation that would include participation at a victim-impact panel, loss of her license for at least one year, and attendance at a safe driving reeducation course. Jane Jones was free to argue for whatever sentence she believed appropriate. A presentence investigation was ordered by the court (to augment the pre-plea investigation that was already submitted) to be completed prior to the sentencing date.

I became personally involved in this case the week prior to the February 22 sentencing date. Mike O'Malley, superintendent of the Rutland Community Corrections Services Center (Probation and Parole), knew of my interest and experience in group conferencing and gave me a draft of the presentence investigation. One condition that the Department of Corrections was considering recommending to the court was that Jane Jones participate in a group conference (after sentencing) if the family of the deceased victim wanted to do this. I recommended to Mike that holding a conference would be a good idea, but that doing so prior to sentencing would be even more compelling than after sentencing. Doing so would potentially give the surviving victims a substantial role in having an impact on the sentence, while simultaneously serving both the interests of the state and the defense.

On February 15, Mike sent the following e-mail to Rutland County State's Attorney Jim Mongeon, the defense attorney and staff of the Department of Corrections associated with the case:

> After reviewing and staffing a recent PSI on a Jane Jones, it became quite apparent that the adversarial nature of the court system was not in the best interest of justice in this case. The victims are looking for closure for this tragedy. They appear reasonable and rational in their requests for closure and reparation from the offender, given the situation. The offender has taken responsibility for her action, would have probably already expressed her remorse for her poor judgement, agreed to victim's wishes for reparation, and the social/psychological healing would have already begun, had she not followed sound legal advice from her legal counsel, which does not always tack and tie with good social/psychological advice. I would like to suggest the following—the use of Group Conferencing as a pre-sentence option.

> As part of our recommendation to the Court on this PSI, we have encouraged the Court to consider employing the group conferencing process as a pre-sentencing tool. This is indeed a compelling option in this case, as it appears likely that the defendant and the family of the deceased, along with other appropriate parties, would voluntarily agree to engage in this facilitated process. The goal would be to arrive at an agreement of reparation, which would be signed by all participants, that would address what needs to happen now as a result of the harm done. The final sentencing decision of the Court would not in any way be obligated by this agreement, but would certainly be, we would hope, informed and influenced by it. If all parties are agreed, the Department of Corrections could organize and hold such a conference in as little as two to three weeks time.

There is no guarantee that a final agreement will be accomplished. However, there are very strong indicators that both parties in this case are excellent candidates to successfully complete this healing process for themselves as well as their community support systems. The ball is now in the hands of the attorneys in this case.

As a result of this e-mail, the defense attorney submitted a request to the Court to extend sentencing to accommodate a group conference. State's Attorney Jim Mongeon was willing to agree to this request so long as Dick Johnson, the deceased victim's father, agreed. Kim Ezzo, Victims' Advocate in the State's Attorney's Office, contacted Mr. Johnson. Kim then called me and suggested I speak to Dick so that he might make an informed decision. I spent over an hour on the phone with Mr. Johnson during the late afternoon of February 19 explaining the process to him. He was very open to the possibility but wanted to discuss it with his wife that night. At 9:00 A.M. the next morning, he called Kim Ezzo and informed her that he and his family wished to participate in the group conference prior to sentencing. With the assent of the state's attorney and the defense attorney, Judge Theresa DiMauro agreed to extend sentencing until April 5.

The Conference

It was agreed that the conference would be held on Saturday, March 17, at 1:30 P.M. This would allow for everyone to be able to attend and would leave the length of time necessary to complete the conference open. A local inn in the victim's town graciously allowed us to use a pleasant space for no charge. The twelve participants at the conference included: Jane Jones (defendant), Frank Jones (her husband), Harriet Franklin (her pastor), Kim Ezzo (victim's advocate), Bob Daily (the driver of the pickup), Thelma Daily (his wife), Dick Johnson (deceased victim's father), Lynne Johnson (Dick's wife), Diane Baker (deceased victim's aunt), Robin Phelps (also an aunt), Ann Hall (cousin), and Jeanne Perry (stepsister). I facilitated the conference and Dyanne Lertola, a corrections services specialist also trained in the process, cofacilitated. Dyanne's role was to help take notes during the agreement phase and to remain in the room to type up the agreement for signatures.

I did all the preconference logistics and participant preparation, which amounted to about twelve hours of work. I personally met with the defendant and her husband, the pick up truck driver and his wife, and the father of the deceased victim and his wife. I spoke with all other participants over the telephone. The only preconference snag worth noting was that Bob and Thelma Daily were thirty minutes late. I had asked the victim contingent to arrive a few minutes early and the defendant contingent to arrive at precisely 1:30 P.M. The victims were shown to the room where the conference was to be held, and the defendant and her two supporters were waiting in the lobby. This half-hour wait seemed interminably long, but at least the two contingents were comfortable and separate from each other.

The conferencing script promoted by the Real Justice organization out of Bethlehem, Pennsylvania (www.realjustice.org), was used almost word-for-word. Slight variations were made to accommodate the situation. For instance, the defendant had no memory of the crash so asking, "What happened?" was replaced by the question, "From what you have been told, what happened?" I also added the following three sentences to the preamble to make certain everyone understood the process: "We will begin by giving everyone the opportunity to speak. Later on in the conference, there will be ample time for discussion and questions as we seek to develop an agreement or understanding about what needs to happen now. During this first part of the conference, however, I would ask that everyone simply listen to whomever is speaking." Since this case involved a fatality, I chose to use the phrase "address the harm" as opposed to the phrase "repair the harm."

The conference itself lasted about three hours, with about forty-five minutes spent "breaking bread" after the formal conference. As one might imagine, it was highly emotional, with many tears and a good deal of anger. All participants remained civil throughout. Toward the end of the conference, Dick shared pictures of Mary, and there was quite a bit of discussion about what she would have wanted to happen in this situation. I believe that what was said in the conference and by whom should remain private. The agreement, however, is part of the official court record and reads as follows:

> We, the undersigned, agree and recommend to the Court that Jane Jones not receive a period of incarceration as a part of her sentence. We do believe that she should not drive for a total period of two years after sentencing. We also believe that the Court should establish a community service component at sentencing to possibly include public speaking, public service announcements, organizing public support to make improvements to the State highway or other appropriate efforts to positively impact the community.

Sentencing

Sentencing was scheduled for 9:00 A.M. on Thursday, April 5. The actual hearing was delayed a bit as the parties were busy developing and agreeing to a "Stipulation to Amend Plea Agreement." At 9:30 A.M., Judge Theresa DiMauro opened the hearing. State's Attorney Jim Mongeon opened with initial remarks and presentation of evidence. He almost immediately referred to the group conference and noted that, to his knowledge, this was the first time such a process has been employed in Rutland County in this type of situation. After presenting some photographs from the crash and other information to the Court, Mr. Mongeon introduced Dick Johnson, the father of the deceased victim, who wished to make a statement. Mr. Johnson's unabridged statement follows:

My name is Dick Johnson. I don't have a lot to say because originally the state was asking for a jail term for Jane Jones and, due to the efforts of John Alexander and Chris Dinnan, they arranged this meeting between Ms. Jones and her family and members of my family. We agreed that Jane going to jail would serve no purpose. It gave us an opportunity to actually meet the Jones and tell them how we feel and why we felt the way we did and just generally discuss the situation, and we all agreed on what the penalty should be for that.

The reason that we didn't think that she should be incarcerated is, first of all, Mary loved children, and I don't believe that she would want the mother taken away from her children. Another reason is that four years prior to that, my niece made the same mistake that Jane Jones made and passed a vehicle there, and the result was that she lost her life in the same spot. Had the situation been different, I don't believe that we would have wanted her to go to jail for it. So, we can relate to it from that angle. The third reason is that I think that the state shares in the responsibility for Mary's death. (This specific state highway) is a disaster and that particular spot is a death trap. The State Department of Transportation is aware of that. They can put up signs and they can paint lines and there's something about that that lures you into believing that you can see all the way up to the intersection, and you can't. A car disappears in that gully for four or five seconds, and you come around that corner and it never occurs to you that there could be a car down there. The state needs to do something about that. They prefer to make a giant project out of it, talking about widening the right-of-way and moving poles and moving cables and doing all sorts of things and making it into a great project and then saying they don't have the money to do it. I believe that a simple fix can save a life. I believe that if they don't do something that someone else is going to die there and another family is going to go through what we went through.

I don't have much more to say other than that I would like to thank John Alexander and Chris Dinnan for their efforts on our behalf and for bringing us together. I think that this is a good program that should be expanded and used wherever possible because it can work. It worked for us.

Following Mr. Johnson's statement, State's Attorney Mongeon asked Mr. Johnson if he supported the plea agreement with the stipulations that had been developed between the state and the defendant. Mr. Johnson indicated that he did. The State's Attorney noted to the Court that he would not have agreed to the stipulated plea agreement without Mr. Johnson's explicit support. Mr. Mongeon thus concluded his opening remarks, and Judge DiMauro gave the floor to the defense counsel.

While the defense knew that they had an agreement with the State's Attorney, there was no guarantee that the Judge would accept the agreement. Thus, over an hour of testimony was presented by the defense to illustrate Jane Jones' remorse and state of mind since the crash and to document the effect of the crash on the entire Jones family, particularly on their son, Steven. Jane's husband, Frank, was called to the stand first. His testimony was followed by a taped deposition from the family's pediatrician, who documented the extent of the injuries to Steven. Steven has severe developmental and neurological problems directly linked to the crash that will most likely lead to the need for extensive lifelong care and assistance. Finally, Jane Jones took the stand.

Following the defense's presentation of this testimony, State's Attorney Jim Mongeon made his closing remarks, followed by the defense attorney's closing remarks. Both recommended that the Court accept the sentencing terms of the stipulated plea agreement. Below are excerpts from Judge Theresa DiMauro's final remarks before sentencing.

> Probably one of the most difficult tasks for judges is sentencing. Some cases are much more clear-cut than others are and it is much easier to accomplish the goals of sentencing, which are punishment, rehabilitation and deterrence of the defendant before the Court and of others who may be before the Court. This is, clearly, not one of those cases.
>
> I . . . have wrestled with what to do this day, having read not only about what happened to Mary Johnson, but what has happened to the Jones family as well. Clearly, we have to start at the point that we have lost Mary Johnson, that her family has lost her. . . . They have had to deal with the suddenness of that loss, with this Court process, which doesn't resolve everything for anyone. Its limitations are apparent and the benefits of the group conferencing are apparent as well.
>
> No one should have to live with the pain the Johnsons have had to live with and no one should have to live with the pain Ms. Jones has to live with.

The comments of Mr. Johnson were very moving and the position that Ms. Jones should not receive any incarceration is a true tribute to the character and strength of the Johnson family. The statement regarding what Mary would want, that she would not want Ms. Jones to go to jail, is a tribute to the kind of person she was.

The benefits, I think, of the group conferencing are apparent in this case and the Court was, when it was proposed, more than willing to try it. The Court has had the experience prior to coming to this Court of attempting and trying alternatives in juvenile cases. It was a similar process where the parties came together to discuss the issues, the case, the child, the needs of the family and what needs to be done to keep the child safe. It was a very, in my mind, successful process. I was very willing to try this and hoped that even if it didn't result in some agreement then at least it would provide an opportunity for the Johnson family to receive some closure here and to meet with Ms. Jones and share their feelings and her to share hers with them in the hopes that it would be of some benefit to the family.

The Court will accept the agreement.

The complete text of the "Stipulation to Amend Plea Agreement" follows:

NOW COMES the State of Vermont, by and through Rutland County State's Attorney James P. Mongeon, and defendant personally through counsel, Attorney Richard Coleman and hereby notify the Court of the following amendment to the written plea agreement dated January 8, 2001.

1. As the direct result of a Conferencing in this matter held by the Vermont Department of Corrections on March 17, 2001 where the victims and the defendant met to review the events and effects of the collision of January 24, 2000 and arrived at an agreement which is attached hereto, the parties hereby enter this amended plea agreement.

2. The State and Defendant jointly recommend to the Court a sentence of 4 years to 12 years all suspended with probation including all special conditions of probation as attached to the original plea agreement except as struck, amended or added herein;

a. Restitution: Struck since all decedent expenses were paid by insurance to the satisfaction of the decedent's family;

b. You shall not operate a motor vehicle for at least TWO (2) years from the date of sentencing and not until reinstated by the Vermont DMV;

c. You shall make arrangements to produce at your own expense and be the announcer on three separate public service announcements for radio broadcast on radio stations throughout Vermont on driver safety, specifically identifying that you were the driver of a car which collided with another, killing that driver, and that speeding and improper passing can kill others, the text and final product subject to the approval of your probation officer in consultation with the Rutland County State's Attorney and the Governor's Commission on Highway Safety;

d. You shall make a presentation for driver education safety to Vermont high schools within a 25 mile radius of your residence based upon these events and effects on the decedent's family, your family and your life, such presentations being made to four (4) high schools each academic year for three (3) years for a total of 12 presentations beginning with the academic year 2001–2002, such presentations being to classes, assemblies or such gatherings as the school administration requests. At least one such presentation will be at (the high school in the town) where the decedent Mary Johnson lived. Such presentation shall be to the satisfaction of your probation officer.

Feedback from Participants

Within a few days of the conference, as there had been no copier available at the inn where the conference was held, I sent a copy of the signed agreement to all twelve participants along with a feedback form and self-addressed stamped envelope. Five participants chose to send the completed feedback form back to me.

Scale: 1 = Lowest Score, 10 = Highest Score

• Please rate your overall satisfaction with the conference:

1   2   3   4   5   6   7   8   9   10

Responses 2-8s, 1-9, 2-10s

• Please rate the process as to how fairly participants were treated during the conference:

1   2   3   4   5   6   7   8   9   10

Responses 1-9, 4-10s

• Please rate your level of satisfaction with preconference preparation efforts:

1   2   3   4   5   6   7   8   9   10

Responses 1-8, 2-9s, 2-10s

• Do you feel the conference properly addressed the offense?

YES   NO

Responses 5 YES

• Did you personally experience any benefits from participating?

YES   NO

Responses 5 YES

Explain:

—"I was impressed with the process and how it was conducted."

—"I had heard rumors that Jane Jones felt no remorse and it was important that I hear, from her, how she has been affected by this. I don't think I could have agreed to the 'no jail time' part if that had been the truth."

—"Just being present for an event like this is beneficial–to witness the opportunity for the truth to be told where people feel safe creates the opportunity for healing. Listening restores wholeness."

—"It gave me an opportunity to express my feelings about my personal loss and also to express my opinion about what the defendant's sentence should be. Strangely, I also found forgiveness in my heart that I didn't know was there."

—"It gave me the opportunity to put 'faces with names' and to express my feelings as to how this tragedy has affected so many people."

• Were you given ample opportunity to have input?

YES   NO

Responses 5 YES

• Did the facilitators do a proper job in leading the conference?

YES   NO

Responses 5 YES

• Would you like to see conferencing used more frequently in the future?

YES   NO

Responses 5 YES

Please explain, including any ideas as to how and in what situations this might be done:

—"I think the offense needs to be taken into account along with the players. I'm not sure this would work well unless all parties are in agreement as to process/rules."

—"I think this avenue should be explored in any situation EXCEPT: 1. Intentional, premeditated, violent crime; 2. Crimes against large numbers of people; 3. Crimes where the defendant might be considered insane or mentally unfit to participate."

—"Certainly, restorative justice conferences are beneficial in situations where the 'victim' and the 'offender' are unknown to each other. I also think they could be beneficial when they do know each other, such as instances of family violence or substance related crimes or sexual abuse, including molestation and rape. Too much television and movie violence leaves out the personal impact and desensitizes us to real pain."

—"I would leave that to others to decide what situations this would work in. I think someone involved in each case should make that determination. It wouldn't work for everyone."

—"I think that any time people need to express feelings in a monitored, informal setting and if [given] the chance to reach an agreement of sorts, [this] would help the parties involved to feel more a part of the process."

• Please take some time to reflect on the experience of being a participant and share your thoughts with us in writing, including what you think was the worst/best thing about this specific conference and how we might improve the process for future applications.

—"I think the fact that it was structured yet the time unlimited were very important factors. It wasn't a free-for-all yet we could take all the time we needed to come to an agreement. I like that everyone had a chance to speak because at sentencing only Jane and Dick would have had the opportunity. I wanted her to know that I (we) didn't hate her and that her children were not the only ones affected by this tragedy. I think a lot of healing happened that day. I also wanted her to know about Mary and was worried that Jane would be too nervous on the day of sentencing to really absorb what was being said. I am now less nervous about the sentencing because no matter what the judge's final decision is – Jane knows how we feel about it. She won't have to walk in there thinking that we are out for revenge. I know that some people were quite angry going in to the conference and I think it was very beneficial to them to see her as a real person who made a horrible mistake."

—"Even though the Johnson family thought that Jane should have contacted them herself, I think this process, because it was guided, was probably more beneficial for everyone concerned. I also think that the amount of time that has elapsed has given everyone a chance to live with their grief so that it is not raw. I don't know how much time usually elapses before these conferences are held. As Robin described the hospital encounter and Dick described Christmas, had this been scheduled in the fall, I'm not sure that it would have resulted in the same outcome. Perhaps it would have called for more preconference preparation. There was still plenty of anger beneath the sadness. I was concerned with the certainty of Bob's memory in regard to Jane's driving habits and where we would go with that. Chris handled that well – because we could have bogged down there. I did feel that a consensus had been reached and Chris could have stepped out a little sooner than he did to write the report. But that was minor. I didn't know whether Kim (the victims advocate with the State's Attorney's Office) was there because the Johnsons asked her to be or if she would normally be there. I was slightly uncomfortable that anyone from the State's Attorney's Office was present. No one was there from Jane's lawyer's office. I hope she maintains strict confidentiality."

—"I went to this conference questioning whether or not I was doing the right thing. I came out of it reasonably certain that it was the right thing to do and that we had accomplished something positive. I guess the best thing about it was the opportunity for my family to meet face-to-face with the defendant and express their anger and sadness and to receive an apology."

—"In our circumstances, I believe that this was very beneficial. Both parties had a lot of feelings that needed to be expressed, and I think that we were all given the opportunity to do so. I don't know if there were any negative aspects to it, at least not where I was concerned."

On Confidentiality

In the majority of conferences I have been involved with as a facilitator, the issue of confidentiality has come up in preconference preparation. Can what is said in a conference be used against the "offender" in further criminal prosecution or civil litigation? What if someone other than the offender, including a victim, reveals involvement in criminal activity? Can participants be subpoenaed and then questioned about what was said and by whom? Is there an obligation on the part of facilitators or others (like officers of the court or social services providers) to report certain information revealed in a conference? In this particular conference, for instance, after all arrangements had been made, I received the following e-mail from the defense counsel:

> Chris: I have a few minor concerns about the "agreement" that Jane will be asked to sign. Does this purport to be a legally binding contract that would involve such things as restitution or other indicators of civil liability? I understand that nothing said in the group conference can be utilized later in a different setting. Is my understanding correct? Please advise.

I replied:

> Especially in a case like this, where the conference is occurring presentence, the "agreement" is really more of an mutual understanding between all 12 participants. Nothing is really binding until the Court determines that it is binding. I have made this clear to all participants and will reiterate this point at the conference.
>
> You bring up the question of restitution. I assume that this will be dealt with in detail during the conference and that part of the agreement will therefore deal very specifically with restitution. I do not suspect that other issues of civil liability will come up. Again, any specifics will ultimately need to either be accepted, modified or rejected by the Court at sentencing.
>
> As to the question of whether or not anything said in the conference could be used in a different setting at a later date, technically it could be. There is no "grant of use" immunity in place here and thus no guarantee that information revealed at the conference cannot be used later. The chances of this happening in this case, however, seem slim at best. As difficult as this situation is, all parties seem intent on having this

meeting. The victims do not appear to be litigious or vindictive in their purpose. I think a face-to-face apology may go a long way to satisfying the needs of the victims in this case.

I appreciate your position as Jane's lawyer. In her state of mind, feeling as guilty as she does, she might be willing to agree to just about anything. While I do not suspect that whatever agreement comes out of this conference will be particularly heavy-handed, you will certainly have the opportunity at sentencing to challenge any aspect of the non-binding agreement.

This issue of confidentiality/immunity apparently varies dramatically between jurisdictions. It also varies depending on whether the offender is a juvenile or an adult, whether the action is criminal or civil, and at what stage in the justice process the conference occurs. In New Zealand, for instance, conferences convened in juvenile cases are strictly confidential while in adult cases, confidentiality is not protected by statute. In Colorado, the generally accepted view is that what is said at a restorative justice conference is not admissible in court because the conferences are viewed as a procedure to settle the case, similar to negotiations in a civil action. Apparently, there are also such protections afforded in Pennsylvania.

In Vermont, it is not clear to me as a practitioner whether protections exist or not or, if they do, to what extent. While there is a great deal of legislation related to confidentiality/rules of evidence, it is a complicated legal issue. Thus, I am inclined to advise participants in any conference that, yes, what is said may be used against them. I go on to say that it most likely will not be, which is easy enough for me to say. Only if a State's Attorney, who has county-wide jurisdiction, were willing to grant "limited use immunity," could any guarantee be offered to participants in a specific conference. This is unfortunate as absolute honesty and candor is so desirable. Assistant Vermont Attorney General Marie Salem is currently in the process of researching this issue for the Department of Corrections to give practitioners a clearer idea of how to proceed and how to best advise participants concerning this issue.

Final Reflections

Given that a central goal of restorative justice processes is to empower victims, this conference was a success. Dick Johnson was days away from making a statement to the Court at sentencing when he was presented with this entirely different option. He was essentially given the choice as to whether he would prefer to proceed with sentencing as scheduled or delay sentencing and participate in the conference. As a result of deciding to proceed with the conference, he was afforded the opportunity to be involved in the sentencing process in a much more substantive manner than simply making a short statement to the court. Five additional members of his family were also empowered by being included in the process, in addition to the driver of the pick-up truck and his wife. Beyond the sentencing aspect, and perhaps more significantly, all victim participants at the conference were also given the opportunity to process this tragedy in a safe and supportive environment. As Dick said to me, "There was an awful lot of anger in that room, but it all seemed to stay there when we left."

While we seek to make restorative justice processes less offender-focused than past practices, the offender(s) obviously still play(s) a vital role. In this case, when Jane learned on her hospital bed that she had passed a vehicle in a no-passing zone and killed a woman, her immediate instinct was to contact the family of the deceased victim. That instinct was quickly thwarted by advice against making such contact. When she finally was provided with the opportunity to meet with the Johnson family, she was able to understand the impact of her actions in an entirely different way than simply being aware that she had done what she did. The human connection had finally been made. Mary Johnson had a face now and a personality and a family. Jane's genuine remorse and acceptance of responsibility led to embraces, initiated by some of the victims, after the formal conference. She had longed for something positive to come out of this tragedy and, as difficult as it was, this conference was definitely "something positive."

Questions

1. What were the advantages of conferencing over a traditional legal trial for:

   a. the offender,

   b. the offender's family

   c. the victim's family

   d. the community.

2. Explain the issues of confidentiality that should be resolved prior to agreeing to a conference.

3. Support your contention that conferencing could or would not work in many cases now handled by traditional legal means and resulting in incarceration. Cite problems that might hinder such conferencing and explain how you might overcome them.

   Note: This question might be handled by dividing the group in half by counting off by twos—the number ones would talk on behalf of supporting the traditional legal and correctional system, and the number twos would talk on supporting group conferencing. After twenty minutes, a spokesperson from each group would presents its conclusion to the whole group.

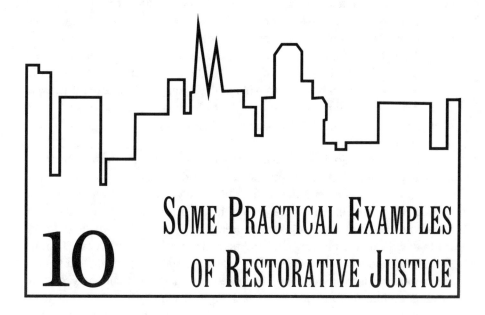

10   SOME PRACTICAL EXAMPLES OF RESTORATIVE JUSTICE

The following fourteen examples of restorative justice may help readers understand how restorative justice can work. As you read through each example, consider how a similar process could be implemented in your community. What would you need to do to make such a process a viable option in your own setting? How difficult would it be to implement such an idea? What would make it easier?

1. Disorderly Conduct in the Cemetery

The case was minor, a disorderly conduct case. A couple of kids coming home from a party cut through the cemetery and knocked over some head-stones. Disorderly conduct is a nonviolent misdemeanor, and the "usual" for that is a $100 fine (less if the kids are poor) and a suspended sentence (the kids had been in trouble before), with probation. That is the justice "system."

The prosecutor and the public defender had been there before, many times. They decided, with a little push from the probation officer, that this was a good case for that new reparative board program. Accordingly, the kids were asked if they wanted to plead guilty to one count of disorderly conduct. If so, they would get probation and have to appear before the board. Of course they agreed—anything to avoid worse.

When the kids came before the board, it was about three months after they had pleaded. One was accompanied by his father, another by his mother.

The board asked them what they were thinking when they knocked over the stones. One of them said, "Nothing. We were just there, and we bumped into them, and one fell over, and we laughed and said 'the dead will rise' and everybody got crazy and we pushed over a whole bunch of them. Then, somebody yelled 'let's get out of here' and we took off."

Then, the board asked the victims what they felt. The victims were represented by an elderly woman, and her daughter, and her daughter. The old woman was dressed in black, with a black shawl and black shoes and she was all bent over. She had not wanted to come to the hearing, because she "didn't speak English so good," but her daughter had prevailed and said she would speak for her.

Sylvia, she said, had come over from the Old Country. Angelo, her husband, had come over in 1928, on a steamer, working his way across, to a job in the granite quarries in Barre. It took him five years to earn enough to pay passage for Sylvia, his bride. He worked in the quarries for Rock of Ages for his whole life. He started as just a laborer, in the pits, and slowly learned the trade of cutting and blasting and drilling and moving the big rocks. Then, he got a break and moved into the sheds, where the slabs were made and the big rocks were cut into stones. And he worked hard and eventually moved up to be an apprentice carver. He had a knack for it. His family in Italy had all been stonecutters, and he moved up to be a sculptor, then head carver, and then master. He had worked in the sculpting shed for thirty years, finally retiring to his garden and his grapes. Like all the masters before him, his crowning achievement was his own headstone. It was ornate almost to the point of being garish, with baby angels and trumpets at the top of an urn, and grapes and grape leaves down the side of the stone.

Sylvia had never spent a day apart from him. When he went into the nursing home, she went there every day and sat beside him. And when he finally died, she went to visit Angelo every day at the cemetery. It was cold that day, Saturday, when she got to the cemetery, and she saw the stone, toppled over and broken off at the delicate base of the urn. The angels were face down in the dirt.

When Sylvia's daughter finished, there was not a dry eye in the room. One of the three boys was sobbing. Another was in his mother's arms. There was a long silence. Finally, one of the boys looked up at Sylvia's daughter. He couldn't look at Sylvia, and whispered, "I'm sorry."

The board talked about what the kids could do to make amends. The assignment was that they would each write a paper, detailing the life story of one of the people whose stones they had desecrated. They were to do the research with the families of the deceased. They were also to do a joint research project, by going up to the Rock of Ages quarry and stone sheds and learn about stone cutting. And they were to write letters of apology to Sylvia.

This was disorderly conduct, a misdemeanor, not a serious crime. There was no need for the state to intervene. It was not worth any jail time. Certainly, it was not worth the front page in the newspaper. This is the difference between restorative justice and what we do now.

Restorative justice is about the harm that has been done. It is about recognizing that crimes do not occur between offenders and the state. Crimes occur between human beings. Human beings do things, wittingly and unwittingly that have harmful effects on other humans. The process of repairing the harm is a human process, not a legal process. How we repair harm is by first understanding the true harm done, and validating that harm was done, and then acknowledging responsibility for that harm. Then, we apologize. After this, we make amends, creating new value to make up for the harm, and taking actions to repair the damage, return the stolen, and clean the besmirched.

Crime response is an opportunity for change. What we do about a crime can be a moment of learning for the offender, and a moment of healing for the victim. It also can be a moment of affirmation for all about why we live and grow in communities.

2. Thirty-two Bad Checks: Identifying All the Harm Done

The woman had pleaded guilty to two counts of writing bad checks, but the affidavit specified that she had written checks all over town, for groceries, for clothes for the children, for rent. When the board chair counted them and said she had written thirty-two bad checks, the woman said she had only pleaded to two counts. "But you wrote thirty-two bad checks!" She acknowledged that she had, and the chair explained that thirty-two people or businesses had been defrauded. The board decided she needed to write thirty-two different letters of apology, and deliver them by hand, and then report back to the board on what had happened, and what she had learned.

Two of the checks were to the bank, and one of the members of the board was an officer of the bank. He asked the woman what she was thinking, and she told him she just needed the things and had simply written checks. After a few minutes of discussion, the banker realized the woman had no idea whatsoever of what a checking account was. She did not realize that you had to put money in the account! She had paychecks, but never deposited them. He then made arrangements for her to come to his office, and spent three afternoons with her, teaching her how to use a checkbook, and how to account for her money.

3. Ben and Jerry's Cow: Understanding the Harm Done

The case involved an accident where Brad, a young man, had failed to stop in time for a herd of cows crossing the road, and had hit one of them. The cow was only injured, and Brad was charged with careless and negligent driving, accident resulting.

When he came to the board, Brad acknowledged his offense and talked about the consequences to himself, swearing that he had learned his lesson. He said he had to pay the $541.50 in court costs (including the contribution to the victim's fund), and $300 to his attorney, and the $250 fine, and that his insurance rate doubled.

The board then asked where the farmer, who had asked to be there, was. The coordinator said, "Milking. He couldn't be here."

The board chair then adjourned the meeting. The next day, the board meeting reconvened, in the barn, in the presence of the injured cow, the farmer, and Brad, with the board chair acting as the mediator. The chair asked the farmer what happened to the cow, and the farmer explained that the cow was not crippled, but that since the accident, she was off her feed, and her milk suffered. Since she was a first-calf heifer, he would probably wait till her calf was weaned and then send her down for slaughter. The chair then asked what the damage was, and the farmer said, "well, I'll probably get about $250 for her, and a first-calf heifer sells for about $1,000, but since I have her calf, I'm probably out about $600."

Brad said he did not realize the farmer had lost that much, and said "I guess I have been thinking more about my own costs than what I did." He agreed to pay the farmer first, and sent him a hundred dollars a month until this debt was paid.

4. Deliverance II: Reaffirming Community Norms

A New Hampshire legislator was visiting his mother in a nursing home in Newport, Vermont, as he did regularly. As he was coming out in the early evening, he looked across the parking lot toward his car and saw a black pickup truck backing into the space behind his car and heard the crunch of metal. Then, the pickup jumped forward again, crashing into another vehicle. After this, the pickup screeched back, turned its lights off, and roared out of the lot. He thought he was in a scene from a movie, and did not dare leave the porch of the nursing home, but he did get a partial plate number. He called the police.

At the reparative board meeting, he told his story. Then, the offender, John, a sixteen-year-old boy, gave his side. He had just gotten his license. He had taken Dad's new pickup to show off to his best friend and pulled into the parking lot to turn around. As he did, he misjudged the distance (Dad had a new oversize trailer hitch on the bumper) and hit the car in front of him. Then, he panicked, threw it into drive and hit the gas and the other car. His friend yelled, "Let's get out of here!" and he drove straight home.

When he got home, he told his mother what had happened. She read him the riot act and marched him right down to the police station, where he told the desk sergeant what had happened.

At the board meeting, when the victim told his story, the boy just hung his head and said, "I'm sorry. I shouldn't have run. I'm sorry I wrecked your car." The boy's parents said their insurance would pay for the damage, and that the boy would be working off the payment, as well as the replacement winch. He also was grounded.

The victim said "Why didn't you just stop and tell somebody? If you had, none of this would have happened?" He told the board he did not want anything more done to the boy, and that he was satisfied with the apology.

The board, however, was not satisfied. They told the boy that they wanted him to make a presentation to the driver education class at Lake Region High School about what he had done and the consequences of his behavior. The boy said "At my school? Couldn't I do it at another school? Everyone there will know me and they won't listen!"

But the board persisted, saying "That's the point. It's your job to make them listen." When he returned for his completion meeting, he had written a letter of apology to the legislator, performed his presentation, and his Dad was letting him drive again.

The legislator was so impressed by the process that he introduced a bill the next session to implement the program.

5. Green River Reservoir: Discovering the Social Contract

Barry moved up from Florida on early retirement. He sold his house for a bundle and built his dream home on the Green River Reservoir on ten acres. The house was a palace by Vermont standards. After moving in, he decided to improve the view of the lake and hired a contractor to cut down a swath of trees that adjoined his property and an access for his boathouse to the water.

The problem was the trees were on state park land. Not only had the trees blocked his view of the lake, they had also blocked everyone else's view of his house. Fishermen, canoeists, and bird watchers were outraged. What used to be a quiet place for contemplation was now New Jersey North. The attorney general issued a press release. The local paper made it the front page for days. The Friends of the Green River Reservoir made it the topic of several meetings and wrote about it in their newsletter. The Friends discussed the offense and decided that the restorative process being used by corrections might have some appeal.

In court, Barry pleaded guilty to unlawful mischief, for destroying state property. The probation agreement was that he would completely restore the site, including replanting the trees, at a cost of some $36,000. He was also to attend a reparative board meeting to determine what amends he would make to the community.

Organizing the board meeting was a challenge. The association appointed some of its members to attend the meeting as victim representatives.

The Fish and Wildlife Department had a presence, as did the Forest and Parks Department. There was extensive coverage of the planned meeting in the local papers, and in the newsletter of the association. The discussion and letters in the association newsletter reached a consensus on what reparations they wanted from the offender. The reparative board rehearsed its process, trying hard to be fair.

The meeting was attended by more than thirty members of the community and the Friends of the Green River Reservoir Association. The board had especially prepared for the meeting, knowing the potential for volatile emotions. The meeting was highly successful. The victims who were present were able to express their feelings about the crime and its impact on them, and the offender clearly recognized that he had "screwed up big time." He acknowledged that he was a newcomer to the area, and had made some big mistakes, and told the assembly that he intended to make it good. The Friends were able to provide their input to the board on what they thought the sanctions should be, and how to make it a "win-win" for all. Several spoke up in defense of the offender, saying that they wanted to be clear that in Vermont, what a man does with his own property should be his own business, but all recognized that there is a community obligation.

The offender not only agreed to all of the suggestions, but went beyond the requirements, and will spend more than the required community service hours working at the park and doing the dirty jobs, like helping dig the latrines, and doing additional planting to screen his boathouse from public view. He presented a very different demeanor than that in court when represented by counsel. What was telling about the outcome was that several of the members of the association volunteered to help him.

6. Hazing on the Team Bus

The soccer team was coming home on the bus from an away game. The varsity guys decided it was time to initiate some of the rookies. Seven of the varsity team went up to the front of the bus and distracted the coach with talk about the game. The other seven went to the back of the bus and stomped the two rookies. One of them had cleat marks and bruises up and down his back, the other had black eyes and bruises. When one of the boy's fathers saw his son, he went ballistic, and the result was a state police investigation and the potential for seven charges of aggravated assault, and major lawsuits against the school, the administrators, and the coach, as well as the kids involved. The media context was a recent major lawsuit lost by the state university for a hazing incident involving the hockey team.

The principal of the high school had recently attended a training on conferencing as an approach to conflict resolution. Working with the parents and the lawyers of the victims and the offenders, with the state's attorney, the state police, and corrections staff, agreement was reached to hold a restorative conference.

We received an e-mail of a letter from the father of one of the victims of the Otter Valley hazing incident about the conference. We asked his permission to use the letter and he said we could, if we used the entire letter, including all of his comments.

> "Dear Family and Friends: Well after what seems like an eternity (a couple of weeks?) of meetings, planning, negotiations, behind-the-scenes string pulling, and a lot of angst, we finally got our Restorative Justice conference tonight (6:30 to nearly 10:00).

> "We estimated that most of the junior varsity team and their parents, ALL fourteen members of the varsity (including the 'evil seven') and their parents, the five or six relevant school administrators, Jake and Sam, and three facilitators were in attendance—a total of nearly ninety people. We met in a 'triangle' in the gym: Sam and Jake and their parents on one side in a single row, seven 'actively involved' varsity players 'opposite' us, with their parents behind them in two rows; two facilitators at the 'hinge' between these two sides, and all the rest of the passive participants and families forming the large/multirow 'end' of the triangle. Sometime we can get specific/detailed about the process, the order of presentations, the 'scripted-ness' of the process, etc. if you are interested. The essential thing is that every 'offender,' 'victim,' 'victim supporter,' (us), and 'offender supporter' was asked a series of questions and could respond at whatever length they felt appropriate. [I, for example, was allowed to say that I was physically sick as a result of the anger I felt for these boys, and that they should consider themselves lucky that they had not picked on a boy whose parent was a psychopath; I then told them that I had been advised, variously, to sue them, expel them from school, treat them as criminals and file charges, and/or abandon the legal process and just beat them. Instead, we chose this process of community healing . . .].

> "This led, in turn, to the question: 'What do you think are the major issues to be addressed?' And finally, 'What are your suggestions for what these boys can do to address these issues?' (Some other suggestions were filed more specifically under a category of what the administrators could take responsibility for).

"Bottom line was that Jake and Sam got their fundamental request(s) met. All the offending players and bystanders showed up and had to acknowledge their role in, and feelings about, what happened on that bus—and do so in front of a large group of pretty unsympathetic people. (I was really kind of stunned at the level of dismay and trauma on the part of the parents of the offenders . . . interesting). J&S also emphasized that what they wanted as a result of this process was remorse on the part of the other players, and respect and civility in the hallways and around school—including being greeted normally and ensuring that the hall talk about what actually transpired was accurate. There was discussion about what this meant, and how the players could live up to that. Also, players let them know that they were already making sure that the 'real' story was making the rounds and that no one was blaming the victims for the craziness and the ensuing penalties.

"The resulting 'Agreement' is a kind of gentleman's agreement that everyone in attendance could live with, the administration will implement with them, and all fourteen varsity players signed. There are five action items (details will be fleshed out later):

— We agree to show respect and civility to Sam and Jake in future daily activities at school.

— We agree to participate in an activity at all five elementary schools [that feed Otter Valley Union High School] and at Otter Valley Middle School to educate younger students about hazing in order to prevent such activity from occurring again in the future.

— We agree to work with the School Board Policy Committee in the revision and further development of the Hazing Policy.

— We agree to participate in future 'team building' activities.

— We agree to work with the administration in the development of a team captain leadership program.

"This might not seem like a lot when you are sitting there reading this, but the fact that everybody was in one place, could see each other's faces, and express their fairly raw emotions was very impressive—and then on top of it to come up with constructive ideas we could agree on was more so. We know going in that we were trading off some things for others (i.e., I had to leave the 'vindictive stick' in the car; on the other hand those boys ate a bunch of humiliation burgers tonight).

"So now I am going to go downstairs and have a beer. Thanks for all your positive energy—it really helped us (and Jake even said so as part of his several very articulate opportunities to speak . . .)."

7. One of Our Own

A board member told us of a case they had in St. Johnsbury. The offender, on his second conviction for driving under the influence of alcohol (DUI), is a well-respected businessman in the community. The board member recognized the name on the paperwork sent to him prior to the case as a good personal friend, and recused himself from the actual board decision, but volunteered to perform the clerical duties at the actual hearing. The offender, when he arrived before the board, recognized several of the members and became extremely embarrassed. He admitted to the board that he had a serious drinking problem, and that he recognized that he had failed his community by violating the law. The board took pains not to differentiate this from other DUI cases, and in fact held him to the standard. He apologized to the board, and will perform community service, and the board, in its turn, will support him in obtaining treatment.

It was clear to the board member who was his friend that this meeting had a powerful effect on the offender, for whom this was not a new problem, and whose friends had not been able to confront him. The board member said that he had a new insight into the use of reparative boards to deal with community members whose behavior is too difficult to deal with one-on-one, or in private, or in social gatherings. He also recognized that the public demonstration of disapproval by the board was powerful, and avoided the destructive effect of punishment.

8. Harassment by Phone: Taking Responsibility

The defendant was a college student. The victim was an African-American who hosted a cable TV call-in show, and who took a fairly strident tone about racial issues, and received a lot of hate mail and harassing calls. As a result, he got caller ID and a recording machine. Most of the calls he got turned out to be from pay phones, but one caller was identified, and when the police checked on it, they found the address to be an apartment rented by a college student. When confronted, he admitted that the call was from his phone, and at arraignment pleaded guilty.

When he came to the board, the victim was there, and he played the tape of the call. The call was vitriolic, nasty, and outrageous. It was hideously cruel. When the tape stopped, the board sat in stunned silence for several moments. Then, one of the members, her voice shaking, said, "How could you do such a thing?"

The student, equally shaken, said, "I didn't do it!" When questioned further, he said that it was his phone, but he was having a party, and some of his friends got drunk and made the call from his phone. "But you pleaded guilty!"

He said, "I know, but my lawyer told me I'd just get probation, and after I graduated it wouldn't count for anything, so I thought it would be easier than to involve anyone else. It was my phone, so I was the only one in trouble."

The board chair told him, "You have a problem." It took him three weeks, but eventually he turned his friends in to the police. When they came to the board and listened to the tape, they were appalled by their own behavior. The board assigned them to make a public presentation of an apology to the ALANA (African, Latin, Asian, and Native American) chapter on campus, and to make a presentation to a student assembly on diversity, and to the sociology class two of them were taking. The university provost said later that it was the best diversity experience he had seen.

9. The Milton Bombers

The Chittenden board heard the first of the Milton "bomb threat" cases. It involved the youngest of the six kids involved (fourteen now, thirteen at the time). Bobby had been processed as a juvenile, but the judge gave his consent for him to see the board.

At the meeting were the principals of the high school, middle school, and elementary school, as well as the guidance counselors from all three schools, teachers, folks from the emergency rescue squad, the fire department, the community police officer, Bobby's social services mentor, and his father.

The case was groundbreaking for us. Not only was this a juvenile case, but it was and is high profile. Before the meeting, two of the board members expressed personal concerns over their own feelings. One was a resident of the town of Milton who felt that he could not be objective, the other a former resident who shared the same fear. We said, "That's the point. You represent the community. The community is a victim here, too."

The meeting was highly emotional. The administrators not only talked about the disruption the bomb threats had on the schools, but on their own lives, one saying that his wife was afraid to say goodbye in the morning for fear she would not see him again. They talked about the traumatic effects on the children and the panic that began to occur as the threats continued.

The board member who lived in Milton said he felt the whole town had suffered a setback in its efforts to become a community in which one could hold his head up. He talked about the impact on the bus drivers, with kids running for their lives during the initial panic, and the fear they would run over someone. The bombing of the Murrah Federal Office Building was brought up several times.

Bobby's father then spoke about his own shame and his fear for his family, with rumors going around that there would be retribution from vigilantes on his son and his family. He then turned to his son and asked the question that was probably what everyone there wanted to know, "Why did you do it?"

The boy's eyes filled with tears, and he mumbled about "going along with the other guys" who wanted to do it to get off from school, but his father pressed him, not satisfied with the answer. Finally he said he was angry at the principal and the kids at school for how they had treated him in the past and that he had not gotten attention when he had wanted it, and he was jealous of the attention others had received. Bobby said he realized now, after listening to all of the people who had spoken that it was not funny, and it was a lot more than just getting out of school for the day, but had hurt a lot of people.

In the discussion over the contract, the board cautioned one another that they did not want to take out their anger over the entire event on Bobby, but had to deal with the broader community fear. They asked the boy to write a letter of apology to the whole community, to be published in the Milton *Independent*. They talked about the "Confidentiality Rules" and decided that everyone already knew who did it. Bobby then agreed to send the letter, stating his name, his age, and confessing to which calls he made, and why he did it. He agreed to send personal letters of apology to the schools, both kids and administration, and to the fire, police, and rescue staff.

The board then discussed the damages in terms of costs to the community, estimated at more than $20,000. They agreed that even if the six kids were to split it up, none of them was able to pay it, and that the burden would most likely fall on the parents. They decided to have Bobby perform forty hours of community work service, but to have it be work at the school, with the janitors, doing year-end work, cleaning out the lockers. They hoped this would impress upon him the amount of effort and pride that the community took in their school and give him a sense of the kids who were threatened by the events.

10. Vandals and Visigoths

The incident was a vandalism spree involving five young men trashing mailboxes, breaking windows, throwing bottles, smashing doors, and generally causing drunken mayhem.

The crimes involved thirty victims and four law enforcement officials. Three offenders were charged as adults (the other two were juveniles) and all three received two-year deferred sentences for unlawful mischief (a felony) contingent on their successful participation in the conference.

The logistics of contacting all the victims and affected parties, as well as the offender families and supporters was a challenge. The victims were all sent a letter describing the offense and their involvement and invited to a community conference that the judge had allowed to determine final disposition, including restitution. The initial response to the letter was not great, so we followed up with phone calls and visits. Ultimately we were able to contact twenty-four of the original victims, and eleven actually came to the conference. The ones who could not come gave the conference staff their statements.

At the conference were the three offenders, ten supporters, including aunts and relatives, eleven of the victims, one of the law enforcement officers, and the conference coordinator. During the conference, the offenders needed coaching to get them to open up. The victims, on the other hand, were biting at the bit to express themselves. They were able to express their emotions at having their mailboxes destroyed, their windows smashed, and their doors damaged. Many of the victims were afraid and angry, and the most common concern was wondering what they had done to deserve the treatment. One older couple was concerned that they were being targeted because their son was a police officer. Another older victim, who was ninety-two and could only get around with a walker, was asleep on the couch when her mailbox came flying through the window.

The conference was highly emotional, with anger and sadness on the part of the victims, that turned to understanding and forgiveness by the end of the meeting. One of the victims was in tears in describing the effect of the offenses on her daughter. The offenders expressed shame, sadness, and ultimate acceptance of responsibility for the impact of their behavior on the lives of so many victims. There were strong expressions of support and love by the offenders' supporters, but also the expression of how hurt and let down they were. The emotions expressed were strong, but the presence of the group restrained any untoward behavior. As the facilitator wrote, "It is a remarkable dynamic when you have an open circle of folks (large or small) working to resolve the conflict. . . ."

A simple agreement was reached as a result of the one and a half hour conference—restitution for damages split three ways and letters of apology to all victims from the three offenders. By all accounts, it was a successful and effective conference, and a case that involved a large number of victims and the community was resolved with satisfaction. Now, it will be up to the offenders to make good on their commitments.

After the conference, the conference coordinator sent a letter to all of the victims, describing the conference and its outcomes, including the agreement that each young man would pay his share of the restitution, and would write letters to all of the victims who were not in attendance.

11. Victim Impact Panel Has an Effect

We received two essays written by offenders who had attended the Victim Impact Panels, one in Randolph, the other in Burlington. The first letter said, in part: "I learned a lot of information surrounding drinking and driving. A small portion of what I learned was the facts of drunk driving. Another portion of what we discussed, was who gets affected by a car accident involving alcohol. The largest and most significant part of the class was drilling into our minds the feelings of losing someone you love. The class was the most depressing thing I have ever gone to in my life. It is something I hope never to be a part of again."

The other writer was more erudite. "Attending the Impact Panel . . . was both an educational and humbling experience. I had several preconceptions about the class that immediately proved themselves wrong. The first thing I noticed was how many people were there. I was shocked. I had been expecting this to be a small class, maybe five or six people at the most. It had never occurred to me before how many people drive while intoxicated. I had never realized what a major problem it is for Vermont."

"It was the second day of classes that really left an impression on me. We had two victims of drunk driving come in to speak with us. For me, the hardest part of listening to the speakers was that they were able to see me and know that I had driven while under the influence of alcohol. I felt ashamed and guilty. As I listened to their stories, I began to feel even worse . . . I don't think I will ever forget the stories that I heard. Since leaving class last Friday, I have retold the stories several times, to my roommates, my parents, and my friends. I know that I will never drive while under the influence of alcohol again. I only hope that by sharing all that I've learned with others that I can influence their choices as well."

12. Rodney and the Teacher

Rodney was a forty-year-old laborer who came before the board for a repeat DLS (Driving License Suspended). Rodney had a lengthy criminal record—nothing serious, nothing violent—and had been in and out of jail for most of his adulthood for violations of probation, for failing to appear, for retail theft, disorderly conduct, and the like. The court he appeared before did not want to put him in jail again, and though the prosecutor knew the reparative boards did not want to take chronic offenders, he decided to give this new program a shot.

Rodney came to the board, and was asked to explain his side of the story, and Rodney did what he always did. He shifted the responsibility to others. "I did it, but it wasn't my fault." He complained about being picked on by the police, being turned in by his neighbors, losing his most recent job because his supervisor had a grudge against him, and on, and on. The board kept after him, confronting him with the affidavit, talking about his lack of responsibility in his life, and he kept dodging.

Finally, a board member who was a retired junior high school teacher raised her hand and said, "Rodney. Rodney." When she had his attention, she said, "Rodney, you're not taking responsibility here. From now on, whenever you are trying to evade responsibility here at the board meeting, I'm going to raise my hand."

For the rest of the meeting, Rodney would start to own up, and then dodge, and she would raise her hand. Every time she did it, Rodney would stop, lower his head, and try another line. Her hand would go up, and Rodney would stop. Pretty soon, all of the board members were raising their hands, showing Rodney they did not believe his lines, either. After an hour of this, they broke through. Rodney began talking about his life and all of the bad choices he had made. When the board pushed him, he took responsibility for his actions.

His contract with the board included getting his license back, and over the next three months, with a little push and a nudge, he did everything he was supposed to do. He filled out all the papers for license renewal, and earned money to pay the fines and the insurance. Then, he went down to motor vehicles to get the license. When he got up to the counter, the motor vehicle examiner started chatting with him, and Rodney told him proudly that he had gotten everything done that he needed, and then the conversation drifted to what else was going on in his life, and he started talking about his job, and then about having gotten into trouble with his boss, again, and how it wasn't his fault, and from the back of the office a voice called out, "Rodney!" and he looked up, and a woman who was also on the board, not the teacher, raised her hand.

Rodney laughed, and said "You mean I have to be responsible everywhere?"

13. Letter from an Offender to Her Dad

Dear Dad,

I don't even know where to begin. I have spent so many years apologizing to you for things that were not serious that now that a serious case has arisen, I don't expect you to accept this. You have dreamed of a polite, successful, well-tempered daughter, and all you received was a juvenile.

You have watched me throw my life and your dreams away and that is not fair to you. You have given me so much and an indescribable amount of love and support that I am forever in debt to you, but I have repaid you quite poorly.

When my name was boldly written in the newspaper, not only were they denoting me, but they were denoting you as well, and I have come to realize that. Raising me was not something you did wrong, or poorly. You can't blame yourself for my actions, and I won't let you. What happened is because I made it happen, not you.

There will come times in my life when I will need your support, faith, and trust, and I can only hope that you will be there to help. I know I have disappointed you and let you down in a way that no daughter should, and I am so unbelievably sorry. I took it way too far. I crossed that line. I don't expect you to take me under your wing and tell me it is ok, because I know that you can't, and I know that it isn't.

I have learned a lesson, and I have promised myself that the mouth of peer pressure will not swallow me anymore. I write this to you, not because I am reported to do so, but as a better way of communicating the fact of how deeply sorry I am. I know that what I did was wrong and stupid and . . . did I mention stupid?

Moving on in life will help me as a step toward the strength I hope to achieve, and I know that no matter what, I have you in my corner. I am so sorry that you almost slipped out of my corner; I won't ever let that happen again, I need you there. For life.

14. Kristi Gets It

Kristi was convicted of possession of a malt beverage and came to the board focused on herself and her own issues. She was cooperative and acknowledged doing the offense, but she was not tuned in to the real impact. During the meeting, she told the board of a friend that had been in a DUI accident, and was in the hospital in Hanover. The board decided she should write an essay on the effects of alcohol, attend a victim impact panel, and spend some time with her friend and write up his thoughts before and after the accident.

She wrote a good, accurate essay on alcohol and its effects on the body, but the paper read like a classroom assignment. It was a research paper, not a personal expression. Then, she went to the victim impact panel. She wrote that up, and it is quite a different paper. "I was left with another whole side of what happens. Many of the students, including myself, could not believe the reality of the severity of the drinking and driving that occurs here, in the state of Vermont."

The classes gave her the facts, but the panel gave her the feeling. "One of the most heart-wrenching hours that I have ever had to sit through. Three individuals offered their life's hardest moments, to teach us the realities of drinking and driving. It was an experience that I feel unable to explain. Having sat in the room with them, and feel the emotion they are living with each and every time they tell the story of their loved ones being taken away from them in an instant, an instant that was completely avoidable, is an experience that can only be explained in the same way by themselves."

Then, she went to visit her friend. Her paper on that experience was profound. She told the story of her friend, and going out back-roading, and getting another six pack, then another, and then deciding to drive to a party. Her friend and his buddies were in a smash up, and they were all hurt. Her friend, who was not driving, had a bad break to the femur. His family was relieved that he was alive, but the break did not heal, and infection set in, and he went through painful treatment, twice a day for two months. But that did not work. Then, he went through a series of bone scrapings every other day, and that did not work, and the leg had to be amputated, with skin grafts that did not take. Now, nine months later, the bone still has not healed, and her friend, "once a bubbly, outgoing person who loved the outdoors and people, he's now depressed and rarely leaves the house."

It is clear from the final paper that Kristi gets it. It seems a safe bet that she will not reoffend.

Questions

1. By going through each essay, explain what types of offenses were handled by restorative justice.

2. Many people see restorative justice as best suited for juveniles. How did the examples show that it should not be limited to juveniles.

3. Other people think that restorative justice is best suited for minor problems. How was it used successfully for major concerns?

4. Do you think there are any issues that would be better suited to a formal legal trial than to a restorative justice solution? Explain.

5. Can you have restorative justice aspects in a traditional legal system? Explain.

6. Why is restorative justice cost effective?

COMMUNITY JUSTICE SANCTIONING MODELS:
11 ASSESSING PROGRAM INTEGRITY

GORDON BAZEMORE, PH.D.
PROFESSOR, DEPARTMENT OF CRIMINOLOGY
   AND CRIMINAL JUSTICE
DIRECTOR, COMMUNITY JUSTICE INSTITUTE
FLORIDA ATLANTIC UNIVERSITY
FT. LAUDERDALE, FLORIDA

DAVID R. KARP
ASSISTANT PROFESSOR OF SOCIOLOGY
SKIDMORE COLLEGE
SARATOGA SPRINGS, NEW YORK

Community justice is taking hold throughout North America and the world. This movement is broadly inclusive of community-based crime prevention programs and community partnerships with various criminal justice agencies including policing, adjudication, and corrections. This chapter examines community justice approaches to sanctioning offenders. Viewed as a whole, the movement toward community justice sanctioning encompasses a wide array of processes, goals, and practical and philosophical rationales. The enthusiasm associated with community involvement in sanctioning as a new response to crime appears to be a result of both crisis and opportunity in the justice system. Advocates of these approaches view them as an opportunity to build support for a justice system frequently criticized as insular and out of touch with community needs and expectations (Bazemore and Day, 1996).

Stated and implicit objectives for community-based sanctioning initiatives include the following:

- giving citizens a greater role in sanctioning
- increasing overall citizen involvement in the justice process
- providing a more meaningful and immediate response to criminal incidents
- encouraging alternative dispute resolution, such as mediation
- reducing fear of crime
- improving the quality of offender monitoring
- increasing awareness of the harm crime causes to the fabric of the community (and conversely the ways in which weaknesses in the community fabric contribute to crime)
- diverting more offenders from the court
- building or strengthening relationships among community members

Underlying philosophies in community justice sanctioning run the gamut from traditional prevention and diversion paradigms to those emphasizing reparation and offender accountability (Bazemore, 1997a; Umbreit, 1995) to various adaptations of shaming (Karp, 2000) and/or reintegrative shaming (Braithwaite and Mugford, 1994; Retzinger and Scheff, 1996). Four emerging models—family group conferencing, community reparative boards, circle sentencing, and victim-offender mediation—share several common characteristics and are generally representative of a community justice approach to criminal sanctioning (Clear and Karp, 1999). As part of a growing, but still emergent and loosely connected national and international movement around "restorative justice" (Bazemore and Schiff , 1996; Braithwaite and Mugford, 1994; Messmer and Otto, 1992; Van Ness, 1993; Van Ness and Strong, 1997; Young,1995; Zehr,1990), these approaches stand as case studies in an effort to give citizens, victims, and community groups an explicit decision-making role in an informal sanctioning process.

Although in-depth descriptions of important differences among the four models is beyond the scope of this paper, the following brief summary illustrates the different trends and themes within this larger movement. Like many other initiatives in community justice (Barajas, 1995; National Institute of Justice, 1996), perhaps the most important shared characteristic of the new sanctioning models is the fact that relatively little is known about their impact, their objectives, or the nature of the process itself. The four models are the context for this examination of critical attributes of community justice sanctioning.

Model One: Family Group Conferences. In cities and towns in the United States and Canada—as well as in Australia and New Zealand—family members and other citizens acquainted with the offender or victim of a crime gather to determine what should be done in response to the offense. Often held in schools, churches, or other facilities, these family group conferences are facilitated by a community justice coordinator or police officer, and are aimed at ensuring that offenders are made to face up to community disapproval of their behavior, that an agreement is developed for repairing the damage to victim and community, and that community members recognize the need for reintegrating the offender once he or she has made amends. Based on the centuries old sanctioning and dispute resolution traditions of the Maori, the modern family group conference was adopted into national juvenile justice legislation in New Zealand in 1989. "Conferencing" is now widely used in modified form as a police-initiated diversion alternative in Australia, and is being rapidly introduced in communities in Minnesota, Pennsylvania, Montana, other American states, and in parts of Canada.

Model Two: Community Reparative Boards. Recently institutionalized by the State of Vermont, in this model, nonviolent offenders meet with local citizen community reparative boards whose members recommend a plan that generally requires that they complete community service, make restitution to the victim, and become involved in educational activities or treatment (Karp and Walther, 2001). At the end of the session, the offender signs an agreement or contract to complete the plan within a specified time period. Community reparative boards, which may be formally coordinated by probation, court, or diversion personnel, are generally composed of five or more local citizens who make dispositional recommendations for eligible cases referred by courts, intake departments, schools, or police officers.

Model Three: Circle Sentencing. In Canadian towns and First Nation communities, and in two communities in Minnesota, residents sit sometimes for hours in a circle listening to citizens, offenders, victims, their advocates, and other community members speak about the impact of specific criminal incidents. When the feather or "talking stick" is passed to them and it is their turn to speak without being interrupted, circle participants may comment favorably on rehabilitative efforts already begun by the offender, who may be a chronic and sometimes violent perpetrator well known to the community. Speakers in these circle sentencing sessions also express concerns for the victim or about the continuing threat posed by the offender and, at the end of the session, attempt to come to a consensus about a rehabilitative plan for the offender and an approach to "healing" the victim and the community. As a recently updated version of ancient sanctioning and settlement practices adapted from the traditions of Canadian aboriginals (Stuart, 1995)—as well as those of indigenous people in the Southwestern United States (Melton, 1995)—circle sentencing was resurrected in 1991 by supportive judges and community justice committees in the Yukon and other northern Canadian communities. These committees and community members are now working with judges, police, justices of the peace, and other supportive criminal justice officials to assume increasing responsibility for offender sentencing and supervision.

Model Four: Victim-Offender Mediation. Throughout North America, in many cities in Europe, and in other parts of the world, crime victims and offenders meet with trained mediators to allow the victim to tell his or her story to the offender, express feelings about the victimization, make the offender aware of the harm caused by his or her crime and get information about the offender and the offense. At the conclusion of most of these victim-offender mediation sessions, the victim and the offender work with the mediator to develop a reparative plan, which ensures that the offender provides appropriate restoration to the victim and/or the community based on direct input from the victim. Originally, and still frequently referred to as Victim Offender Reconciliation Programs, mediation is still unfamiliar to some mainstream criminal justice audiences and marginal to the court process in many jurisdictions where they do operate. However, mediation programs now have a long and respectable twenty-five-year track record, and more than 300 programs now serve victims and offenders in Canada and the United States (Umbreit, 1998; Umbreit and Coates, 1993).

Although there is a long tradition of evaluation research on community-based programs, research on community sanctioning is in its infancy. Relevant recent studies for the most part offer findings on specific applications of selected restorative justice sanctions and processes. Primarily, this research has been focused on one model, victim-offender mediation (Umbreit and Coates, 1993; Umbreit, 1994), and one sanction, restitution (Bazemore and Schneider, 1985; Butts and Snyder, 1991; Schneider, 1986; 1990).

Research focused on describing and evaluating the new community sanctioning approaches is critical for several reasons. On the positive side, these new models represent some of the most promising approaches for changing the nature of the sanctioning function in criminal justice (Bazemore and Umbreit, 1995; Karp and Clear, 2002). Some have suggested that meaningful citizen involvement in decisions about the disposition of offenders is an important "gateway" to broader and deeper participation in all aspects of the response to crime (Bazemore and Day,1996; Braithwaite and Mugford, 1994). On the negative side, the movement to devolve justice to the neighborhood level is fraught with dangers such as concerns about net-widening (Polk, 1994), power imbalances for young offenders and adults in conferencing settings (Umbreit and Stacy, 1996), insensitivity to victims (Braithwaite and Parker, 1999), and concerns about the "tyranny of community" in cases when community dynamics result in a variety of abuses such as vigilantism or discrimination (Griffiths and Hamilton, 1996; Karp, 1999).

While these emerging and informal justice decision-making models present some unique challenges to researchers, at this stage, the primary obstacle to meaningful evaluation of these approaches is neither technical nor methodological. Rather, a first step is to get clear about *what* it is the new models are trying to accomplish and *how* they are trying to accomplish it. What is needed is an evaluation protocol that defines the intended outcomes in community sanctioning, describes intervention inputs, and provides theoretical rationales that link inputs, sanctioning processes, and outputs.

Toward this end, our focus in this chapter is limited to the "independent variable" in community justice sanctioning. Currently, there is little common knowledge about how the four models described actually work in practice and the underlying principles that guide the informal decision-making processes employed. Although it is important to also articulate the intended outcomes of these and other similar approaches, the primary purpose of this paper is to suggest the *dimensions* of variation that can help to define the appropriate research questions and propositions for assessing the "integrity" of community sanctioning interventions (Karp and Clear, 2000).

The Independent Variable in Community Justice Sanctioning: Defining Dimensions of Variation

For purposes of this discussion, we will divide what could be a wide range of dimensions for classifying the inputs of community justice sanctioning into four conceptual categories. First, several dimensions of variation reflect the concern for community partnership with criminal justice agencies in community justice. These are classified here under the larger conceptual category of *community involvement*. Second, several characteristics have to do with the environment in which sanctioning is undertaken, such as if offenders are treated fairly and with dignity or if line staff in agencies are given the discretion to be responsive to immediate problems that arise in the sanctioning process. These dimensions are grouped according to their concern for the justice system's *accessibility* to the public. Third, several dimensions reflect a community justice approach to sanctioning, emphasizing offender accountability for the victim and community restoration. These dimensions are categorized by their emphasis on *repairing harm* caused by crime. Finally, we use the category *reintegration* to refer to dimensions focused on managing the reintegration of the offender into the community.

Each category adds theoretically and practically important evaluation criteria that can be used in defining the inputs or independent variables in community sanctioning. In describing these dimensions, we use family group conferences, community reparative boards, circle sentencing, and victim-offender mediation as ideal types to illustrate the general range of variation in community sanctioning inputs.

Community Involvement

Community justice has been defined as:

> . . . all variants of crime prevention and justice activities that explicitly include the community in their processes and set the enhancement of community quality of life as an explicit goal. Community justice is rooted in the actions that citizens, community organizations, and the criminal justice system can take to control crime and social disorder. Its central focus is community-level outcomes, shifting the emphasis from individual incidents to systemic patterns, from individual conscience to social mores, and from individual goods to the common good (Clear and Karp, 1999, p.25).

The new practice and emerging theory of "community justice" suggest a preference for neighborhood-based, more accessible, and less formal justice services that to the greatest extent possible move the locus of the justice

Table 1: Community Involvement

	Key Concerns	Research Questions	Circle Sentencing
Community and Stakeholder Identification	Identification of the relevant community and stakeholders	Who is affected by the criminal incident? What are the community boundaries (geographical and social)? What parties should be involved in the sanctioning process?	Correspondence of incident and stakeholder residence; staff/citizen views of affected parties and relevant parties for participation
Stakeholder Participation	Participation of key stakeholders of the criminal events: victims, offenders, "onlookers," community institutional representatives; participation of marginalized groups	To what extent do stakeholders participate in the sanctioning process? What is the quality of stakeholder participation? How much authority, responsibility, and accountability is given to stakeholders? Are marginalized groups brought to the table?	Number of active stakeholders; stakeholder knowledge of volunteer opportunities; nature of recruitment activities; extent of participation by stakeholders; indicators of authority, responsibility, and accountability; who staff view as their client; how citizens view their role
Community Partnership	Power sharing by community groups with criminal justice agencies	What is the criminal justice agency response to power sharing? To what extent is the process driven by system needs? What arrangements secure parity? What systems of accountability apply to community groups?	Nature of agreements between community groups and criminal justice agency; views of relevant parties regarding parity; instances of accountability processes

response closest to those affected by crime (American Probation and Parole Association, 1999). What community justice adds that is unique is a change in the *role* of the community in the justice process. This change has three important dimensions: identifying those who should be part of the sanctioning process; eliciting their participation; and clarifying the relationship between community organizations and criminal justice agencies in community justice partnerships. These dimensions are here labeled Community and Stakeholder Identification, Stakeholder Participation, and Community Partnership (*see* Table 1).

Community and Stakeholder Identification

The first dimension, identify who should be involved in the sanctioning process, has been a conceptually problematic area in all neighborhood or community-based interventions. "Community" is often an amorphous concept that is unfortunately used more often to obfuscate rather than to clarify issues of citizen involvement in government-sponsored processes. How the community and key stakeholders are operationalized for purposes of community justice sanctioning—who is at the table—will have tremendous importance for all other key dimensions of community justice (Bazemore, 1997b). Critical questions about community involvement include the following. Who is affected by the criminal incident? How do they define their community and are those people included in the sanctioning process? Are the representatives of community institutional leaders included? Who do agency representatives believe should be included?

While the community may be defined *de facto* as anyone who "shows up" for a community sanctioning meeting, the specific definition of community in each model runs the gamut from the most restricted focus on the victim-offender dyad in traditional victim-offender mediation, to a highly inclusive definition in circle sentencing, to the rather hand-picked "community" of reparative board members present in community reparative boards. In comparing two models such as victim-offender mediation and family group conferencing, for example, one may examine outcomes to determine the impact of the participation of what would be viewed as "third parties" in victim-offender mediation (for example, family members, friends), but essential participants in the family group conferencing or circle sentencing process. Or, one may compare sanctioning processes where the victim was not present with those where they were involved.

Stakeholder Participation

The second dimension in community justice, stakeholder participation, has to do with the extent to which the community is not only granted a seat at the table, but assumes a significant role as participant in justice processes (Clear and Karp, 1997; Griffiths and Hamilton, 1996; Pranis, 1996). Such designations as "coparticipant," "stakeholder," or "partner" suggest meaningful input into as well as significant responsibility for the response to crime (Barajas, 1995; Bazemore and Day, 1996; Stuart, 1995). In particular, we are concerned with the role of key stakeholders, victims, and offenders. Additionally, we are concerned with those who are connected less directly such as "onlookers" (witnesses to the event or family and friends of the key stakeholders) and community institutional representatives such as civic leaders, justice agency staff, school staff, and so forth.

One of the most important tasks for empirical research concerned with this dimension will be to examine the extent to which citizens wish to participate in community sanctioning. While systematic surveys by the Vermont Department of Corrections prior to establishing community reparative boards answered this question in the affirmative for that state (Dooley, 1996; Perry and Gorczyk, 1997), other initial questions included the extent to which a community sanctioning process really invites participation, how volunteers are recruited, the clarity of expectations for citizen participants, and how much authority, responsibility, and accountability are given to stakeholders.

Particularly important is the issue of democratic representation. Are community members who are typically marginalized brought to the table? Indeed, in practice, subtle differences exist along this continuum of involvement that may be driven both by the nature of the specific sanctioning intervention and by the willingness of justice professionals to assume the role of collaborator and facilitator, rather than the primary provider of services (Bazemore, 1997a; McElrae, 1993). Community sanctioning approaches may therefore be ranked along a continuum that attempts to assess intensity and type of participation.

Examining the four models, community reparative boards are the only one of these interventions that tend to formalize participation, generally by appointing a group of semipermanent board members. Other models rely more or less on word of mouth and hope to sustain enough interest to attract interested participants. Some examples of Australian family group conferences have suffered from an apparent lack of commitment to ensuring citizen, and especially crime victim, participation (Alder and Wundersitz, 1994), while New Zealand conferences appear to have devoted resources to ensuring that "communities of concern" are present (Maxwell and Morris, 1993). Circle sentencing relies heavily on word of mouth with apparent success, at least in Aboriginal communities (Griffiths and Hamilton, 1996; Stuart, 1995), although it is possible that committee members themselves are often the core participants. Victim-offender mediation depends on victim and offender participation, but does not usually recruit family and other community members.

Community Partnership

The third community involvement dimension is characterized by concepts such as "power sharing," "community empowerment," "active collaboration," "devolution of justice decision-making" (Griffiths and Hamilton, 1996), and citizen "ownership" over a process that is to some degree outside the absolute control of the formal justice system. One practitioner, Pranis (1996), has described this dimension as an evolving relationship between justice systems and communities in which the government role slowly changes in relation to the community role.

This change in the system role from "expert" crisis manager with no need for community input to partner with the community occurs as citizens take on more responsibility and provide more input in an emerging collaborative process. Stages along the way may reflect intermediate steps in which the justice system attempts to become more "information-driven" (Clear, 1996) and community-focused (a stance in which information is seen as valuable, and interventions focused on community level outcomes; citizen involvement, for example, is seen as important goal) before reaching the highest level of collaboration in which the system may be said to be "community-driven."

One specific component of this relationship is the extent to which the sanctioning intervention or program is dependent on courts or other government agencies for referrals. While some relationship with the formal system is almost always necessary, what is at issue here is the extent to which the process is driven by system needs—for example, to reduce court dockets or divert offenders—or by the needs of citizens, victims, and offenders (Van Ness, 1993).

The issues of discretion and gate-keeping also raise questions about the degree of power sharing in decision making and the role of the formal system in the process. Unintended consequences of collaboration with formal agencies include a cooptation of the community justice process (Bazemore and Griffiths, 1997; Griffiths and Hamilton, 1996), while extreme independence, on the other hand, may lead to irrelevance and marginalization.

The four sanctioning models vary significantly on the partnership dimension. For example, do community members decide what kinds of offenders are eligible for participation in the program? Notably, eligibility varies from minor first offenders to violent, chronic offenders (in the case of circle sentencing). While each model can claim some discretion for citizens, only circle sentencing allows citizens control over admission. New Zealand family group conferences legislatively require local sanctioning conferences to dispose of cases for adjudicated delinquents or those admitting guilt for all offenses except homicide, rape, and aggravated assault.

Therefore, the New Zealand conferences are the only other approach that frequently admits more serious delinquents. New Zealand family group conferences also allow citizens to decide the need for custody, and because of their broad legislative mandate, have the only truly significant impact on court caseloads.

In victim-offender mediation, the victim is in one sense the primary gatekeeper because victim participation is totally voluntary, but most programs are dependent on court, probation, and diversion programs for referrals. Their relative independence and commitment to the victim and offender as the client, however, may be driven in part by whether the victim-offender mediation program operates as a unit of the court or probation or if they can function as independent community agencies (Belgrave, 1995).

Accessibility

While community involvement is centrally concerned with bringing stakeholders to the table, another criteria concerns how the process is conducted around the table. For many, the various dimensions of community involvement are central. Citizens cannot easily experience justice from a distance, and they are unlikely to participate if the process is too complex, unfriendly, or too formal. As the experience with community corrections shows, simply placing courts and other agencies in neighborhoods, without a process that makes community involvement meaningful, often results in isolated programs that are in but not of the community (Byrne, 1989; Clear, 1996). Commenting on how much participation and involvement occurs in community courts today, Rottman infers that simply adding new programs and staff to improve accessibility of justice services is a one-dimensional approach to community justice:

> The demand (of citizens for personal involvement) is not met by adding more legal aid centers and more pro bono work by attorneys. What people want challenges the professionalization of the court and their dominance by lawyers—forces that originally contributed to the drift from community ties. Court and community collaboration today consequently depends on balancing the role of lawyers and the formalism they bring that militate against the influence of extralegal factors on the one hand and public expectations for user-friendly, problem-solving courts on the other (Rottman, 1996, pp. 50-51).

Four dimensions reflect making the justice system more accessible to the public: location/proximity, flexibility, informality, and sensitivity (*see* Table 2).

Table 2: Accessibility

	Key Concerns	Research Questions	Indicators
Location/ Proximity	Distance as barrier to receiving service; neighborhood location of sanctioning process	Does neighborhood location increase participation?	Distance of stakeholders to sanctioning location
Flexibility	Limited operating hours; narrow range of services; rigidity of staff roles; "compartmentalization" of functions; decentralization of staff authority and accountability	Do hours and services meet community needs? Do staff "work to rule" or do they show initiative and have autonomy? Is staff trained sufficiently for multitasking and independence?	Participant's views of flexibility of process; array of services offered; staff willingness and ability to meet diverse needs; staff training; stakeholder's views of fairness, equality
Informality	Adversarial and administrative rules/procedures as barriers; failure to address emotional needs and other concerns	Are informal dispute resolution processes available? Is the process open to expressing of participant concern or is it "rule-driven"? Is process consensus-based?	Time allowed for process; focus on resolution, participant's needs and obligations rather than blame and punishment
Sensitivity	Stakeholders are treated as individuals—personally, respectfully; acknowledgment of rights, dignity	How are victims treated? How are offenders treated? What types of relationships evolve between stakeholders? What is the staff role?	Stakeholder's satisfaction with process; stakeholder's views of treatment

Location/Proximity

The community justice movement is explicitly concerned with the quality of neighborhood life. Yet, most justice functions operate at levels which aggregate neighborhoods, and often fail to address concerns at the local level. The assumption underlying the concern with location is that distance is a primary barrier to participation in and satisfaction with justice services. This assumption at various periods in recent history has prompted a movement to physically decentralize justice services. Decentralization often occurs with a special focus on those inner-city neighborhoods thought to need these services most. Such decentralization is a primary motivator for community-based corrections, team and neighborhood policing, neighborhood dispute resolution, and foot patrol. This theme is also heard within the community sanctioning movement—though it is clearly only one of several themes that address lack of access.

Assessing variation in proximity as an independent variable involves measuring to what extent distance varies for individuals involved in a community sanctioning process. Where was the incident in relation to the sanctioning process? What is the relationship between stakeholders' residence and the sanctioning process? Does distance affect participation and/or overall satisfaction with the process?

Turning to the four community sanctioning models, each takes place in neighborhood locations such as in community centers, schools, churches, and other informal settings. Actual proximity to most users is not known. It has not been discussed or investigated in existing evaluations, though, in practice, some models like victim-offender mediation seem less concerned with neighborhood location than others. They may even hold mediation sessions in centralized locations (near courthouses, for example) to attract more participants, or, in the victim's home if agreed to by all stakeholders. While advocates of all models express preference for holding community sanctioning sessions close to participants, only community reparative boards view neighborhood setting as a key concern.

Flexibility

The flexibility dimension refers to efforts to adapt working hours, staffing patterns, and the nature and range of services to the needs of residents in local neighborhoods (Rottman, 1996; Stone, 1996). One component of this dimension may include decentralization (Clear, 1996). This may occur because an objective of such efforts may (but does not necessarily) allow and encourage managers to reorganize agencies to avoid multiple units, narrow specializations, and compartmentalization (Schorr, 1997). Moreover, decentralization reflects a flexibility in accommodating the concerns of citizen stakeholders who are seeking a significant role in the sanctioning process. Bureaucratic systems add to the difficulty citizens have in understanding (and thus accessing) the justice process. They also limit the capacity of professionals to respond to the diverse needs of communities. This dimension is frequently mentioned by advocates of community sanctioning (McElrae, 1993; Stuart, 1995), and by more mainstream advocates of court reform (Edwards, 1996).

One of the most theoretically interesting aspects of the flexibility dimension refers to the ability of justice professionals to adapt their professional role definitions to various and often diverse community needs outside of their job description. Community policing initially provided the prototype for this "role stretch" or "role blurring." This occurred when officer assignments included service provision, prevention, capacity-building and problem-solving (Moore and Stephens, 1991). Such role transformations require new sets of expectations on autonomous initiative and personal accountability. This is indicated by individual attitudes and performance, and also by agency expectations and agency support and training for these role changes. Ultimately, such role adaptations are measured by stakeholders' interactions with line staff—the front line representatives of the justice system to the public.

Practitioners of each model attempt to adapt the process to meet local needs, but role stretch occurs primarily in circle sentencing. Here, police officers, judges, and prosecutors, after fulfilling their legal responsibility (for example, reading the charges), begin to play the role of a citizen participant in the circle process (Bazemore, 1997b). In two of the models, victim-offender mediation and community reparative boards, justice system professionals are involved in only the most distant sense, usually as sources of referral. Family group conferences using the Australian (or Wagga Wagga) model involve police as facilitators of a sanctioning process. The nature of this role may vary depending on the extent to which the officer views his or her function as more of a coordinator and facilitator rather than one who administers sanctions and leads a "shaming" process (Alder and Wundersitz, 1994; Umbreit and Stacy, 1996).

Informality

Informality may also affect community involvement if it offers a process that limits formal legalistic barriers and procedures that alienate many citizens from courts and other justice agencies. The informality dimension may include the following:

- getting away from rules and procedures

- providing a wide array of nonlegal or paralegal services not typically provided by courts (for example, counseling or victim support)

- offering an array of informal mediation and problem-solving options, which allow citizens to speak, and which seek to enhance the human and humanistic qualities of the process (National Institutes of Justice, 1996; Zehr, 1990).

In principle, informality speaks to the concern that justice is a function of the community rather than the state. It is meant to resolve disputes in human relations rather than technical discrepancies between behavior and legal codes.

The level of informality can be measured in part by the number and range of nonadversarial processes offered. It also can be assessed by observing how services are provided and the extent to which the process itself is rule and procedure-driven or informal. We also would consider whether informal dispute resolution processes are available, if the process is responsive to immediate and unexpected concerns of stakeholders, and the extent to which the process is driven by consensus decision making over Robert's Rules of Order.

On the dimension of formality, in comparing the four models (with the exception of most community reparative boards, which tend to deliberate cases), decision making occurs more or less by consensus of participants (including victim and offender). In no case is there anything resembling an adversarial process. While all models are informal in focus, process and protocol vary substantially. They range from ancient rituals involving passing the feather or talking stick, to the "script" of the family group conferences, to the nondirective and facilitative approach now taught to many, if not most, mediators in victim-offender mediation (Umbreit, 1994).

The amount of time allowed in the decision-making process is also an indicator of the extent to which the process is driven by court case processing or caseload requirements. A central critique of the formal court process among advocates of victim-offender mediation, for example, has been the primary emphasis on speed and efficiency. Mediation practitioners insist on ensuring that time allowed in victim-offender mediation is based primarily on the needs of what are for them the primary clients of justice processes—the victim and the offender.

Sensitivity

A fourth dimension of accessibility reflects the capacity of those engaged in the sanctioning process to treat one another with sensitivity. Sensitivity means that the justice process takes seriously the rights and dignity of individuals. It treats them with respect and acknowledges them as persons who are members of the community. This is not simply "justice with a smile," for the interactions embedded in the various sanctioning models tend to take a serious tone, and the damage done by offenders is not to be made light. Rather, it is based on the Kantian imperative that:

> Persons are not merely subjective ends whose existence as
> an effect of our actions has a value for us: they are objective
> ends—that is, things whose existence is in itself an end. . . .
> Act in such a way that you always treat humanity, whether in

your own person or in the person of any others, never simply as a means, but always at the same time as an end (quoted in Lukes, 1973, p. 49).

The Kantian imperative is exemplified in a sanctioning process where an offender easily can be vilified (Braithwaite and Mugford, 1994; Garfinkel, 1956). Sensitivity is a response to a human tendency toward degrading offenders and minimizing the plight of victims. It serves as an alternative to the traditional justice system's responsiveness to this problem by demanding impartiality and routinization. The community justice approach invokes a higher standard of communal engagement in which stakeholders meet in a face-to-face process without denying the severity of the offense or the "personhood" of the offender. Thus, this process dimension is characterized by the emotional sensitivity stakeholders and facilitators bring to the sanctioning process that links the parties together by an "ethic of care" rather than a cold "logic of justice" (Gilligan, 1982).

The essential questions for the sensitivity dimension have to do with the treatment of stakeholders.

- How are victims and offenders treated?

- What types of relationships evolve between stakeholders?

- What roles do staff coordinators and facilitators play in managing the emotional process?

Such questions have taken particular prominence in discussions of the dynamics of shaming that appear to be embedded in informal sanctioning processes (Karp, 2001; Moore and McDonald, 1995; Scheff, 1996; Tomkins, 1992).

Repairing Harm

Community justice sanctioning takes a cue from the problem-oriented perspective of community policing in emphasizing the resolution of specific problems caused by crime and problems that are the antecedent causes of crime (Goldstein, 1990). Taking a second cue from the philosophy of restorative justice, community sanctioning begins with value statements about the primary goal of intervention and the process itself. Specifically, because crime is defined by its harm to individual victims and communities, the justice intervention is focused on repairing this harm through a problem-solving process (Karp, forthcoming; Van Ness et al., 1989; Zehr, 1990). The process itself necessarily elevates the role of the victim. It focuses attention on the victim's needs, while allowing for victim, offender, and community input and involvement in a process that is focused on finding common ground and attending to the mutual needs of each coparticipant.

Despite the prominent and elevated role of the victim, restorative justice cannot be reduced to a "victim rights" agenda, and interventions are certainly

Table 3: Repairing Harm

	Key Concerns	Research Questions	Indicators
Offender Accountability	Offender takes responsibility for crime; offender participates in sanctioning process; offender makes commitment to opportunity for restoration	Does the offender acknowledge the damaging consequences of the crime? Does the offender take responsibility through active participation in the process? Is there correspondence between the criminal harm and the reparative tasks?	Nature of reparative agreements; offender's view and role in process; use of apology and other demonstrations of responsibility and remorse
Victim Restoration	Victim input on reparative needs and the sanctioning process	What is the victim's role in the process? Do victims define harm and means for reparation? Do victims influence the offender reintegration process?	Effects of victim's contribution to the process; stakeholder views of victim's role; victim satisfaction
Community Restoration	Problem-solving and capacity building at community level; focus on group versus individual offender intervention; use of creative community service	Are community effects of crime measured? Do sanctioning interventions "build community?" To what extent is community service tied to offense and to community needs?	Efforts to measure community effects; linkages between sanctioning agreements and community-level needs; staff effort in capacity building

not limited to victim services or a focus on victim impact alone. From a restorative perspective, the emphasis on victim healing and reparation itself, in fact, implies a critical, though at times indirect, role for offender and community. The theory underlying restorative justice is that neither offenders nor victims are well served when the needs of the other, and of the community, are neglected. Justice is best served when the needs of each are addressed and all are involved in crafting the response to crime (Van Ness,1993; Zehr, 1990). Community justice therefore provides three unique dimensions of variation in repairing harm: offender accountability, victim restoration, and community restoration (*see* Table 3).

Currently, when a crime is committed, two primary questions are asked: who did it and what should be done to the offender? The latter question is generally followed with another question about the most appropriate punishment. Viewed through the restorative "lens," however, crime is understood in a broader context than what is suggested by the questions of guilt and what should be done to punish (or sometimes treat) the offender. Zehr (1990) argues that, in restorative justice, three very different questions receive primary emphasis. First, what is the nature of the harm resulting from the crime? Second, what needs to be done to repair the harm? Third, who is responsible for reparations?

Community justice sanctioning has a strong emphasis on providing alternatives to incarceration, yet ones that are symbolically expressive in condemnation of the crime (Kahan,1996). Accountability is defined in terms of offender commitments to obeying the law and offender appreciation of the damage wrought by the crime. Primarily, offenders are held accountable by making restitution to their victims and providing meaningful service to repay the debt to their communities. For offender accountability, critical questions include:

- Does the offender admit responsibility for the crime, particularly by acknowledging its harmful consequences?
- What role does the offender play in negotiating reparative agreements?
- What is the correspondence between the damage done and the reparative tasks assigned—is there proportionality and symbolic linkage between the offense and community service tasks?

Answering Zehr's third question, concerning responsibility for repairing harm, requires that the process focus on the future in ensuring that these obligations are fulfilled. While formal restitution programs have devoted extensive effort to documenting harm and to developing clear and workable payment schedules (Schneider, 1985; 1990), much more observation of the various community sanctioning processes is needed to determine the extent to which obligations and action steps are identified and follow-up occurs. Community sanctioning processes are perhaps best situated to engage citizens in the monitoring and follow-up process. Each seeks this desirable goal of having citizens assume responsibility for monitoring and enforcing obligations. Typically, restorative sanctions include apology, mediation, restitution, and community service (Karp, forthcoming). Little is known about the ability of most of these processes to ensure that reparative agreements are carried out, however.

Victim Restoration

Although victim restoration is not the only dimension of restorative justice (Bazemore, 1996; Bazemore, and Maloney, 1994; Van Ness,1993), it is the victim's central, essential, and elevated role in the justice process that perhaps most distinguishes community justice sanctioning from traditional approaches. For the victim, community justice offers the hope of restitution or other forms of reparation, information about the case, the opportunity to be heard, and expanded opportunities for involvement and influence.

Assessing this dimension in evaluation could involve a range of observation, interviews, and victim-impact surveys aimed at tapping the extent to which the process is attentive to victim needs and concerns, provides for the victim's safety, allows victims to express their feelings, meets victims" needs for information, and explores the extent to which the victim feels that these things have occurred. In this regard, Umbreit (1997), for example, has developed a "restorative justice" continuum, which focus on the victim's experience in various justice processes, with a special focus on the victim-offender dialog.

The victim's role, the emphasis on preparation, and the nature of the process indicate a primary concern with this dimension in the victim-offender mediation protocol. While victims speak first in victim-offender mediation and extensive preparation is focused on ensuring that the victim's concerns are addressed, community reparative boards and some implementations of family group conferences, for example, appear less structured to do so. Circle sentencing, on the other hand, provides at least equally extensive pre- and post-session work directed at victim concerns. It is the only approach that provides for a victim support group (Stuart, 1995).

It is possible, however, that the broader concerns of both circle sentencing and family group conferences, which include a focus on offender "healing," and "shaming and reintegration" of the offender, respectively, may overwhelm the focus of the process where offender's needs appear to be extensive. These are all empirical questions, however, which should be addressed in a comparison of these processes in achieving victim, offender, and community satisfaction and other outcomes.

Community Restoration

As Byrne (1989, p. 10) has noted, "offender-based control strategies are incomplete, since they take a closed system view of correctional interventions: change the offender and not the community." The third reparative dimension of community justice sanctioning is the extent to which the object of intervention includes not only the offender or victim, but also the community and community groups. This approach underscores the principle that communities as well as individuals are harmed by criminal incidents.

Such interventions seek to strengthen the capacity of the community, community groups, and socializing institutions to control and prevent crime (Barajas, 1995; Bazemore and Schiff, 1996; Clear and Karp, 1999). Such changes follow the innovations of community policing, which alters the emphasis from arresting individuals to working with community members in problem-solving and capacity-building (Sparrow, Moore, and Kennedy, 1990). The focus of community restoration begins with offenders and community service, but extends beyond this to a close assessment of local problems and collective efforts to improve the quality of community life.

In contrast to the microlevel concerns of victim restoration and offender accountability, a primary aspect of community restoration is preventative. Efforts to prevent and control delinquency and crime from this perspective focus less on remedial and ameliorative services, and more on proactive efforts to change conditions in neighborhoods and institutions believed to be criminogenic; less, for example, on targeting individual delinquents and more on institutional change to promote positive youth development and personal growth for all young people (Lofquist, 1983; Pittman and Fleming, 1991; Polk and Kobrin,1972).

Much more information is needed on what interventions focusing on community rather than individual change actually *look like* in practice. Yet, in assessing variation on this dimension, it is possible to distinguish commitment to the idea of community as a target of intervention in part by how community sanctioning staff view and operationalize their role. A primary measure of this dimension might be the amount of time that is spent doing individual casework rather than organizing sanctioning panels, developing victim support groups, offering offender community service opportunities, and other such tasks that link the sanctioning process to community quality of life outcomes.

The content of the intervention directed at community change differs substantially from simply attempting to increase the number of citizens participating in community reparative boards. It includes involving residents in a reintegrative shaming process in family group conferences (Braithwaite and Mugford, 1994). Intervention also may differ in scope as shown in the contrast between the holistic efforts of circle sentencing where participants promote "community healing," and "peacemaking," and in building capacity for increased involvement (Bazemore, 1997b; Stuart, 1995). Such interventions include the more micro and incidental efforts of victim-offender mediation staff to involve community by recruiting additional volunteer mediators. What differences in specific outcomes for the victim, the offender, and the community would we expect as a result of the more macro-circle sentencing focus compared with the more specifically targeted intervention of victim-offender mediation? The latter is concerned first with victim outcomes, the second with offender outcomes, and only very indirectly with the community.

Reintegration

To this point, community sanctioning has been discussed in terms of bringing community members to the table (community involvement), showing how the setting matters for active participation (accessibility), and investigating toward what end the sanctioning should be directed (repairing harm). Community justice is also explicitly concerned with the capacity of a community to maintain a quality of life that is at once inclusive and safe. The perspective of community justice maintains that outcasting and exile are last resorts for offenders; alternatives to incarceration are sought wherever possible.

Therefore, the sanctioning process must consider the implications of sanctioning for offender recidivism and public safety. Reintegration assumes that offenders are operating at the margins of community life and need to become better tied to conventional social institutions and role models. Three

Table 4: Reintegration

	Key Concerns	Research Questions	Indicators
Offender Supervision and Public Safety	Risk management; offender violations of reparative agreements; public trust in the system	What risks do offenders pose to the community? Are offenders monitored? What are the sanctions for agreement violations? Is the community willing to reintegrate offenders? What are the offender's conventional ties to the community?	Types of offenders in the community; risk assessment criteria; mechanisms of supervision; adherence to noncompliance procedures; extent of conventional mentoring and support
Competency Development	Long-term viability of offender reintegration; development of conventional competencies and social support	Is the offender capable of succeeding in the legitimate social world? What are the competencies of the offender? What opportunities are provided for competency development?	Risk and protective factors; array of programs available for competency development; success rates of programs
Decertification of Deviant Status	Earned redemption; full acceptance by the larger community of the offenders	Do offenders escape consequences of stigma and outcasting? What rituals exist for decertification of deviance?	Offender beliefs and attitudes, community trust, community rituals

dimensions are especially important for the successful reintegration of offenders. The first refers to the needs for offender supervision and public safety, the second dimension refers to competency development, and the third refers to processes that remove the criminal label from offenders who have successfully completed sanctioning agreements, that is, the decertification of deviant status (*see* Table 4).

Offender Supervision and Public Safety

A community justice model is equally concerned with the impact of crime and criminal justice decisions on the quality of life in the community as it is with individual outcomes for the key stakeholders. Its first questions with regard to public safety ask about the recidivism risk of offenders. This is not simply a decision about incarceration, for the same question remains for the offender on parole. Reintegration is viewed as a process of regaining a place as a member of the community after violating its normative standards. The public needs to gain trust in the offender and faith in the sanctioning process managed by the criminal justice system. This trust is based on assessment of offender risk and the mechanisms of community and criminal justice supervision.

Risk assessment is based on considerations of personal characteristics of the offender and situational factors that make reoffending more likely (Clear and Karp, 1999). Part of risk assessment requires close observation of the offender's participation in the sanctioning process. Do they demonstrate commitment by acknowledging responsibility and complying with reparative agreements? A second part revolves around the offender's conventional ties to the community that can be cultivated as resources for monitoring offender activity and providing social support. Risk intervention by the criminal justice system requires substantial systems of monitoring and supervision by agencies in partnership with the community. These may include regular home visits, drug testing, or Big Brother/Big Sister-style mentoring. Such systems are necessary to instill faith in the community that offenders, although present, are not dissociated from socializers and enforcers of community norms.

Competency Development

A second dimension of reintegration is the traditional concern for offender rehabilitation. Does the offender have the educational, employment, and social skills necessary to succeed in community life without resorting to crime? From a community sanctioning perspective, services provided to the offender such as drug counseling or job training are best done within the framework of victim and community restoration. For example, while engaging in community service as part of a reparative agreement, additional efforts would be made by the justice system to provide occupational training, which would benefit both the service project and the future capacity of the offender to gain employment.

Competency development is particularly important in three arenas (Clear and Karp, 1999). First, offenders need to gain mastery of basic educational and employment skills that will serve them in the job market. Second, offenders need to be able to cooperate with others and sustain meaningful relationships without resorting to violence or withdrawing from the social relationships that undergird the community structure. Third, offenders need to be able to exercise self-control in the gratification of immediate interests and show empathy for the needs of others. These competencies support the offender's capacity to act as a contributing member of a democratic community where citizenship is defined by the ability to work for the common good in addition to the pursuit of self-interest.

Decertification of Deviance

The third dimension that concerns offender reintegration marks the final stage of the sanctioning process—the point at which the offender is no longer stigmatized by the offense and is fully accepted as a member of the community with all of the rights and responsibilities accorded other members. In theory, the criminal justice system is designed so that once offenders "pay their debt" to society, their slate is clean. In practice, however, reintegration is quite uncertain. Braithwaite (1989) argues that oppositional culture formation is a direct result of offender outcasting by the community. What is needed, in Braithwaite's terminology, are "ceremonies of reintegration" that "decertify" the offender status (Braithwaite and Mugford, 1994).

In a community sanctioning model, decertification is a dynamic process responsive to offenders' demonstrations of remorse and reparation. Thus decertification follows from a process of "earned redemption" (Bazemore, 1998). Critical questions about the decertification process include the following:

- Are offenders stigmatized and outcast?

- What demonstrations are necessary for the community, especially victims, to entertain forgiveness and inclusion of the offender into daily community life?

- What concrete strategies or rituals are employed to mark the offender's acceptance and reintegration?

Conclusion

In outlining four categories of dimensions that may influence outcomes in community justice sanctioning processes, our goal has been to suggest a systematic way of classifying independent variable influences, which have empirical and theoretical coherence. At this early stage in the development and evaluation of community sanctioning models, it is critical to establish theoretical and value-based criteria for answering the question "how do we know it when we see it?" For example, how do evaluators know that a process referred to as a family group conference, for example, has been carried out in a way consistent with the community justice principles which inform it? Can evaluators know that when an offender recidivates two months after participating in such a conference, or when the victim feels dissatisfied, the theory of intervention underlying this approach was incorrect or inappropriate? Or was this apparent failure due to the fact that the conference was inadequately implemented?

The first concern with determining whether an intervention has actually occurred is an issue of the utmost importance in evaluating any new initiative. The possibility of multiple interpretations of the meaning of terms like "mediation," "shaming," and even "involvement" leave new processes open to the phenomenon by which the name of status quo practices is simply changed to fit new trends (for example, community policing, restorative justice), with little or no actual change in the content of interventions. To avoid situations in which relabeled traditional practices are evaluated as "restorative justice" or "community justice" programs, it is important to establish common definitions and criteria for determining whether and to what extent an intervention has occurred.

Because programmatic consistency with underlying principles in processes such as victim-offender mediation varies dramatically (Umbreit, 1998), it is important in evaluation to have access to common criteria that allow for valid and reliable assessment of intervention integrity. Such criteria would reflect one or more dimensions of practical and theoretical importance to practitioners and participants in the implementation of a sanctioning model, and they could be used in comparing different implementations of the same model or contrasting different models.

A shortcoming of this paper's singular focus on dimensions for defining independent variables in community sanctioning has been our failure to discuss impact measures. While the importance of an effort to develop clear outcome measures for community justice processes cannot be disputed (Bazemore, 1997a), before jumping to impact evaluation, it is important to get a better sense of what it is citizens and professionals are doing (and believe they are doing) in community sanctioning. Specifically, before evaluators impose outcomes and impact designs on interventions we do not fully understand, we should think carefully about whether we can describe inputs, processes, and *intended* outputs. Then, we will be in a position to build theoretically informed impact evaluation protocols.

References

Alder, C. and J. Wundersitz. 1994. *Family Group Conferencing and Juvenile Justice: The Way Forward or Misplaced Optimism?* Canberra, ACT: Australian Institute of Criminology.

American Probation and Parole Association. 1999. *Community Justice: Concepts and Strategies*. Lexington, Kentucky: American Probation and Parole Association.

Barajas, Jr., E. 1995. Moving Toward Community Justice. *Topics in Community Corrections*. Washington D.C.: National Institute of Corrections.

Bazemore, G. 1996. Three Paradigms for Juvenile Justice. In Joe Hudson and Burt Galaway, eds. *Restorative Justice: International Perspectives*. Monsey, New York: Criminal Justice Press.

————. 1997a. What's New About the Balanced Approach? *Juvenile and Family Court Journal*. 481: 1-23.

————. 1997b. The "Community" in Community Justice: Issues, Themes and Questions for the New Neighborhood Sanctioning Models. *The Justice System Journal*. 9: 193-228.

————. 1998. Restorative Justice and Earned Redemption. *American Behavioral Scientist*. 41: 768-813.

Bazemore, G. and S. Day. 1996. Restoring the Balance: Juvenile and Community Justice. *Juvenile Justice Journal*. December, 3: 3-14.

Bazemore, G. and C. Griffiths. 1997. Circles, Boards, Conferences and Mediation: Scouting the New Wave in Community Justice Decision-Making. *Federal Probation*. 59: 25-37.

Bazemore, G. and D. Maloney. 1994. Rehabilitating Community Service: Toward Restorative Service Sanctions in a Balanced Justice System. *Federal Probation.* 58: 24-34.

Bazemore, G. and M. Schiff.1996. Community Justice/Restorative Justice: Prospects for a New Social Ecology for Community Corrections. *International Journal of Comparative and Applied Criminal Justice.* 20, 2: 311-335.

Bazemore, G. and P. Schneider, eds. 1985. Research on Restitution: A Guide to Rational Decision-making. Chapter 5 in *The Guide to Juvenile Restitution* a training manual for restitution program managers, Washington, D.C.: Office of Juvenile Justice and Delinquency Prevention, U.S. Department of Justice.

Bazemore, G. and M. Umbreit. 1995. Rethinking the Sanctioning Function in Juvenile Court: Retributive or Restorative Responses to Youth Crime. *Crime and Delinquency.* 41 3: 296-316 .

Belgrave, J. 1995. *Restorative Justice.* Discussion Paper. Wellington, New Zealand: New Zealand Ministry of Justice.

Braithwaite, J. 1989. *Crime, Shame, and Reintegration.* Cambridge, U.K.: Cambridge University Press.

Braithwaite, J. and S. Mugford.1994. Conditions of Successful Reintegration Ceremonies. *British Journal of Criminology.* 342: 139-171.

Braithwaite, John and Christine Parker. 1999. Restorative Justice is Republican Justice. In Gordon Bazemore and Lode Walgrave, eds. *Restorative Juvenile Justice: Repairing the Harm of Youth Crime.* Monsey, New York: Criminal Justice Press.

Butts, J. and H. Snyder. 1991. *Restitution and Juvenile Recidivism.* Pittsburgh: National Center for Juvenile Justice.

Byrne, J. M. 1989. Reintegrating the Concept of Community Into Community-based Corrections. *Crime and Delinquency.* 35: 471-99.

Clear, T. R. 1996. Toward a Corrections of "Place": The Challenge of "Community" in Corrections. *National Institute of Justice Journal.* (August): 52-56.

Clear, T. R. and D. R. Karp. 1999. *The Community Justice Ideal.* Boulder, Colorado: Westview.

Dooley, M. 1996. Restorative Justice in Vermont: A Work in Progress. In *Community Justice: Striving for Safe, Secure, and Just Communities*, pp. 31-36. Washington, D.C.: National Institute of Corrections.

Edwards, L. P. 1996. The Future of the Juvenile Court: Promising New Directions. In *The Future of Children*, pp. 131-139. Los Angeles: Center for the Future of Children, David and Lucille Packard Foundation.

Garfinkel, H. 1956. Conditions of Successful Degradation Ceremonies. *American Journal of Sociology.* 61: 420-424.

Gilligan, C. 1982. *In a Different Voice: Psychological Theory and Women's Development*. Cambridge, Massachusetts: Harvard University Press.

Goldstein, H. 1990. *Problem-Oriented Policing*. New York: McGraw-Hill.

Griffiths, C. T., and R. Hamilton. 1996. Sanctioning and Healing: Restorative Justice in Canadian Aboriginal Communities. In Joe Hudson and Burt Galaway, eds. *Restorative Justice: International Perspectives*. Monsey, New York: Criminal Justice Press.

Kahan, D. M. 1996. What Do Alternative Sanctions Mean? *The University of Chicago Law Review*. 63: 591-653.

Karp, D. R. 1999. Community Justice: Six Challenges. *Journal of Community Psychology*. 27: 751-69.

⸺. 2000. The New Debate About Shame in Criminal Justice: An Interactionist Account. *Justice System Journal*. 21: 301-322.

⸺. Forthcoming. Harm and Repair: Observing Restorative Justice in Vermont. *Justice Quarterly*.

Karp, D. R. and T. R. Clear, eds. 2000. Community Justice: A Conceptual Framework. In *Boundaries Changes in Criminal Justice Organizations*. Volume 2 in *Criminal Justice 2000*, p. 323-368. Washington, D.C.: National Institute of Justice.

⸺. 2002. *What is Community Justice? Case Studies of Restorative Justice and Community Supervision*. Thousand Oaks, California: Pine Forge Press.

Karp, D. R. and L. Walther. 2001. Community Reparative Boards in Vermont. In Gordon Bazemore and Mara Schiff, eds. *Restorative Community Justice: Repairing Harm and Transforming Communities*, pp. 199-218. Cincinnati: Anderson.

Lofquist, W. A. 1983. *Discovering the Meaning of Prevention: A Practical Approach to Positive Change*. Tucson, Arizona: AYD Publications.

Lukes, S. 1973. *Individualism*. Oxford: Basil Blackwell.

Maxwell, G. and A. Morris. 1993. *Family Participation, Cultural Diversity and Victim Involvement in Youth Justice: A New Zealand Experiment*. Wellington, New Zealand: Victoria University.

McElrea, F. W. M. 1993. A New Model of Justice. In B. J. Brown, ed. *The Youth Court in New Zealand: A New Model of Justice*, pp. 1-14. Auckland, New Zealand: Legal Research Foundation.

Melton, A. 1995. Indigenous Justice Systems and Tribal Society. *Judicature*. 703: 126-133.

Messmer, H. and H. U. Otto. 1992. Restorative Justice: Steps on the Way Toward a Good Idea. In H. Messmer and H. U. Otto, eds. *Restorative Justice on Trial*, pp. 28-31. Dordrecht, Netherlands: Kluwer Academic Publishers.

Moore, D. B. and J. M. McDonald. 1995. Achieving the Good Community: A Local Police Initiative and its Wider Ramifications. In K. Hazlehurst, ed. *Perceptions of Justice: Issues of Indigenous and Community Empowerment*, pp.199-229. Brookfield, Connecticut: Ashgate.

Moore, M. H. and D. W. Stephens. 1991. *Beyond Command and Control: The Strategic Management of Police Departments*. Washington, D.C.: Police Executive Research Forum.

National Institute of Justice. 1996. *Communities: Mobilizing Against Crime: Making Partnerships Work*. August. Washington, D.C.: National Institute of Justice.

Perry, J. G. and J. F. Gorczyk. 1997. Restructuring Corrections: Using Market Research in Vermont. *Corrections Management Quarterly*. 1: 26-35.

Pittman, K. and W. Fleming. 1991. A New Vision: Promoting Youth Development. Testimony to House Select Committee on Children, Youth and Families. Washington, D.C. : Academy for Education Development. September.

Polk, K. 1994. Family Conferencing: Theoretical and Evaluative Questions. In C. Alder and J. Wundersitz, eds. *Family Conferencing and Juvenile Justice: The Way Forward or Misplaced Optimism?*, pp. 155-168. Canberra, ACT: Australian Institute of Criminology.

Polk, K. and S. Kobrin. 1972. *Delinquency Prevention Through Youth Development*. Washington, D.C.: Office of Youth Development.

Pranis, K. 1996. Communities and the Justice System: Turning the Relationship Upside Down. Paper presented before the Office of Justice Programs, U.S. Department of Justice, Washington, D.C.

Retzinger, S. and T. Scheff, 1996. Strategy for Community Conference: Emotions and Social Bonds. In B. Galaway and J. Hudson, eds. *Restorative Justice: International Perspectives*, pp. 315-336. Monsey, New York: Criminal Justice Press.

Rottman, D. 1996. Community Courts: Prospects and Limits in Community Justice. *National Institute of Justice Journal*. Washington, D.C.: U.S. Department of Justice.

Scheff, T. 1996. Crime, Shame, and Community: Mediation Against Violence. Unpublished Manuscript.

Schneider, A., ed. 1985. *Guide to Juvenile Restitution*. Washington, D.C.: Office of Juvenile Justice and Delinquency Prevention.

————. 1986. Restitution and Recidivism Rates of Juvenile Offenders: Results from Four Experimental Studies. *Criminology*. 24: 533-552.

————. 1990. *Deterrence and Juvenile Crime: Results from a National Policy Experiment*. New York: Springer-Verlag.

Schorr, L. B. 1997. *Common Purpose: Strengthening Families and Neighborhoods to Rebuild America*. New York: Doubleday.

Sparrow, M., M. Moore, and D. Kennedy. 1990. *Beyond 911: A New Era for Policing*. New York: Basic Books.

Stone, C. 1996. Community Defense and the Challenge of Community Justice. *National Institute of Justice Journal*. August: 41-45.

Stuart, B. 1995. Circle Sentencing, Mediation and Consensus—Turning Swords into Ploughshares. Unpublished Paper. Territorial Court of the Yukon.

Tomkins, S. 1992. *Affect/Imagery/Consciousness*. New York: Springer.

Umbreit, M. 1994. *Victim Meets Offender: The Impact of Restorative Justice in Mediation*. Monsey, New York: Criminal Justice Press.

————. 1995. Holding Juvenile Offenders Accountable: A Restorative Justice Perspective. *Juvenile and Family Court Journal*. 46: 31-41.

————. 1999. Avoiding the Marginalization and "McDonaldization" of Victim Offender Mediation. In G. Bazemore and L. Walgrave, eds. *Restoring Juvenile Justice: Changing the Context of the Youth Crime Response*. Monsey, New York: Criminal Justice Press.

Umbreit, M. and R. Coates. 1993. Cross-Site Analysis of Victim-Offender Conflict: An Analysis of Programs in These Three States. *Juvenile and Family Court Journal*. 431: 21-28.

Umbreit, M. and S. Stacy. 1996. Family Group Conferencing Comes to the U.S.: A Comparison with Victim-offender Mediation. *Juvenile and Family Court Journal*. 47: 29-39.

Van Ness, D. 1993. New Wine and Old Wineskins: Four Challenges of Restorative Justice. *Criminal Law Forum*. 42: 251-276.

Van Ness, D., D. Carlson, T. Crawford, and R. Strong. 1989. Restorative Justice Practice. Monograph. Washington, D.C.: Justice Fellowship.

Van Ness, D. and K. H. Strong. 1997. *Restoring Justice*. Cincinnati: Anderson.

Young, M. 1995. Restorative Community Justice: A Call to Action. Washington D.C.: Report for National Organization for Victim Assistance.

Zehr, H. 1990. *Changing Lenses: A New Focus for Crime and Justice*. Scottsdale, Pennsylvania: Herald Press.

Vocabulary and Questions

- community sanctioning

- community justice

- family group conferencing

- community reparative boards

- circle sentencing

- victim-offender mediation

1. Why is evaluation of the following models needed:

    a. community involvement

    b. repairing harm

    c. reintegrating offender into the community

2. What is meant by community and stakeholder identification?

3. What are the dimensions of community responsibility?

4. What can be done to improve accessibility on the following dimensions?

    a. location

    b. flexibility

    c. informality

    d. sensitivity

5. Please define and give an example of the following terms:

    a. repairing harm

    b. victim restoration

    c. community restoration

    d. offender reintegration

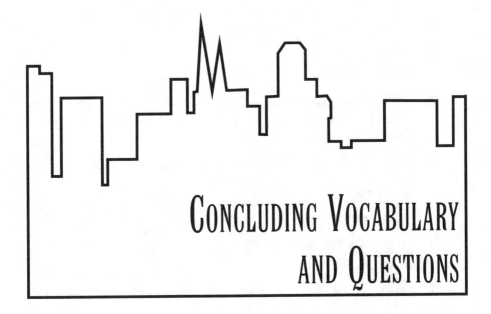

CONCLUDING VOCABULARY AND QUESTIONS

Discuss each of these terms in light of how it relates to or is impacted by restorative justice.

- recidivism

- victim's rights

- shame

- youth courts

- drug courts

- mediation

- conflict resolution

- accountability for harm caused

- restitution agreement

Answer the following questions in groups or individually.

1. Do you agree that restorative justice is "a revolution?" Support your answer.

2. Explain whether restorative justice is better suited for the juvenile system than the adult system.

3. Explain what types of crimes, if any, you would exclude from the restorative justice system and why.

4. What cost-benefits would accrue from using restorative justice? Would there be any long-term hidden costs?

5. Because many of the concepts of restorative justice stem from tribal or aboriginal sources, does this make it harder to accept in an urban environment. Why?

6. What type of training do facilitators need for each of the following:

   a. victim-offender mediation

   b. reparative boards

   c. family group conferencing

   d. circle sentencing

7. Explain why restorative justice is called a "win-win" solution. In your answer provide at least three examples.

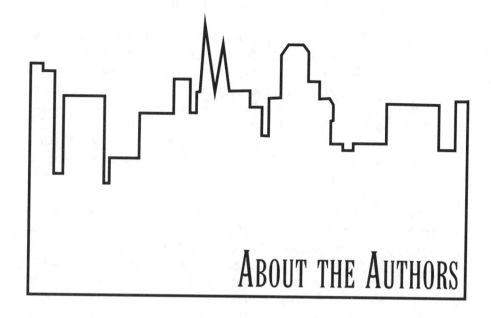

ABOUT THE AUTHORS

Lauren Abramson is a psychologist who has worked with children and families in communities for the past twenty years. She is currently Assistant Professor in the Department of Psychiatry and Behavioral Sciences at Johns Hopkins University and is the coordinator for community conferencing efforts in the City of Baltimore as well as for the state of Maryland. Dr. Abramson focused attention on community conferencing in Baltimore in 1966 and has published this work in national and international publications. For several years she has collaborated with the Australian developers of the process to help elucidate the theoretical explanations for the success of conferencing.

Gordon Bazemore is currently Professor of Criminology and Criminal Justice and Director of the Community Justice Institute at Florida Atlantic University. His recent publications appear in *Justice Quarterly, Youth and Society, Crime and Delinquency, The Annals of the American Academy of Political and Social Sciences, The Justice System Journal,* and the *International Journal of Victimology*. Dr. Bazemore has completed two books, *Restorative Juvenile Justice: Repairing the Harm of Youth Crime* (co-edited with Lode Walgrave) (Criminal Justice Press) and *Restorative and Community Justice: Cultivating Common Ground for Victims, Communities and Offenders* (co-edited with Mara Schiff) (Anderson Publishing). He is currently principal investigator of a national study of restorative justice conferencing funded by the National Institute of Justice and the

Robert Wood Johnson Foundation, and a national action research project funded by the Office of Juvenile Justice and Delinquency Prevention to pilot restorative justice reform in several juvenile court jurisdictions.

John Braithwaite is the Meyer Visiting Research Professor at the New York University Law School and a member of the Centre for Restorative Justice in the Research School of Social Sciences, Australian National University. His books include *Restorative Justice and Responsive Regulation*, *Shame Management through Reintegration* (with Eliza Ahmed, Nathan Harris, and Valerie Braithwaite), *Restorative Justice and Civil Society* (edited with Heather Strang), *Restorative Justice and Family Violence* (edited with Heather Strang) and *Not Just Deserts: A Republican Theory of Criminal Justice* (with Philip Pettit).

Ron Claassen is codirector of the Center for Peacemaking and Conflict Studies established in 1990 at Fresno Pacific University. He is a member of the Fresno Pacific University faculty and devotes 60 percent of his time to teaching in the Master of Arts in Conflict and Peacemaking Program and 40 percent to community training, consultation, and intervention. He is also the founder and former director (1982-1999) of the Fresno County Victim Offender Reconciliation Program, the first VORP in California. He has written a VORP organizing training manual and participated in the establishing of more than fifty VORPs throughout the United States and Canada. Mr. Claassen has extensive experience in mediation including victim/offender (ranging from petty theft to negligent homicide), contract disputes, racial and sex discrimination, employee disputes, wrongful termination, school site disputes (parents, teachers, administrators), church disputes, and public policy issues. He has trained thousands in conflict resolution and mediation training events. He is also the author of numerous articles and training manuals related to the constructive management of conflict, including "Restorative Justice Fundamental Principles" adopted May 1996 by the Alliance of Nongovernmental Organizations Working Party on Restorative Justice and included in the American Correctional Association's *Corrections Compendium*, "Restorative Justice Handbook," December 1998, Volume 23, Number 12.

Chris Dinnan has worked for the Vermont Department of Corrections for more than twelve years, presently as a Community Resource Coordinator. He holds a master's degree in public administration from the University of Vermont. He believes that "conferencing" is an underutilized tool in the criminal justice system. Mr. Dinnan hosts an internet discussion list on the subject (http://lists.doc.state.vt.us/mailman/listinfo/conferencing), which is open to anyone who wishes to join.

David Karp is an Assistant Professor of Sociology at Skidmore College in Saratoga Springs, New York, where he teaches courses in criminology and criminal justice. He conducts research on community-based responses to crime and has given workshops on restorative justice and community justice nationally. Currently, he is engaged in a qualitative research study examining Vermont's community reparative probation boards and is a member of the New York State Community Justice Forum. He is the author of more than thirty academic articles and technical reports and three books: *Community Justice: An Emerging Field, The Community Justice Ideal* (with Todd Clear), and *What is Community Justice: Case Studies of Community Supervision and Restorative Justice* (also with Todd Clear).

Dr. Paul McCold is the Director of Research for the International Institute for Restorative Practices, Bethlehem, Pennsylvania, where he is currently evaluating restorative practices in a variety of settings. Dr. McCold authored *Restorative Justice: An Annotated Bibliography*, and he was the principal investigator in the Bethlehem Experiment. He is active in the International Network for Research on Restorative Justice for Juveniles (Belgium) and represents the Friends World Committee on Consultation of the Religious Society of Friends on the Alliance of Non-Governmental Organizations (NGOs) on Crime Prevention and Criminal Justice (New York), where he was a member of Alliance's Working Party on Restorative Justice from 1995-2000.

David B. Moore is the Director of Transformative Justice Australia. He studied in Australia and Germany and holds degrees in languages and political science, political economy, and social theory. He taught politics and history at the University of Melbourne and Charles Sturt University in New South Wales, where he headed the justice studies program, and was centrally involved in the Australian pilot of community conferencing. Mr. Moore subsequently worked on policy in the Queensland premier's department. He has published extensively in justice and related fields. He co-founded Transformative Justice Australia in 1995 and travels widely working in the area of conflict transformation. He lives with his wife, daughter, and son in Sydney, Australia.

John M. McDonald is the Director of Transformative Justice Australia. He studied education in Wollongong and industrial relations and philosophy at the University of New South Wales. He received his Ph.D. from Griffith. He worked as an educator for ten years in Sydney, then worked in Europe, before returning to Australia where he worked for ten years as the Principal Adviser to the New South Wales Police Commissioner, and consultant to the Australian Federal Police and the Australian National University. In 1996, he received a Vincent Fairfax Award for Ethics in Leadership. He is a founding director of Transformative Justice Australia and travels widely working in the area of conflict transformation. He is married, has five children, and lives in Sydney, Australia.

John G. Perry has worked for twenty-four years for the Vermont Department of Corrections and has been the Director of Planning since 1983. Prior to coming to corrections, he was a guidance counselor and teacher in rural Vermont. He is the author of the 1993 Bureau of Justice grant proposal that restructured corrections in Vermont, creating the two-track system of correctional services and integrating the concepts and practices of restorative justice into adult corrections. The Vermont Reparative Probation program was a 1999 winner of the Ford Foundation's Innovations in American Government competition. He is the author of numerous articles on corrections focusing on the use of private-sector thinking in government.

Francis Schweigert has written several articles on restorative justice and community development, with particular attention to moral learning through community practices, and is active in local community restorative justice programs. He is currently serving as a community liaison in the Community Ventures Program at the Northwest Area Foundation, leading teams in helping communities reduce poverty through long-term partnerships. Prior work includes teaching at the University of St. Thomas and the University of Minnesota, church-based education and organizing. He holds a Ph.D. in educational foundations from the University of Minnesota. He resides in St. Paul, Minnesota with his wife Kathy and four children.

Mark Umbreit is a professor and founding director of the Center for Restorative Justice and Peacemaking at the University of Minnesota, School of Social Work in St. Paul. Dr. Umbreit is an internationally recognized speaker, trainer in restorative justice practices, and author of more than 130 publications. His most recent book is *The Handbook of Victim Offender Mediation: An Essential Guide to Practice and Research* (Jossey-Bass Publishers). Dr. Umbreit initiated the first cross-national study of victim offender mediation in Canada, England, and the United States and has just recently completed the first multisite empirical study of the impact of victims of severe violence who request to meet with the offender in prison.

Benjamin Wachtel is the media and technology coordinator for the Community Service Foundation, the nonprofit human services agency that founded the Real Justice program. Ben is an experienced conference facilitator and a certified Real Justice trainer. He was a research associate in the Bethlehem Pennsylvania Police Family Group Conferencing Experiment and coauthor of the final report.

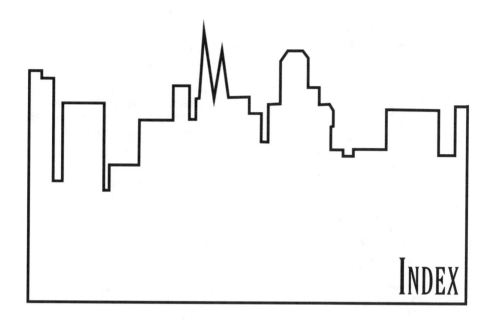

INDEX

*In this index, the use of **bold** indicates a full-chapter treatment of the subject.*

A

Aboriginal Community Council, 58
Aboriginal Consumer Education Fund, 58-59
aboriginal people. *See* indigenous/aboriginal people
Abramson, Lauren. *See also* conferencing (community) Baltimore case study
connected emotional transformation model, 115
"The Psychology of Community Conferencing," **123-38**
transformative process, 13
accessibility in community participation
comparison of components, 195f
decentralization, 23, 196-97
flexibility, 195f, 196-97
informality, 23, 195f, 197-98
introduction, 194-95
location/proximity, 23, 195f, 196
sensitivity to individual dignity, 195f, 198-99
time, 198
accountability (offender)
adversarial system and, 3, 10
classroom example, 144

in crime reduction, 46
Maori (New Zealand), 26-27
reintegration and, 14-15
in repairing harm, 200f, 201
trust and, 144, 145
accountability versus punishment, 144
acknowledgment (offender)
reconciliation through, 9
in tribal/indigenous cultures, 27
victim empowerment from, 9
adversarial system. *See also* justice system (traditional)
accountability (offender) in, 3, 10
conflict maximization and, 117, 124
informality versus, 198
Native American system versus, 27
victims demeaned by, 3
affective sequence of emotion stages, 135-36
Alexander, John, 154, 158
alternatives (juvenile justice)
circle sentencing, 78-81
community relationships in, 98
conferencing (family group), 75-78
reparative boards, 72-75
victim-offender mediation, 69-72, 69f
alternatives (prosecution)
case study example, 157-61
family group conferencing (Australia), 187

in tribal/indigenous cultures, 26
victim-offender mediation, 70
Victim Offender Reconciliation Program
  Conferencing, 148-49
Wagga Wagga model of family
  conferencing, 75-76
amends. *See* restitution
American Bar Association, 72
American Friends Service Committee, 30
American Kennel Club, 3
American revolution, 5
Anglo-Saxon law, 5
antigang programs, 60, 61
apology
  crucial nature of, 114
  pressure to offer, 85
  in tribal/indigenous cultures, 26-27
Aristotle, 21, 33
Assembly of Manitoba Chiefs on conflict
  resolution, 27
Australia. *See also* conferencing (Australian
    pilot program)
  compliance statistics, 62
  conferencing history, 109
  conferencing programs, 118-20
  family group conferencing, 187
  Transformative Justice Australia, 107,
    116, 118-19

B

Baltimore Community Conferencing
  Center, 126
Baltimore neighborhood conflict case
  study. *See* conferencing (community)
    Baltimore case study
Bayley, David, 57
Bazemore, Gordon
  "A Comparison of Four Restorative
    Conferencing Models by the Office of
    Juvenile Justice and Delinquency
    Prevention," **67-105**
  "Community Justice Sanctioning
    Models: Assessing Program
    Integrity," **185-211**
  processes of restorative justice, 8
belonging in community, power of, 25, 27-28,
  42, 137, 144
biblical justice, 5-6, 28-30, 145
Braithwaite, John
  on community empowerment, 7
  Crime, Shame and Reintegration, 109
  criminal subculture of community, 42
  "Linking Crime Prevention to
    Restorative Justice," **55-65**
Burford, Gale, 63

C

California, Victim Offender Reconciliation
  Program, 146-49
Canada
  circle sentencing, 78, 187-88
  compliance statistics, 62
  family group conferencing, 76, 187
  Widening the Circle video, 62-63
case studies in restorative justice. *See also*
    examples of restorative justice
  Baltimore neighborhood conflict, **126-33**
  Grossly Negligent Operation with Death
    Resulting, **153-67**
Charitable Intent (Williams), 119
Christie, Nils, 23, 26
the circle of community, 26-28, 32
circle sentencing, **78-81**, 82f, 85
  background, 78
  community involvement, 86f
  described, 78, 187-88
  example of, 80f
  focus on offender, 202
  goals/outcomes desired, 79, 87f
  implementation considerations, 79
  for juvenile crime, 78-81
  monitoring/enforcement in, 87f, 89-90
  offender role, 78, 79, 89, 96
  participants/participation options, 78,
    86f, 96, 194
  preparation, 86f, 89-90
  process/administration, 78, 82f
  reading recommendations, 81
  research findings, 80
  restoration component of, 202
  as role stretch for participants, 197
  traditional justice system relationship,
    79, 86f, 96, 194
  victim's role, 85, 86f, 87
Claassen, Ron, 15, 45
Claassen, Roxanne, 143-45, 150
collective responsibility
  individualism versus, 41
  Native American traditions, 27
Colonial Mutual Life, 58-59, 63
Colorado, confidentiality in conferencing,
  166
community. *See also* conferencing
    (community); empowerment
    (community)
  circle as symbolic of, 32
  criminal subculture of, 42
  microcommunity within, 44-49, 143-45
  in retributive model, 6
community, defined
  by belonging, 41
  in circle sentencing, 86f

in community conferencing, 125
in community justice initiatives, 39-40
in community policing, 39, 42-44
in family group conferences, 48, 86f
by itself, 49
by police officers, 44, 48
relationships in, v, 7, 25, 40-42
by reparative boards, 86f
in restorative justice, 11, 44-46
in victim-offender mediation, 86f
community (collective)
in compliance, 12, 61-62
creating healthy, 137
debt owed to victim/offender, 12
geography as, 41-43, 45, 49
governmental roles versus, 45
individualism versus, 41
microcommunity versus, 44, 45, 48
moral authority of, 12, 13, 25, 49
power/responsibility of belonging, 25,
  27-28, 42, 137, 144
reciprocity in creating, 6-7, 11, 15-16
reconciliation/reintegration
  responsibilities, 15f
in social control, 11-13, 26-27, 42, 44, 48
as stakeholder, 45
community conferencing. See conferencing
  (community)
community development. See also
  community weakening
conferencing a test of, 96-98
by conferencing (ice house example),
  47-48
conflict resolution in, 23-24
reintegration in, 22
community involvement
accessibility. See accessibility in
  community participation
conferencing model comparisons, 83,
  86-87f
efforts to increase, 90-91
new initiative requirements, 95-96
pros and cons of, 189
community involvement in sanctioning
components compared, 191f
concerns regarding, 23, 191f, 192-93
influences, 199
introduction, 190-91
offender accountability components, 201
stakeholder in, 191-92, 191f
system collaboration and, 193-94, 198
community justice
biblical justice systems, 28-30
defined, 39-40, 190
emerging theory of, 190-91
goal of, 23, 42

history, 22-23, 24-25
iniatives of, 39-50
interdependence in effectiveness, 42
restorative impact ranking, 94f
in tribal/indigenous cultures, 6, 25-28
Community Justice Conference (Fresno), 148
community justice initiatives, 39-42. See
  also community policing
community justice theory, 190-91
community-offender relationship, 3, 7, 12
community policing. See also police officers
  as facilitators
community definition in, 39, 40, 42-44
community involvement, 43-44
education/training for, 43
"Effective Cautioning Using Family
  Group Conferencing," 110
effectiveness, 40, 43, 57
emphasis, 202
goals/objectives, 40, 43
Innovative Neighborhood Oriented
  Policing (INOP), 43
participation roles, 43
problem-oriented policing versus, 43-44
community-policing syndrome, 99
community reparative boards. See
  reparative boards
community-victim relationship, 8
community weakening. See also community
  development
crime in, v, 42, 97
restorative justice practices in, 45
complete justice, 33
compliance
community responsibility in, 12, 61-62
ensuring in reparation, 88, 89, 201
followup circles, 78
in Victim Offender Reconciliation
  Program (VORP), 148
conferencing
in correctional settings, 119
and crime prevention, 57-63
dramatizations of, 119
restorative, 68, 96-98
conferencing (Australian pilot program). See
  also Australia
administrative responsibilities, 110
"Effective Cautioning Using Family
  Group Conferencing", 110
history, 109
hypothesis reformulation, 116-17
political impetus for, 109-10
conferencing (community). See also conflict
  transformation in conferencing
affective sequence of emotion stages,
  135-36

apology in, 114
appropriate use of, 125
conflict resolution versus, 117
defined, 123, 125, 126
facilitator role, 108
focus in, 125
food (refreshments) component, 26, 130
history, 109-11
outcomes, 137
principles of, 108, 126
process stages, 108
psychology of, 123-37
relationship building via, 137
restorative justice process versus, 117
sequence of participation, 112-14
stages of emotion, 115
in tribal/indigenous cultures, 25-28
vulnerability moment (collective), 113, 115
conferencing (community) Baltimore case
    study
    aftermath, 130-33
    decision, 129-30
    deliberation, 128-29
    manifestation, 126-27
    preparation, 127-28
    refreshments, 130
conferencing (family group). *See also*
    Grossly Negligent Operation with
    Death Resulting case study
    for additional information, 77-78
    Australia, 193, 197
    community defined, 48
    confidentiality in, 165-66
    described, 75-76, 187
    "Effective Cautioning Using Family Group
        Conferencing," 110
    example, 75f
    focus in, 202
    goals/outcomes desired, 76-77, 87f
    implementation considerations, 77
    for juvenile crime, 75-78
    microcommunity perspective in, 47
    monitoring/enforcement in, 87f, 88-89
    New Zealand, 193, 194
    offender role, 76
    participants/participation options, 48-49,
        76-77, 86f
    police officers as facilitators, 47, 75-76
    preparation, 86f, 88-89
    process/administration, 76, 82f
    rehabilitation effectiveness and, 61
    reintegrative shaming in, 203
    research findings, 77
    restoration component in, 202
    sequence of participation in, 76

traditional justice system relationship,
    86f, 95
in tribal/indigenous cultures, 187
victim role, 76, 84-85, 86f
Wagga/Real model, 40
conferencing model introduction
    circle sentencing, 78-81, 80f
    family group conferencing, 75-78, 75f
    reparative boards, 72-75, 73f
conferencing models compared
    administration, 81, 82f
    community involvement, 83, 86-87f
    preparation/follow-up
        circle sentencing, 89-90
        family group conferencing, 88-89
        reparative boards, 88
        victim-offender mediation, 88
    process, 81, 82f
    summary, 91-92, 98-99
    victim's role
        circle sentencing, 85, 86
        family group conferencing, 84-85
        reparative boards, 84
        victim-offender mediation, 83-84
conferencing (victim-offender). *See*
    mediation (victim-offender)
confidentiality in conferencing, 179
conflict, defined, 24
conflict (community) Baltimore case study
    aftermath, 130-33
    decision, 129-30
    deliberation, 128-29
    manifestation, 126-27
    preparation, 127-28
    refreshments, 130
conflict identification, 133
conflict minimization/maximization, 117,
    124-25
conflict resolution
    appropriate use of, 124
    circle sentencing in, 80
    community conferencing versus, 117
    community development via, 23-24
    identification of conflict in, 133
    police officers/policing practices in, 44,
        46-47
    in tribal/indigenous cultures, 23, 27
"Conflicts as Property" (Christie), 23, 124
conflict transformation in conferencing
    appropriate use of, 124-25
    community conferencing as, 117-18, 120,
        135
    defined, 124
    emotional expression as central to, 13,
        117-18, 120, 133-37

connected emotional transformation model, 115
conscience of the individual, 21, 42
constructive commitment components, 145
contracts for reparation. *See* reparation agreements
A Conversation (Williams), 119
cooperation, learning through conferencing, 137
crime
  defined, 199
  emotional consequences of, 142-43
  individualism as cause of, 41
  statistics (U.S.), 3
crime prevention
  community restoration in, 202-03
  conferencing in, 57-63
  goals/objectives, 43
  Innovative Neighborhood Oriented Policing (INOP) in, 43
  by victim-offender mediation, 71
crime prevention failure causes
  court system limitations, 58
  follow-through, 61-62
  motivation, 56-57
  plurality of deliberation, 57-61
  resources, 57
crime reduction, 42, 46
Crime, Shame and Reintegration (Braithwaite), 109
Criminal Justice Ethics, 109
criminal justice system. *See* justice system (traditional)
criminal subculture of community, 42
cultural influences. *See* social practices

D

Dane law, 5
Danzig, Richard, 22-23
debt. *See also* accountability
  community to victim/offender, 12
  offender to victim/community, 10
decentralization in community participation, 24, 196-97
decision making in Native American cultures, 27
deflation (collective vulnerability), 113, 115
Department of Corrections (New South Wales), 119
Department of Education and Training (New South Wales), 119
Department of Juvenile Justice (New South Wales), 118
Department of Social Security (Australia), 59
deviant status recertification in reintegration, 204f, 205-6

dignity of the individual. *See also* respect for persons
  accessibility in, 195f, 198-99
  in biblical justice traditions, 30
  in Eskimo culture, 27
  Habitat for Humanity project example, 22
  restorative practices in, 33
DiMauro, Theresa, 154, 157, 159
dispute resolution. *See* conflict resolution
dispute resolution centers, 90
distributive justice, 32-33
drug courts, 90

E

educational system, VORP in the classroom, 143-45, 149-50
"Effective Cautioning Using Family Group Conferencing," 110
Eglash, Albert, 21
elders roles, 11, 27, 28
emotion. *See also* specific emotions, for example, shame
  of crime, 142-43
  deflation, 113
  empathic guilt, 112
  guilt, 111
  hope, 14, 143
  microsociology of, 111-12
  in motivation, 133-34
  as regulators of social conduct, 111-13
  sequence of in conferencing, 135-36
  transitional collective experience, 115-16, 117-18, 120, 135-36
  trust, 142, 144, 145
  of victims, 8
  vulnerability moment (collective), 113, 115, 135-37
emotional affect system, 134-35
emotional expression in conflict transformation, 13, 117-18, 120, 133-37
emotionality model, 114
emotional transformation model, 115
empowerment (community)
  of conferences (ice house example), 47-48
  conflict resolution in, 23-24
  by participation, 15
  restorative justice in, 46
empowerment (offender), 46
empowerment (victim)
  by offender acknowledgment, 9
  by reparation control, 46
  victim-offender mediation, 83
Enlightenment theory of criminal justice, 24
equality before the law, 56
Eskimo, conflict avoidance practices, 27

Evaluation of restorative justice. *See* Restorative justice—evaluation of examples of restorative justice. *See also* case studies in restorative justice

Australian insurance fraud, 58-60

Ben and Jerry's Cow, 171-72

circle sentencing, 80f

classroom example, 143-45

community reparative board session, 73f

Deliverance II, 172-73

Disorderly Conduct in the Cemetery, 169-71

driving accident fatality, 9-10

family group conferencing session, 75f

Green River Reservoir, 173-74

Habitat for Humanity project, 22

Harassment by Phone, 177-78

Hazing on the Team Bus, 174-77

Hollow Water community, 60

ice fishing houses vandalized, 47

Kristi Gets It, 183-84

Letter from a Board Member in Springfield, 12f

Letter from an Offender to Her Dad, 182-83

Milton Bombers, 178-79

One of Our Own, 177

Raskol gang programs (Papua, New Guinea), 60

Rodney and the Teacher, 181-82

Summer Home, 9f

Thirty-two Bad Checks, 171

Vandals and Visigoths, 179-80

Victim Impact Panel Has an Effect, 181

victim-offender mediation session, 69f

examples of restorative justice (juvenile)

Deliverance II, 172-73

Disorderly Conduct in the Cemetery, 169-71

Hazing on the Team Bus, 174-77

Letter from an Offender to Her Dad, 182-83

Milton Bombers (example), 178-79

Vandals and Visigoths (example), 179-80

Exodus 21: 26-27, 29

F

Face to Face (Williams), 119

facilitators

in circle sentencing, 79

conferencing role, 76, 108

police officers as, 44, 46-47, 75-76

Victim Offender Reconciliation Program (VORP), 146

family group conferencing, 75-78, 82f, 84-85, 88-89

family sharing of responsibility

rehabilitation effectiveness with, 61

in tribal/indigenous cultures, 26-27

fear reduction in victims

community validation in, 8, 9

conferencing in, 77, 135

Finland, compliance statistics, 62

First Nation communities, 187-88

Fitzgerald, Marie, 137

fixing windows concept, 14

flexibility components in community participation, 195f, 196-97

followup circles, 78

forgiveness

basis for, 145

biblical justice systems, 28-29

in conferencing, 109

importance, 109

Japanese practice of, 26

pressure to, 85

in reconciliation, 145, 148

as transformation versus reintegration, 109

formality barrier to community participation, 195f, 197-98

Friends of the Green River Reservoir, 173-74

friends sharing of responsibility, 27

Fuller, Lon, 58

G

gang programs, 60-61

geography as community, 41-43, 45, 49

Gibbs, James, 26

Girard, Rene, 31

God's role in justice, 29-30

Goldstein, Herman, 43-44

Gordon, Diane, 3

government

community versus, 45

crime prevention resource allocation, 57

need for community authority, 49

roles/responsibilities, 45, 48-49

as victim, 45

grace, experiencing through VORP, 148

Great Britain, compliance statistics, 62

Grossly Negligent Operation with Death Resulting case study, **153-67**

the conference, 156-57

feedback, 161-64

the incident, 153-54

the presentence, 154-56

reflections, 166

the sentencing, 157-61

H

harm done to others. *See also* examples of
restorative justice
  Ben and Jerry's Cow (example), 171-72
  emotional stages in repairing, 135-36
  obligation recognition in, 10
  realization moment, 136
  repairing through solutions, 21, 198-203,
    200f
  resolving community, 124-25
  shared definition of, 10-11
  Thirty-two Bad Checks (example), 171
  validation in repairing, 8
Hawkiaha, Matt, 148
healing
  in biblical justice traditions, 30
  microcommunity in, 46
  Native American emphasis, 27
  shame in, 136
healing circles, 60, 78
Hollow Water, Manitoba, 60
hope, desire for, 14, 143

I

incarceration
  conferencing in correctional settings, 119
  consequences, 4
  criminal risk prediction for, 4
  demand (supply and demand law), 3, 4
  prisons as source of restoration, 14
  recycling prison graduates, 3, 24
  restorative justice process versus, 13-14
  as sacrificial rite, 31
  statistics, 2, 3, 26
incarceration economics, 2-3
indigenous/aboriginal people. *See also*
    specific groups, for example, Maori;
    tribal cultures
  community involvement practices, 11-12,
    193
  conflict avoidance practices, 27
  elders role in justice process, 11
  justice process, 5-6, 11, 26-28, 94
  sacrificial rites to restore harmony, 31
  sanctioning/healing practices, 78, 188
individualism versus community, 41
informality in community participation, 23,
  195f, 197-98
initiatives for restorative justice
  accountability in decision making, 93-96
  community building as test of, 95-98
  community involvement importance,
    95-96
  impact ranking, 94f
  implementation considerations, 92-93
  integrity/consistency in, 92

  juvenile justice system in, 97-98
  power sharing issues, 93-96
  progress evaluation/measures, 92-93
  traditional justice system impact on,
    95-96
injustice recognition in justice, 147-48
Innovative Neighborhood Oriented
  Policing (INOP), 43
INOP (Innovative Neighborhood Oriented
  Policing), 43
interdependence
  in crime reduction, 26, 42, 46
  importance of, 137
  Japanese practice of, 26
  in social control, 42, 48
Inuit justice model, 5

J

Japan, community justice system, 26
Jesus' role in justice, 30
just acts, 30
justice
  affordability components, 4
  fairness components, 4
  injustice recognition in, 147-48
  for offender equals victim, 9
  purpose, traditional, 25, 30
  restoration as, 32-34
  the social contract and, 11
justice (divine), 28-29
Justice Juggernaut, 3
justice system (traditional). *See also*
    adversarial system; prosecution
    alternatives
  circle sentencing relationship, 79, 86f,
    96, 194
  community conflict resolution versus, 23
  community involvement with, 193-94, 198
  emphasis, 200
  family group conferencing and, 86f, 95
  focus of, 83
  history, 24
  initiatives for restorative justice impacted
    by, 95-96
  job security in, 3
  offender role, 23
  polycentric problem resolution ability
    of, 58
  reintegrative shaming in, 115-16
  reparative boards relationship, 86f, 96
  restorative justice versus, 45, 200, 201
  retributive model for, 3-4
  role in restorative process, 13-14
  victim-offender mediation relationship,
    86f, 95
  victim role, 23

juvenile justice system
    confidentiality in conferencing, 166
    examples of. *See* Examples of restorative
        justice (juvenile)
    initiatives for restorative justice, 97-98
    in Oregon, 97
    reparative boards in, 72-75
    victim-offender mediation in, 69-72, 69f
juvenile justice system (alternatives)
    circle sentencing, 78-81
    community relationships in, 98
    conferencing (family group), 75-78
    reparative boards, 72-75
    victim-offender mediation, 69-72, 69f

K

Kantian imperative, 198-99
Karp, David R.
    "Community Justice Sanctioning
        Models: Assessing Program Integrity,"
        185-211
Kaveny, Malvina, 32
Kelling, George, 14
Kpelle (Liberia) village moot, 26

L

Law Enforcement Assistance Administration,
    90
Laws of Ethelbert, 21
Lertola, Dyanne, 156
Liberia, Kpelle moot, 26
location/proximity in community
    participation, 23, 195f, 196-97
Lowy, Michael, 23

M

MacDonald, John, 13
Manitoba, Canada
    circle sentencing, 78
    Hollow Water community, 60
Maori (New Zealand)
    communal accountability practices, 26-27
    justice model, 5
    sanctioning/dispute resolution model,
        75, 187
Marshall, Tony, 46
Matthew 5: 28-29, 38-42
McCold, Paul, 11
    on community, 7
    "Community Is Not a Place: A New Look
        at Community Justice Initiatives."
        39-52
McDonald, John M.
    "Community Conferencing as Conflict
        Transformation," 107-21

McElrea, Fred, 148
mediation
    conflict minimization and, 124
    police officer abilities, 44, 46-47, 75-76
    in tribal/indigenous cultures, 25-28
    victim-offender mediation versus, 70
mediation (victim-offender)
    for additional information, 72
    community involvement practices, 193
    described, 20, 70, 188-89
    empowerment/freedom in, 20-21
    goals/outcomes desired, 70, 87f
    implementation considerations, 71
    for juvenile crime, 69-72, 69f
    mediation versus, 70
    the mediator in, 20, 71, 88
    monitoring/enforcement in, 87f, 88
    moral authority of, 21
    offender role, 70
    participants/participation options, 71,
        83, 86f
    preparation, 86f, 88
    process/administration, 70, 82f
    research findings, 71-72
    restoration component in, 202
    role stretch for participants, 197
    statistics, 69-70
    system partnership in, 194
    traditional justice system relationship,
        86f, 95
    victim-offender dialog, 70
    victim role, 70, 83-84, 86f
Megan's Law, 2
Mennonite religion, 30
mentoring programs, 90
microcommunity, 44-49, 143-45
Mills, John Stuart, 32
mimetic theory/mimesis, 31
Minnesota
    Australia, 187
    circle sentencing, 78, 187-88
    family group conferencing, 76, 85
    victim-offender mediation endorsement,
        72
Minnesota Department of Corrections, 98
Mongeon, Jim, 154-55, 157-59
Montana, family group conferencing, 76, 187
Moore, David B., 13, 44
    "Community Conferencing as Conflict
        Transformation", **107-21**
    "The Psychology of Community
        Conferencing", **123-38**
moral authority
    community as source of, 49
    community in social contracts, 12, 13, 25
    of conscience, 21
    customary/tribal law in enforcing, 28

of mediation, 21
moral foundations of restorative justice.
   See also social contract of society
   biblical justice, 5-6, 28-30, 145
   conscience of the individual, 21, 42
   dignity of the individual, 22, 27, 30, 33,
      195f, 198-99
moralnets, 25
motivation
   in crime prevention, 56-57
   emotion in, 133-34
   for participation in mediation, 71-72
   restitution as, 71-72

N

Native Americans. *See also* specific groups,
      for example, Navajo
   circle sentencing, 187-88
   conflict resolution traditions, 27
   justice models, 5
   sanctioning/healing practices, 78
neighborhood boards. *See* reparative boards
neighborhood in community, 41, 42-44
neighborhood justice centers, 90
networks, relational, 25, 137. *See also*
   relationships
New Guinea, Raskol gang programs, 60
New South Wales
   conferencing history, 109
   youth justice conferencing program,
      118-19
New Zealand
   compliance statistics, 62
   conferencing history, 109
   confidentiality in conferencing, 166
   family group conferencing, 75, 77, 187
   limitations to restorative justice, 63
   restorative conferencing in, 68
Nichomachean Ethics (Aristotle), 21, 33
non-European cultures and community
   justice, 25-28. *See also* individual
   countries, for example, Tanzania
Normal rule of law, 5

O

obligation recognition, 10. *See also*
   accountability (offender)
offender. *See also* accountability (offender);
      acknowledgment (offender);
         empowerment (offender);
            reintegration (offender)
   behaviors resulting from punishment, 4
   community debt owed to, 12
   criminal risk prediction for, 4
   criminal subculture of, 42
   incarceration as sacrificial rite, 31

   retributive system in obligations of, 10
   as stakeholder, 45
   as victim, 3, 45
offender, role of
   circle sentencing, 78, 79, 89, 96
   family group conferencing, 76
   in restorative process, 10-11
   in traditional systems, 23
   victim-offender mediation, 70
offender-community relationship, 3, 7, 12
offender outcasting, 205
offender-victim relationship, 4, 7
   adversarial system and, 3
Old Testament justice model, 5-6
O'Malley, Mike, 154-55
Oregon, change in juvenile justice, 97
outcasting of offenders, 205

P

parole, statistics, 2
partial versus complete justice, 33
participant satisfaction
   family group conferencing, 77, 85
   victim-offender mediation, 71, 84
   Victim Offender Reconciliation Program
      Conferencing, 149
   youth justice conferencing program, 118
participants/participation options
   circle sentencing, 78, 86f, 96, 194
   family group conferencing, 48-49, 76-77,
      86f
   reparative boards, 86f
   victim-offender mediation, 71, 83, 86f
   Victim Offender Reconciliation Program
      Conferencing (Fresno), 149
participation sequence. *See* sequence of
   participation
peace, building through victim offender
   reconciliation, **141-51**
peacemaking circles. *See* circle sentencing
Peacemaking Model, 145, 149-51
peacemaking practices of Skokomish, 27
Pennell, Joan, 63
Pennsylvania
   confidentiality in conferencing, 166
   family group conferencing, 76, 85, 187
   Real Justice program, 157
Perry, John G., "Challenging the
   Assumptions," 1-17
personality theory of emotion, 115, 134
plea bargaining, 3, 10. *See also* adversarial
   system
police officers as facilitators, 44, 46-47,
   75-76
policing. *See* community policing;
   restorative policing

political system
power role in restorative theory of
justice, 33-34
Restorative Justice statute (Vermont), 13f
role in restorative process, 13-14
polycentric problem resolution, 58-59
power issues
in community justice, 23
in implementation of new models, 94-96
problem-oriented policing in, 44
in restorative theory of justice, 33-34
Pranis, Kay, 41, 49
prayer tradition of Maori, 27
prison. *See* incarceration
probation
recycling of offenders, 3, 24
Reparative Probation Program
(Vermont), 14-15, 74
statistics, 2
victim-offender mediation requirements,
70
problem-oriented policing, 43-44
problem resolution, polycentric, 58-59
procedural justice, 33
prosecution alternatives
case study example, 157-61
family group conferencing (Australia), 187
victim-offender mediation, 70
Victim Offender Reconciliation Program
Conferencing (Fresno), 148-49
Wagga Wagga model of family
conferencing, 75-76
psychology of community conferencing,
123-37
punishment. *See also* retribution/retributive
justice; retribution/retributive justice
accountability versus, 144
in biblical justice systems, 28-29
in community conferencing, 125
efficacy of, 4-5
Enlightenment theory of, 24
as motivator, 42
recidivism and, 4
restorative justice process versus, 13-14

R

Raskol gang programs (Papua, New
Guinea), 60
reading recommendations
circle sentencing, 81
community reparative boards, 75
Real Justice (Bethlehem, Pennsylvania), 157
recidivism, incarceration related, 2, 3
recidivism prevention
circle sentencing, 80
victim-offender mediation statistics, 71

recidivism reduction
Victim Offender Reconciliation Program
Conferencing (Fresno), 149
youth justice conferencing program, 118
recidivism risk and reintegration, 204-05
reciprocity/reciprocal behavior, 6-7, 11,
15-16
reconciliation, defined, 142
reconciliation (victim-offender). *See also*
Victim Offender Reconciliation
Program (VORP)
community responsibilities, 15f, 142
components of, 14-15
history, 30
by offender acknowledgment, 9, 14
reparation component, 14
recycling of offenders, 3, 24
redemption in biblical justice traditions,
29-30
rehabilitation programs
effectiveness in conferencing, 61
in reintegration, 204f, 205
reification, 8, 16
reintegration (offender)
accountability and, 14-15
in biblical justice traditions, 30
classroom example, 144
community responsibilities, 11, 15f
components of, 204-5, 204f
dignity of the individual in, 22
emotional transformation in, 13
Letter from a Board Member in
Springfield, 12f
Native American emphasis, 27
reintegrative shaming in, 55, 203
restitution/restoration in, 11
sanctioning components in, 203-6, 204f
trust component, 204
reintegration (victim)
community responsibility for, 12
emotional transformation in, 13
sentencing participation in, 14-15
reintegrative shaming, 55-56, 110, 115-16,
203. *See also* shame
Re-Integrative Shaming (RISE) experiment,
56
relational justice, 40
relationships. *See also* specific, for example,
victim-offender
in biblical justice traditions, 30
conferencing in building, 137
creating healthy, 137
in defining community, v, 40-41
remorse, 11
reoffending. *See* recidivism

reparation
  apology in, 114
  in biblical justice traditions, 29-30
  empowerment from control of, 46
  Green River Reservoir (example), 173-74
  Japanese cultural emphasis, 26
  offender responsibilities, 15f
  reintegration and, 14-15
  restitution versus, 21
  symbolic as crucial, 114
reparation agreements
  completion compliance, 61-62, 88, 89
  described, 187
  family group conferencing, 76
  monitoring/enforcement, 88, 201
  sentencing in, 14
  victim-offender mediation, 188
reparative boards, 82f, 84
  for additional information, 75
  authority, 72-73
  community involvement, 86
  described, 72, 187
  effectiveness, 74
  example, 73f
  goals/outcomes desired, 73, 87f
  implementation considerations, 74
  for juvenile crime, 72-75
  monitoring/enforcement by, 87f, 88
  participants/participation options, 14, 86f
  preparation, 86f, 88
  process/administration, 73, 82f
  reading recommendations, 75
  restoration component in, 202
  role stretch for participants, 197
  traditional justice system relationship, 86f, 96
  victim role, 84, 86f
Reparative Probation Program (Vermont), 14-15, 74
respect for persons. See also dignity of the individual
  in civil communities, 143
  classroom example, 143-45
  constructive commitment components and, 145
  Japanese cultural emphasis, 26
  moral duty of, 22
  restorative practices in, 33
  restoring through VORP, 144
restitution
  completion statistics, 71
  as constructive versus destructive activity, 8-9, 21-22
  creative/self-determined, 21-22
  dignity of the individual in, 22
  history of practice, 21

as motivator for victim participation, 71-72, 84
offender responsibilities, 6
in reintegration process, 11, 22
reparation versus, 21
in tribal/indigenous cultures, 6, 27
victim-offender mediation success statistics, 71
restoration, 30, 32-34, 202-3
restoration agreements, 144, 148
restoration (community), 27, 200f, 202-3
restoration (victim)
  the community in, 12
  constructive versus destructive activity, 8-9
  offender responsibilities, 15f
  as reintegration contingency, 11
  in repairing harm, 200f, 201-2
  sentencing participation in, 14-15
  in tribal/indigenous cultures, 27
restorative justice. See also initiatives for restorative justice; moral foundations of restorative justice
  board, 12, 14-15
  characteristics, 6-7
  defined, 4, 46
  emphasis, 200
  evaluation of, 92-93
  examples of. See examples of restorative justice; examples of restorative justice (juvenile)
  foundational elements, 19-20, 30
  philosophy of the circle of community, 26-28, 32
  purpose, v, 32, 33, 68
restorative justice system. See also initiatives for restorative justice
  community conferencing versus, 117
  efficiency of process, 9
  historical basis for, 5-6
  parties of, 45
  processes/process efficiency, 7-8
  retributive justice system versus, 7f
  traditional justice systems versus, 45, 200, 201
Restorative Justice Unit (New South Wales), 119
restorative policing, 46-48. See also police officers as facilitators
restorative theory of justice, 33-34
retribution/retributive justice. See also justice system (traditional); punishment
  alienation of victims/offenders in, 42
  behaviors resulting from, 4
  in biblical justice systems, 6, 28-29

in Eskimo culture, 27
history, 4, 5-6
purpose of, 32
restorative justice system versus, 7f
safety of victim from, 4
social practices of, 31-32
Retzinger, Suzanne, 111
RISE (Re-Integrative Shaming) experiment, 56
risk assessment/prediction, 204-5
   incarceration related, 2
   pro-criminal associates component, 4
risk intervention for reintegration, 205
ritual
   of apology and forgiveness, 111
   ceremonies of reintegration, 6, 205
   communal, 32
   sacrificial rites to restore harmony, 31

S

safety of victim from retaliation, 8
Salem, Marie, 166
sanctioning models
   circle sentencing, 187-88
   community reparative boards, 187
   family group conferencing, 187
   objectives, 186
   philosophies underlying, 186
   research challenges, 189
   victim-offender mediation, 188-89
sanctioning variables
   accessibility
      comparison of components, 195f
      decentralization, 196-97
      flexibility, 195f, 196-97
      informality, 195f, 197-98
      introduction, 194-95
      location/proximity, 195f, 196-97
      sensitivity to individual dignity, 195f, 198-99
      time, 198
   community involvement
      comparison of components, 191f
      concerns regarding, 191f
      introduction, 190-91
      stakeholder in, 191-93, 191f, 192-93
      system collaboration and, 193-94, 198
   reintegration
      comparison of components, 204f
      competency development/
         rehabilitation, 204f, 205
      decertification of deviant status, 204f, 205-6
      introduction, 203-4
      offender supervision and public safety, 204-5, 204f

repairing harm
   comparison of components, 200f
   introduction, 199-200
   offender accountability, 200f, 201
   restoration in, 200f, 201-3
   summary, 206-7
Saskatchewan (Canada), circle sentencing, 78
satisfaction of participants. See participant satisfaction
Scandinavia, conflict resolution, 23
scapegoat practices, 31
Scheff, Thomas, 111
school use of VORP, 143-45, 149-50
Schweigert, Francis
   "Moral and Philosophical Foundations of Restorative Justice," 5-6, **19-36**
scientifically guided society model, 110
self-guiding society model, 110
sentencing circles, 78. See circle sentencing
sequence of emotion (affective), 135-36
sequence of participation
   in conferencing, 76, 84, 112-14
   emotions in the, 111-13
   in transformation, 113-16
   in victim-offender mediation, 83
shalom, 30
shame. See also reintegrative shaming
   collective experience of, 109, 115-16
   guilt versus, 111-12
   psychological element in conferencing, 109, 111-13, 135
   purpose of, 111, 136
   and ritual of apology and forgiveness, 111
   triggers for/causes of, 134, 136
   Victim Impact Panel Has an Effect (example), 181
"Shame Forgiveness and Juvenile Justice," 109
shame for social control. See also reintegrative shaming
   belonging desires as factor in, 42
   family group conferencing process, 84
   regulatory function of, 111
   in tribal/indigenous cultures, 26-27
Shearing, Clifford, 57
Skokomish Community Peacemaking Panel, 27
Skokomish peacemaking practices, 27
social contract of society. See also moral foundations of restorative justice
   classroom example, 143-45
   community enforcement of, 11-13
   Green River Reservoir (example), 173-74

moral authority of, 12, 13, 25
persons acting on behalf of the group, 22
respect as a moral duty in, 22
in restorative model, 7
social control
community in maintaining, 11-13, 26-27,
42, 44, 48
interdependence in, 42, 48
shame for, 26-27, 42, 84, 111
social practices
emotional responses influenced by,
134-35
individual versus collective
responsibility, 41
of retributive justice, 31-32
scapegoat in restoring harmony, 31
scientifically/self-guided society models,
110
social intervention, biblical traditions
of, 30
social practices (tribal/indigenous cultures)
in community development, 22-23
community justice, 25-28
sacrificial rites to restore harmony, 31-32
shame for social control, 26-27
Soft on Crime!, 2
South Australia, family group conferencing,
75, 85
South Dakota, Habitat for Humanity project,
22
stakeholder
community representatives as, 49
defined, 45
sanctioning and the, 191-93, 191f
statistics
compliance, 62
conviction rates (Japan), 26
crime (U.S.), 3
incarceration dollars (U.S.), 2
incarceration (Japan), 26
incarceration (U.S.), 2, 3
probation/parole (U.S.), 2
recidivism reduction, 71
restitution obligation completion, 71
victim-offender mediation programs,
69-70
· VORP participation/growth, 147, 149
story telling (reification), 8, 16
Stuart, Barry, 80
supply and demand (law of), 3

T

Tanzania, 6, 23, 26
three strikes and you're out, 2, 3
Tomkins, Silvan, 115, 133-34
transformation (emotional), 13, 109

transformation of conflict. See conflict
transformation
transformative justice, 40
Transformative Justice Australia, 107, 116,
118-19
transitional collective experience of
emotion, 135
tribal cultures. See indigenous/aboriginal
people
Tri-Global, 59
trust, developing, 145, 148, 204

U

Umbreit, Mark
"A Comparison of Four Restorative
Conferencing Models by the Office of
Juvenile Justice and Delinquency
Prevention", 67-105
processes of restorative justice, 8
United Kingdom, conferencing in
correctional settings, 119

V

Van Ness, Daniel, 21
vengeance
adversarial system and, 3
as basis for retributive justice, 31
Vermont. See also Grossly Negligent
Operation with Death Resulting case
study
confidentiality in conferencing, 166
family group conferencing, 76
reparative boards, 72, 84, 187
Reparative Probation Program, 14-15, 74
Restorative Justice statute, 13f
Vermont Department of Corrections, 74
victim. See also empowerment (victim)
adversarial system and, 3
community debt owed to, 12
emotions of, 8
focus in restorative justice, 8-10, 45
motivation for mediation participation,
71-72
in retributive model, 6
society versus individual, 45
as stakeholder, 45
stigma of being a, 8, 12
validation of harm, 8
victim, role of
circle sentencing, 85, 86f, 87
family group conferencing, 76, 84-85, 86f
reparative boards, 84, 86f
in restorative process, 8-10, 27
in traditional systems, 23
victim-offender mediation, 70-71, 83-84, 86f

victim (community as), 48, 178-79
victim-community relationship, 8
victim offender mediation, 69-72, 82f, 83-84
Victim Offender Reconciliation Program Conferencing, 147
Victim Offender Reconciliation Program Conferencing (Fresno), 148-49, 149
Victim Offender Reconciliation Program (VORP), 141-51
  applications and limitations, 150-51
  approach, 142-45
  change in, 15
  classroom example, 143-45, 149-50
  facilitator responsibilities, 146
  monitoring/enforcement, 148
  Peacemaking Model and, 145, 149-51
  process/preparation, 146-47
Victim Offender Reconciliation Program (VORP) Fresno, 146-49
victim-offender relationship, 3, 4, 7
violence as basis for retribution, 31
VORP (Victim Offender Reconciliation Program). *See* Victim Offender Reconciliation Program (VORP)
vulnerability (collective) moment in conferencing, 113, 115, 135-37

W

Wachtel, Benjamin, 11
  on community, 7
  "Community Is Not a Place: A New Look at Community Justice Initiatives," **39-52**
Wagga/Real Justice model, 40, 47
Wagga Wagga, New South Wales, 109
Wagga Wagga model, 75-76, 89
Wagga Wagga Police Department, 75-76
Wahrhaftig, Paul, 23
West Germany, compliance statistics, 62
Widening the Circle (video), 62-63
Williamson, David, 119
Wilson, James Q., 14

Y

Yazzi, Chief Justice, 5
youth courts, 90
youth justice conferencing program (New South Wales), 118-19
Yukon Territory (Canada) use of circle sentencing, 78, 188

Z

Zehr, Howard, 68
  restorative justice model of, 7